902839549 0

D1351370

AROUND THE WORLD
IN 80 TRAINS

AROUND THE WORLD IN 80 TRAINS

A 45,000–Mile Adventure

Monisha Rajesh

BLOOMSBURY PUBLISHING
LONDON · OXFORD · NEW YORK · NEW DELHI · SYDNEY

BLOOMSBURY PUBLISHING
Bloomsbury Publishing Plc
50 Bedford Square, London, WC1B 3DP, UK

BLOOMSBURY, BLOOMSBURY PUBLISHING and the Diana logo are trademarks of
Bloomsbury Publishing Plc

First published in Great Britain 2019

A catalogue record for this book is available from the British Library

Library of Congress Cataloguing-in-Publication data has been applied for

ISBN: HB: 978-1-4088-6975-8; eBook: 978-1-4088-6978-9

2 4 6 8 10 9 7 5 3 1

Typeset by Newgen KnowledgeWorks Pvt. Ltd., Chennai, India
Printed and bound in Great Britain by CPI Group (UK) Ltd, Croydon CRO 4YY

MIX
Paper from
responsible sources
FSC® C020471

To find out more about our authors and books visit www.bloomsbury.com
and sign up for our newsletters

For Ariel, without whom this book would
have been published a year ago

Contents

I

The 14:31 to Paris

Leaning against the window, I looked up at the iron ribcage arched across the roof of St Pancras, blue sky blazing between its bones. It appeared to be rolling back, when I realised it was we who were moving. The 14.31 Eurostar to Paris hummed out of the station, and I sat back, warm spring sunshine flashing into the carriage. As London fell away, I tried to breathe in as much of the city as I could, hoping to hold it in my chest until we met again in seven months' time. A long journey lay ahead, a journey that would take me around the world. Exactly five years ago to the day, I'd stepped off the *Charminar Express* in Chennai, marking my eightieth train journey around India. With nothing but a three-month rail pass, an outdated map, and hopeless naivety, I'd travelled 25,000 miles – the circumference of the earth – reaching the four points of the country's geographical diamond. In between hanging from doorways, squatting on steps and snoozing on piles of laundry, I'd come to understand why Indian Railways is known as the 'Lifeline of the Nation'.

Having narrowly avoided a number of scrapes, I'd sworn never to take on anything so ambitious again. Little did I know that the railways had followed me home – their dust in my hair, their rhythm in my bones, their charm infused in my blood. Slowly, the symptoms began to manifest: I'd linger on bridges watching freight thundering below. On warm afternoons, I'd buy round-trip tickets just to sit in the window and read, and at night, I'd lie awake listening to distant horns sound through the darkness. It became a sickness, one that had no cure. At least, no cure that I'd find in London. I had to get back on the rails – but I couldn't just pack up and leave. After returning from India I'd eased back into the swing of London life, working as the subeditor at *The Week* magazine, and, by all accounts, the job was the stuff of dreams: I swanned in at ten o'clock, and spent the day reading newspapers and drinking tea, with Coco the office dachshund asleep in my lap. In essence, I was being paid to do what most people did on a lazy Sunday. And now there was someone else to consider, my fiancé Jeremy, who had proposed a few months earlier, next to a bin outside St John's Wood tube station. Knocked out of the way mid-proposal by a group of Japanese tourists wearing waterproofs and wellies, he had asked me to marry him, in the rain, on the very spot where we had met for our first date.

Dismissing the idea of leaving, I carried on with the humdrum of daily life, suppressing the urge whenever it rose, until I finally gave up the fight: there was too much to discover on the rails, and the trains were waiting – but not for long. Train travel is evolving at high speed: bullet trains are multiplying, long-distance services running out of steam. Sleeper services are being phased out, and classic routes fading away. According to economists and pessimists, the romance of the railways is dying a swift death, but I refused to believe it was true. Nowhere in the world could rival India's railways, but I knew that every country's network would possess a spirit of its own, it just needed a prod and a poke to unearth. Trains are rolling libraries of information, and all it takes is to reach out to passengers to bind together their tales.

After a final cup of tea, I patted Coco goodbye, and bade farewell to *The Week*. Jeremy – better known as Jem – agreed to join me for a month along the way, and I set about organising the trip. Hanging a world map on the living-room wall, I punctured it with pins, and tied coloured string from one to another, watching the next seven months of my life unwind around the globe. Surrounded by stacks of guides and maps, I sat cross-legged on the floor of our flat, poring over routes, flagging up significant events, and planning with as much precision as such a journey would allow for. One of the greatest mistakes a traveller can make, is to believe a journey can be controlled – least of all one of this magnitude. Nothing but disappointment can result in such a fallacy, and I'd made allowances for delays, cancellations, and general tardiness on my part. When I'd travelled around India, the plan was to have no plan, which had served me well within the confines of a single country; but this adventure had too many cities, countries and crossings for me to ride by the seat of my pants. As the day of departure approached, Jem grew ever more quiet, until one morning he sat down next to me.

'Are you going to be okay for seven months on your own?'

'Yes,' I said, in a small voice that surprised me.

'Are you sure?' He stared at the map. 'There are some pretty hairy places under those pins. Iran? Uzbekistan?'

'I'll be fine.'

The truth was that I wasn't sure I'd be fine. In India, I'd been groped on a night train, cornered in a station, chased down a platform, stared at, leered at, spat at, shouted at, sworn at, and spent numerous nights crouched in hotels after dark with my bags piled up against the door. Above all, I didn't want to leave Jem behind. What a waste it would be, to travel around Europe, Russia, Mongolia, China, Vietnam, Thailand, Malaysia, Singapore, Japan, Canada, and America, with no one to build and share memories.

Now, as I looked at the passenger in the seat next to me, I knew we'd made the right decision. Jem had quit his job, bought his first rucksack, and was accompanying me for the entire journey. Alarmed by his suggestion that all he needed for the next seven months was a new pair of boat shoes and a couple of jumpers, I'd taken off his Tag Heuer, handed him a Swatch, and marched him to Blacks for waterproofs and socks. Having grown up in the backwaters of Cobham, Surrey, Jem wasn't used to bags that weren't on wheels, and I suspected we were in for an interesting time. That morning, I'd made a last-minute dash to Stanfords in Covent Garden to pick up a notebook for the trip. Turning it over, I stroked the newness of the leather, and opened it up to document the first of eighty trains, sliding the ribbon into place. Looking out of the window, I saw that the train was approaching the Channel Tunnel; I took a deep breath as we went underground and England faded from sight.

Contrary to what they implied, Eurail passes were perfect for people who planned, people who lacked spontaneity, people who knew exactly where they would be having dinner and at what time, ninety days in advance. I am not one of those people, and was rapidly finding the one-month rail pass a hindrance to our travels. For fixed itineraries it was fine, paying itself off within five or six long-distance journeys. But for people like us who woke in Paris wanting lunch in Barcelona, it didn't work to our advantage. Each booking incurred a supplement fee, a cancellation fee or an administrative fee, and I spent the first week in Europe indoors, standing in stationary queues, waiting for refunds.

While I'd been filling in forms and moving from one counter to another, Jem had come up with a list of sights and cities that he wanted to visit, handing it to me over lunch in a cafe in the Marais.

'Gaudí's House … Valencia … Lourdes? Really?' I asked, as the waiter placed a basket of freshly sliced baguette on our table along with two paper placemats and a carafe of water.

'Yes,' said Jem, trying to spread hard white butter across the bread, and tugging it apart.

'But you're not religious.'

'I know, but I'm curious. You know how you hear about places when you're a kid and you imagine them to be a certain way, I've always wondered what Lourdes is like.'

Amid the din of conversation and scraping chairs, I looked around the cafe with a growing admiration for the way in which the French cared for nothing else when it came to meal times. Over a *pichet* of wine, they tore bread, wiped it in cream, cracked crème brûlée, sipped dark, perfect coffee, and drew out the afternoon as though it were a Saturday instead of the middle of a working week. No one seemed to have a job to go to, turning up with coiffed canines, manicures and perfect tans – the women were well turned out, too. Lifting a crisp, sticky chunk of *confit de canard*, I thought about going to Lourdes, and decided that it wouldn't hurt to find salvation along the way.

After lunch, we boarded the train to Limoges from where we were continuing the journey to Clermont-Ferrand, then Béziers – one of the longest single lines of track through France, known for the views over the Massif Central. While waiting around for the connection in Limoges, we shared a Coke and paced the cool, empty station, listening to the squeak of our footsteps and admiring the domed roof, the interior of which was engraved with four partly clothed women: Le Limousin, La Bretagne, La Gascogne and La Touraine. Circled in wreaths, carrying chestnuts and overlapped with acorns, oak leaves and vines, the allegories represented the four regions served by the train. Ropes of oak leaves snaked towards the dome, culminating in a circle of stained glass. For such a provincial town, the station was unusually ornate. Curious about its exterior, we wandered out into the forecourt, unable to see the roof from where we stood. Over the road, we found a seat on the wall of a fountain from where we could take in the full splendour of the art deco building and its clock tower. Of the stations we were to pass through in Europe, Limoges-Bénédictins turned out to be one of the loveliest, a haphazard and serendipitous discovery – thanks in no part to our rail pass.

France's TGVs – *Trains à Grande Vitesse* – have revolutionised train travel across Europe for commuters, but for idlers like us whose sole intention was to spend the afternoon gazing out of windows, the high-speed trains served little purpose, reducing the views to a blur. There were few passengers on the slow trains from Limoges to Clermont-Ferrand, and Clermont-Ferrand to Béziers, most of whom moaned about the heat, fell asleep in the heat, then jumped off within a couple of hours, leaving us to wind down the country alone.

'Look what they've missed out on,' said Jem, edging to the window as the train rumbled across a canyon, at the bottom of which were children playing in dinghies and leaping off limestone rocks into the water. Stopping their games, they looked up and waved paddles as we crossed the bridge. Over the next three hours, we crept through the depths of dark forests, silver trails of water whispering by. With the windows open, the clean smell of pine filled the carriage, as we rocked our way south to Béziers. An alert sounded on Jem's phone and he glanced down.

'I should have been going into a weekly meeting right now,' he said, leaning back with his eyes shut, a small smile on his lips.

From Béziers a connection via Toulouse brought us to Lourdes just in time for the evening procession. We ambled down the hill with the tributaries pouring into the sea of pilgrims making their way towards the Grotto. Expecting a quiet town with a few nuns scattered around a trickle of water, I felt like I was caught up in the aftermath of a football match. Rammed with pizzerias, kebab houses, and bars outlined in neon, Lourdes looked like the Magaluf of Christendom. Souvenir shops with names like 'A La Grâce de Dieu' and 'Mystères de Marie' lined the pavements, each one trying to out-flash the other with commemorative teacups, fans, doorstoppers, and cigarette lighters shaped like Jesus. Wandering around in bemusement, Jem pointed at a foot-high fluorescent statue of the Virgin Mary rising over us.

'Imagine waking in the middle of the night and seeing that staring at you.'

'Would you like your car to smell like the pope?' I asked, finding a collection of car fresheners that purported to smell like different saints.

'What does Joan of Arc smell like? Charcoal?'

Each one of these supermarkets of religion was stacked with postcards, rosaries, snow globes, paintings, incense, and bottles of holy water – their prices rising by a few euros at a time the nearer we got to the Grotto.

Among the crowds heading towards the procession were children in wheelchairs, haggard parents pushing them along. The sight filled me with frustration. I'd once considered myself a Hindu, accepting the religion into which I'd been born with very little thought – largely because it didn't require me to do much but treat others as I'd hope to be treated, and eat *barfi* and biryani during festivals. Happy to go along with the idea that there was an unknown entity above, I'd mutter the odd prayer from time to time: in the moments before sleep, at a temple, or while perched on a back-row pew in Hampstead Parish Church in the quiet midweek. However, after my travels around India in the company of a self-confessed 'devout' atheist, I began to question the existence of a higher power and my need for religion as a whole. Time and again I encountered so-called 'godmen' exploiting the poor and vulnerable, priests extracting money for nothing, and blind faith leading to disappointment. By the end of my journey I concluded that the existence of a god went against all logic and reasoning and that I had no need for any kind of religion. Feeling freer and more awake than ever before, I found myself unable to ever pray or consider god again. Now, as I watched sick pilgrims streaming towards the grounds, carrying expensive candles and cans to collect water, I felt a renewed sense of my own conviction. Even if the experience brought peace to the needy, knowing others were profiting from their desperation wasn't something I could accept. However, at the last minute I bought a tiny bottle, with a gold lid shaped like a flower, to fill with water and keep as a souvenir, if nothing else.

Arriving at the sanctuary gates, Jem and I moved to the side as patients were wheeled in from a nearby hospice, their beds layered with blankets to stave off the evening chill. The sky had darkened and a deep purple bruise glowered over the Byzantine Rosary Basilica, as it loomed above the thousands holding candles and murmuring prayers. Taking our chance to slip away to the Grotto, we joined the queue, passing a man with a suitcase filling up plastic tubs of holy water. In silence, we edged through the tunnel, the trickle and drip echoing around. Beneath the statue of Our Lady, the rock wall glistened with water running down from her feet. From behind, impatient pilgrims stretched their arms over my head to touch the cold surface, bringing their fingers to their necks, lips moving in quiet prayer. As resistant as my feelings were, I was surprised by the calm that overcame me as we left the passage. On the way out, I had stopped to fill my water bottle, screwing the lid tightly shut and placing it in my pocket, when I noticed Jem lingering around the Grotto.

'If it's okay, I'd like to light a candle for Dad,' he said. We chose a tall, slim gold candle and placed it in the holder together, watching the flame dart sideways in the wind, before walking back towards the thoroughfare, where the procession was well under way.

One Sunday, aged fifteen, Jem was polishing his father's Church's brogues – a weekly ritual – when he saw him break out into a sweat. It was a cold January day and Jem eyed him with unease, knowing that something was wrong. Within a few minutes his father was leaning over the arm of the sofa, clutching his chest, before collapsing on the floor with a heart attack. Jem watched on helplessly as his father died before his eyes, aged just forty-four. Losing a parent at such a young and formative age jilted his entire outlook on life. The suggestion that his father's death was god's will insulted him, and he rejected others' attempts to use religion to find reasoning in such an unjust event. Instead, he made a pledge to himself that every day from then on would be lived to the fullest, with career and money taking a backseat in favour of making the most of his time with friends and loved ones.

The next two weeks passed by in a blur of high-speed trains. Leaving Lourdes, we travelled to Toulouse, then Barcelona, shooting across to Madrid, looping down to Valencia, and curving back up the coast to Barcelona. From there we'd crossed the south of France and Monaco, coming to rest in Italy. There were twenty-eight countries available with the rail pass – almost one for every day we had in Europe – but it was impossible to devote a significant amount of time to any one place. Narrowing it down to a few old favourites, we chose to travel through cities that were havens of glorious food, better wine and even better beaches – but the trains were proving a disappointment. No one spoke, everyone slept, and there was little to differentiate one journey from the next. Efficient, punctual and easy to use, Europe's trains served no greater purpose than to take passengers from one stop to the next, with a few pretty pastures in between. In the absence of sleeper services, these short hops didn't lend themselves to the high-octane adventure we'd been hoping for.

Sitting in a cafe in Milan, I scanned the list of trains we'd already taken. Every time I bent down to write, the sound of mopeds distracted me, as young women with legs like Bambi put-putted past in sandals and summer dresses, revving over the cobbles like something out of a Dior advert.

'I'm the one who's supposed to be leering, not you,' said Jem, pressing his beer against his cheek.

'I can't help it. Italian cafes are designed for leering. Everyone's drinking and you're sitting on the pavement with your back to the restaurant with no one to look at but pretty girls in pretty dresses. Anyway, it's not like those transition lenses are fooling anyone. I can see you perving behind them.'

Jem looked put out. 'Don't make fun of my lenses.'

'You know, we've already taken fifteen trains.'

'Feels like more,' said Jem, offering me a piece of melon draped with sweet, stringy Parma ham.

'I'm pretty sure we've spent most of our seven-month budget on bookings and fees,' I said, watching the owner flap his cloth across a table, and kiss a couple of regulars on both cheeks. Italian agents in Rome had refused to change tickets that I'd booked two days earlier in Monaco through French agents, who had refused to amend a booking made two days before that in Valencia by Spanish agents. Each insisted the other company was responsible for voiding the tickets that were no longer needed, and declared that any refunds had to be requested by post – for a fee. I'd been directed towards a queue, which turned out to be a queue for tickets for a second queue that was for refunding pre-bought tickets, at which point I gave up – which was probably what each company hoped passengers would do. Binning the whole load, I decided it was time to leave Europe before I lost the will to live.

'Don't forget we need to pick up our laundry,' Jem reminded me as we finished lunch and walked back towards the hotel.

The bell of the laundromat gave a happy tinkle as we arrived to collect our clothes. The strong smell of laundered sheets hit me as we closed the door, and I immediately began sweating from the heat of the dryers. The iron hissing beneath her weight, Vittoria waved and put her glasses onto her nose, looking down her clipboard, before lugging a plastic-wrapped pile onto the counter. Vittoria didn't speak a word of English, and we didn't speak any Italian, yet with the combination of sign language and good faith, we'd managed to explain that we wanted everything chucked into one machine, and by the looks of things, she'd done a perfect job. Running my finger down the edge of our clothes, I waited for her to tap the total into a calculator. Hovering with his hands in his pockets, Jem handed me a twenty-euro note, as Vittoria turned the calculator around and took off her glasses, which hung from her neck by a chain. The screen read €109. Every inch of my skin prickled with horror, the tips of my ears turning hot. Looking up at Vittoria without saying a word, I felt my mouth fall open. She looked down, then laughed, shaking her head. I sighed with relief and, turning to Jem with my eyes wide, mouthed *she'd forgotten the decimal point*.

Only she hadn't.

Vittoria had forgotten to add an additional €9 for a pair of knickers, and the total came to €118.

I turned to Jem in a panic. 'She wants €118 for our laundry!'

'That can't be right.'

'I'm not paying that for a bunch of clothes that were shoved in a bloody washing machine.'

Vittoria laid out the sheet on which she'd listed our eight T-shirts, two pairs of jeans, three cotton dresses, four pairs of socks, a stack of underwear, and a cardigan that was now missing a button – I saw that she'd listed the prices on a sheet from a nearby five-star hotel. Wagging a finger in front of her, I shook my head. 'No, not paying,' I said.

Pulling out her phone, she began speaking into her Google Translate app before showing me the screen, which now read: *What would you like to do?*

'Tell her you want to burn down her shop, the thieving …'

'Shush, hang on,' I said to Jem.

'No way, I'm not letting this woman fleece us. Tell her she can keep our crap. In fact, it would probably cost less than that to replace it all at H&M.'

'It would cost less than that to fly home.'

Jem seized her phone. 'We are not paying this,' he said into it.

Vittoria pursed up her mouth and read the screen, turning on the sound. Laughing, she shrugged in the infuriating way that only Italians can do, and tapped a new figure into the calculator, knocking twenty euros off the total.

'We are not paying that. You are cheating us.'

Vittoria listened to the deadpan automated voice, and smirked, throwing both hands in the air before speaking into the app.

'There is an ATM down the road,' came the voice.

It was like listening to C-3PO and Stephen Hawking having the most passive-aggressive argument I'd ever witnessed. Tapping at her watch, Vittoria was not about to budge, and her shop was about to close. Offering a further ten-euro discount, she moved our clothes out of reach, at which point I was ready to explode, knowing that Vittoria had exploited the vulnerability of two foreigners unable to speak her language. Sweating from the steam in the shop and the steam in my ears, I dragged Jem out onto the pavement and went in search of the ATM.

'We have to pay it, she's never going to give our clothes back otherwise.'

'Fine, but I'm going to come back after dark and put a brick through her window.'

★

After the laundry episode, we had blown our budget for Europe, and had no option but to leave under a dark cloud, winding our way up through Switzerland and Germany, crossing through Lithuania and Latvia, from where we were due to board the train to Moscow from Riga. On the train from Milan to Zurich, I found myself sitting at a table opposite an imposing figure dressed head to toe in black and drinking wine. It was the middle of June and he was wearing a black T-shirt and a pair of drop-crotch black trousers. With his grey beard and dark eyes, he looked like a film noir in human form. Glancing up a couple of times, I could see he was obviously listening with undisguised interest to our musings over Russia. Mark was from Stoke Newington, and was on his way to shoot a story for the *Sunday Times Style* magazine.

'Are you going to Moscow, then?' The tone of his voice didn't inspire me with hope.

'Yes, we've never been before. Have you?'

'Ha!' Mark threw back his head and laughed, folding his arms across his chest. 'I haven't been since 1987 when I went on a joint trip from school with my film studies classmates.' He visibly shuddered. 'The history studies group came too and the two groups hated one another. It was an awful trip. I ended up being pursued by Russian urchins after they were arrested in our room.'

'Wait, what? Why were they in your room?'

'These two lads appeared from the shadows and asked if we wanted anything: flags, champagne, fur hats, all black-market stuff.' Mark poured out the rest of his wine, shaking the last drops into the glass. 'So, me and my mate Andre arranged a party in our room, basically an impromptu bazaar of the army uniforms and accessories they had touted to us, and said we'd take a cut of the sales. The rest of our film studies group bought tons. Anyway, the police turned up and they had to do a runner, so we held on to all their stuff in a few suitcases.'

'That's a bit harsh.'

'We did get it back to them after they stalked us around Moscow for three days, trying to catch hold of us in the street, and loitering around the hotel.'

'We don't have that much time in Moscow,' said Jem, 'just a couple of days, as we're taking the Trans-Mongolian to Beijing and it only departs on certain days of the week.'

'Probably not a bad thing,' said Mark, narrowing his eyes. 'Russians don't tend to be particularly warm towards, how should I say it, people of your ...'

'Colour?' I prompted.

'Precisely,' said Mark, looking relieved.

'You're not the first person to tell us that,' Jem replied.

Jem's mother is Malaysian and his father half Scottish, half Lithuanian. However, the Malaysian side of the family won the gene war, and he is as black-haired and brown-eyed as I am.

'Who knows though, things change,' said Mark. 'We did the train from Moscow to Leningrad. I remember it was boiling,' he said. 'I was so depressed, lying in my bunk, hearing a party next door, where I knew the boy I adored was. I was in a constant bad mood all week and spent a long time weeping as I was madly in love with him, and he slept with a girl. I remember lying there in my ridiculous cashmere John Flett coat, full of unrequited love. Oh, my god that train!' Mark buried his face in his hands as my enthusiasm for Russia slowly dissolved into nothing. 'I remember our pathetic little plastic bags of boiled eggs and weird stuff that we bought at the train station. We thought we were going to die of malnutrition, and lived off a family assortment of biscuits that my friend Ceri brought. I think I blocked it all out, but now that I recall, she also had a single orange, and we were granted one segment each.'

'Was the food that bad on board the train?' I asked.

'Black bread, and eggs swimming in oil. Make sure you buy your own food. I remember Ceri slapping my hand away from the Peek Freans, and screaming "Stop! We need to ration them!"' Mark sat back and looked out of the window. 'I also remember sending a message home to my dad asking him to meet me at the airport with Perrier and freshly squeezed orange juice, neither of which I could find in Russia. I still can't drink mango juice because it's all they had and it reminds me of that long,

long, long week. I did come back with a luxuriant rabbit fur hat though.'

The thought of five days on board a train eating nothing but black bread, oily eggs and biscuits, drinking nothing but mango juice, was enough to make me nauseous, and I made a mental note to stock up on food before boarding the Trans-Mongolian.

'My lasting memory of the trip was how fucking depressing Moscow is. The city, I understand, is still a shithole. I've not been able to bring myself to go back since. One of the history studies group wrote a feature about it, and it ran as a full page in the *Daily Mail*. I have it somewhere.'

A few nights later, Jem and I were lying like dead fish, rocking in the darkness as the train from Riga sped towards Moscow. My blanket drawn up to my chin, I stared at the berth above my head where a skinhead in a vest was asleep, his wrist hanging over the side. It was almost the girth of my thigh. Staring at the wrist as it swung with the motion of the train, I began to dread the next few days, praying that Mark was wrong about Moscow. He hadn't been there for almost thirty years and it had to have changed since then.

Neither of us slept, knowing that we would soon be arriving at the border for customs and passport checks, but we were too scared to talk in case we woke our companion. Slowing for what felt like an eternity, the train finally creaked and juddered to a halt. Muffled voices and footsteps approached immediately, and a torch flashed through the window. A woman screamed as a German shepherd straining on a leash came panting up the aisle, throttling itself, lurching up at Jem, then snuffling around my berth. Jem froze against the wall, his blankets on the floor. A torch shone into my eyes, and a voice said something I couldn't understand. Handing over our passports, we sat still as the dog tugged at the leash, and another pair of footsteps clumped up the aisle. A guard stopped at our berths, crossed both forearms in the air and gestured for us to get up. Throwing all our bedding to the ground, he lifted up the berths, checked inside to where our bags were stored and rummaged around before signalling for us to move back. Returning our passports, the first guard gave us both one last look, then tugged at the dog and moved on to the next carriage.

'We were the only people they checked,' whispered Jem.

'We're the only brown people on board,' I whispered back.

Jem's hands were like ice. He hated dogs, and although I adored them, even I had felt my bowels loosen at the heat and smell of the sniffer dog's saliva in my face. As the train squealed and began to move on into Russia, the snores from above deepened, and I eventually turned on my side and allowed myself to fall asleep. We'd wanted adventure, and I could tell it was about to begin.

2

A Small World

Bombing trains is rife in Moscow. Commuter services and
metro carriages are prime targets, particularly new stock that has
just been rolled into use. It takes nerve, skill and speed to bomb
trains: there's a high risk of being arrested, but the adrenaline rush
and respect from other crews fuels the addiction. Planning takes
precision. Crews check police schedules, study train timetables,
and scout out hiding places, plotting escape routes in case things
go wrong. One grey afternoon, we got bombed on the way
back from Kubinka to Moscow. Groaning to a halt in between
stations, the train was seized by masked men who scaled the sides
with SAS stealth, bolting from one end of the carriage to the
other. Amid the faint rattle and hiss of spray cans, I could smell
the fumes of fresh paint. Before we realised what was happening,
the train's guards jumped down and chased them away, but not
before the group had tagged the carriage with chunky neon
letters spiked with black.

Russian graffiti writers are part of a growing community of
street artists, many of whom use their work to express their
dissidence. Government authorities are quick to conceal the art,
which makes train-bombing more attractive to writers who use
the carriages as mobile galleries, watching with pride as their
work tours the city. The ubiquity of graffiti by train lines never
failed to darken my mood as we crossed the country. From time
to time I would spy a wittily placed tag, but overall it rarely
extended beyond misogyny or vandalism – the adult equivalent
of using a compass to scratch a cock and balls into a school desk.

As we waited for the train to proceed, I noticed – alongside a bulging, angry 'SLUT' – the same UTOP tag that had appeared a number of times along the route. Wondering if it was a political movement or the Russian slang for whore, I looked it up and found a two-minute music video of the UTOP crew, in which the writers used power tools and metal cutters to remove a grille and drop into a metro tunnel. Overnight they painted an entire carriage orange, writing their name in neat, bold lettering, with a pair of eyes peering cheekily through a slit. Not only did they document themselves at work, they made sure that one of their crew was on the platform the next morning to film the train arriving in all its glory. Considering the potential repercussions at the hands of the Russian government, it was an impressive stunt.

That morning, we'd taken the commuter service to Kubinka to visit Patriot Park, Putin's latest provocation. Dubbed a 'military Disneyland', the park had opened two days earlier and had been featured on news around the world, with footage of children clambering over tanks, missiles, and rocket-propelled grenade launchers. It had looked like the ideal way to spend a couple of hours, so we had taken the metro to Belorussky station, an asylum-green kingdom of domes and spikes, and caught the train seconds before it left. At once I knew that we were making a mistake: the inside looked like an old school bus, with seats harder than concrete, and faces harder than the seats. Even the rust flaked with rust. We ought to have abandoned the trip, but the whole point of travel is to do things you would never normally do, so the fatalist in me sat tight as the train creaked and left the station. For the next hour we passed unbearable poverty, rolling by rough sleepers, hungry-looking children and makeshift homes covered in plastic. Unsure if these were Russians or Ukrainian refugees who'd fled the violence in Donetsk and Luhansk, I sank into my seat, the unease growing in direct proportion to our distance from Moscow.

Life had not been kind to people here, their knuckles cut and calloused by labour, their slip-on shoes unfit for the rain. Pale eyes stared out of bloodless faces – not subtle glances, but fixed, purposeful staring. Folded arms revealed fading green tattoos; downturned mouths were marked with cold sores. Shrinking myself into a corner, I stared out of the window, avoiding eye contact, wishing we'd stayed in the capital. Over an hour and a half, the crowded carriage dwindled to two men and an old woman. Dressed in vests and tracksuit bottoms, the men turned around every few minutes, wrapping biceps around the back of the seats as they watched us.

'Should we change carriages?' Jem whispered.

'Maybe. I'm praying they get off first.'

'At least the old lady is still in here. They won't do anything if she's sitting behind us.'

I glanced round to look at her. 'She hasn't moved for an hour and I think she's soiled herself.'

The train slowed and I saw with relief that the platform of Kubinka station was approaching. Wailing and banging her head back and forth on the seat in front of her, the woman had woken up and begun hurling indiscriminate abuse, urine puddling around her feet. The men were the least of our problems, but as we crossed the footbridge they followed closely, spitting at my legs as they passed.

'Why are we here? Let's just get the train back to Moscow,' I said, stepping over the glob.

'We've come this far, let's find the park, have a quick nose round, then head back. We can take an Uber back to Moscow if you like.'

No one seemed to have heard of 'Patriot Park'. Even though the Russian translated as 'Park Patriot' and we'd written down the Cyrillic, wilful ignorance – paired with open hostility – made our attempt to find a taxi impossible, until a driver in fatigues herded us into the back of his car and sped off towards the motorway.

'Is this an actual taxi?' Jem asked, scrabbling for the seatbelt. 'There's no meter.'

'I'm too scared to ask.'

The driver seemed to know where he was going and accelerated down the slip road and onto the motorway, weaving around cars, tearing past trucks and lorries, before turning around to ask questions in Russian. With nothing but a free app downloaded onto his iPhone, Jem attempted to hold it against the driver's ear. Smacking away the phone with a paw-like hand, he pulled off onto a road that led to a huge car park.

'Park Patriot,' he said, slamming the brakes.

There was nothing to see but a convention centre and a couple of tanks. Strains of communist music played through speakers.

'This can't be the place, there's nothing here.'

'Park Patriot,' he repeated, thumping the steering wheel with each syllable. Throwing open the door, the driver lumbered off as though looking for information, then disappeared into a pink portaloo.

'Shall we sack it off and go back to the station?'

'Probably best.'

Wiping his hands on his shirt, the driver got back in and tore away from the kerb, careering around the empty car park. Leaning forward with his app, Jem asked the driver to go back to the station.

'Electrician?' he asked.

'No. Station. Train,' said Jem, making wheel motions with his arms.

'Electrician?' the driver shouted, turning a purplish hue.

Jem turned around. 'Why does he keep saying electrician?'

'I have no idea, let's just go back to the station.'

Holding up a finger and nodding, the driver appeared to have got the message and swung out of the car park and back onto the motorway as Jem yanked his seatbelt back on. 'What's this weird add-on bit on the belt? It looks like it's been ...'

'Cut out by emergency services?'

'That's what I was thinking.'

Our driver overtook every car in sight, then cut across three lanes, clipping the bumper of a Lada as we veered off onto a slip road.

'He's going to kill us,' Jem said.

'Hang on, we didn't come this way.'

Bumping down a dirt track flanked by fields, our driver had brought us to the nearby Kubinka Tank Museum. As the taxi pulled up outside, we wound down the window and saw a shirtless teenager on a stool having his head shaved. A couple of girls were selling Stalin and Lenin fridge magnets.

'Right, we're going back to the station,' I said.

'Electrician?'

'Why does he keep saying electrician?!'

'I have no idea, but make the train gesture and maybe he'll get it.'

Muttering, the driver reversed, almost hitting a small girl on her bike, then sped back to the station where he pulled up in front of a stall, knocking over the awning. He turned around with barely concealed fury as the shop owner banged on the windscreen. Activating the central locking system, he flashed his hands twice.

'Jesus, he wants 2,000 roubles.'

'Give him three if it means we get out in one piece.'

Counting out the notes, Jem handed over an extra 500 and the locks popped up. A crowd had gathered behind the shop owner, who wrenched open the passenger door as we scrambled out and ran towards the platform where the train back to Moscow was already waiting.

That evening, we sat in bed reading all the hype on Patriot Park. The park was still under construction and was currently being used as a venue to hold conferences and exhibitions; the footage had come from 'Army-2015', nothing more than a military exhibition that showcased equipment. However, in the process of our research we came across a word of warning on the Kubinka Tank Museum website:

A difficult system of the local trains network and the lack of ads in Russian can lead to the fact that a tourist without knowledge of Russian language can be in a different location remote from Moscow. Sometimes being in the platform of the RR station and even inside of the local train wagons (*elektrichka*) as unaccompanied way may not be safe. Especially the Asian type tourists from China, Malaysia, Japan. Foreigners are very attracted to crime. For your security it is recommended to use a Russian speaking escort or the car with the English speaking driver (or guide).

Jem stared at me. 'Foreigners are very attracted to crime?'

'I think it means foreigners are a clear target.'

'Could you not have found this before we set off?'

'You're only half Malaysian.'

'Great, so we had only half a chance of being victims of racist crime.'

'Ha! He wasn't saying "electrician" he kept saying *elektrichka*, which is the commuter train.'

'Don't dodge the topic.'

'I'm not. Anyway, I wouldn't worry about it, from tomorrow we'll be fine. The Trans-Siberian is famous; there'll be plenty of foreigners on it.'

'You are the first English people I have ever met on board this train,' said Aleksandr. 'And you are the first English people that *he* has ever met on board this train,' he continued, pointing to his room-mate, who was also called Aleksandr.

That afternoon we had boarded the Trans-Siberian, the godfather of trains. Strictly speaking the Trans-Siberian is not a train, but a route, spanning more than 5,700 miles from Moscow to Vladivostok. Featuring high on bucket lists, the train is the benchmark by which rail enthusiasts measure one another. If you say you haven't taken it – but that you will one day – their eyes glaze over as you cease to exist. In fact, we were travelling on the Trans-Mongolian, a more interesting route that drops down through Mongolia and ends in Beijing. Riding all the way to Vladivostok held no appeal other than that we could then tell people we'd ridden all the way to Vladivostok. There was nothing we wished to see at the end of the line, and the last thing we wanted to do once we'd arrived was turn around and come back. On the other hand, the Trans-Mongolian opened up far more opportunities for onward travel than simply wandering around the edge of the world map looking at Orthodox churches. We'd already stood in awe overlooking the Disneyland domes of St Basil's Cathedral on Red Square, and from then on, all other architecture was underwhelming. In spite of being one of the most familiar images in existence, the presence of the colourful domes – like big beautiful swirls of gelato – striped, latticed and topped with gold crosses, was glorious to behold. Via the Trans-Mongolian route, Jem and I could break up the journey in Irkutsk for two nights, then carry on to Ulaanbaatar in Mongolia, before eventually arriving in Beijing – eleven days after leaving Moscow.

After our first Russian train experience, we had boarded the Trans-Mongolian with trepidation, anticipating a mix of Russians, backpackers, students, weirdos, train geeks, and retired couples ticking off their bucket list. Met with familiar stares, we quickly realised we were the only foreigners on board. Having looked through travel-agency photos of the 'Rossiya' service, we'd expected air-conditioned cars with soft berths, power sockets and flat-screen TVs, only to find ourselves staring down a grubby hard sleeper with a broken window and a condom wrapper under the seat.

No one else entered our compartment until early evening, when a middle-aged man with grey hair and a slight squint had looked inside the door. Carrying a small gym bag and a black case, he'd placed them underneath his berth and then, ignoring us both, sat by the window staring at birch trees for four hours. As a gesture of goodwill, we had bought him a Magnum ice cream, which he accepted, then laid on the table in front of him. We'd sat at the edge of the berth quietly licking our own ice creams, wondering what would happen next. The temperature was pushing forty degrees and the ice cream began to melt. Few exercises were as excruciating as sitting in silence, watching a rejected ice cream melting. To give him space, we'd taken ourselves off to the dining car, returning an hour later, only to find the Magnum exactly where he'd left it, weeping into a wet patch. He hadn't even thrown it away, leaving it as a silent, but clear, rejection of friendship. Taking out his phone, Jem opened up his Russian-language app and tried to chat to our companion, who had misunderstood everything we had tried to say, and in reply, taken out his own phone to show us photographs of him carrying a hunting rifle. We soon began to wonder what was in the black case.

It was at that moment that 'Aleksandr I' had peered into our compartment and bellowed: 'Do you have a problem?' Convinced that if we didn't before, we certainly did now, I shrank at the sight of this blond giant in an Adidas vest. It turned out that Aleksandr II had walked past the door and seen us trying to use the app to chat to our room-mate. Knowing that Aleksandr I spoke English, he had sent him to our compartment to help us translate. Trouble averted, we then caused a genuine fight by offering to buy the Aleksandrs a couple of pints by way of thanks; the gesture implied that we thought they were too poor to afford their own drinks. Cultural differences settled, all four of us then moved to the dining car where we were now forging a friendship over tankards of Hoegaarden, pleased to be free of our room-mate. Aleksandr I and Aleksandr II were amused to see us on board their train, confirming our suspicions that we had indeed been booked onto the slower, poor-quality service for Russians – our home for the next five days.

Aleksandr I was a young lawyer who used the train to attend court hearings in Kirov once every two weeks, a seasoned traveller on this route. He was translating for Aleksandr II who was on his way home to see family in Chita. Over the jarring sound of techno-house, I strained to catch the discussion between the two men – not that I stood to glean much, knowing fewer than four Russian words, but it catered to the illusion that I was involved in the conversation. An elderly waitress named Oksana had taken a shine to me and Jem. Each time she wheeled her trolley past our table, she reached out to stroke my hair, before shouting and shaking a finger at the Aleksandrs.

'Why is she angry?' I asked.

'She thinks that because you are buying us drinks we are taking advantage of you. She is telling us not to scam you,' said Aleksandr I.

Relieved to have an ally on board, I smiled at Oksana who flashed a toothy grin then snarled at the Aleksandrs. 'Please tell her that's not the case.'

'I can't say anything more. Anyway, what would you like to discuss? What would you like to know about Russian people?'

'What's the Russian opinion of English people?' Jem asked.

'That is direct. You want to know the popular opinion? Okay. Britain is a very conservative country, pro-America, with an arrogant opinion towards any other country, even within the European Union. The UK is portrayed like a spy of the USA inside the EU, placed to split the European nations.'

This, too, was direct – and frighteningly incisive given that the Brexit vote was yet to take place. Aleksandr II was slumped on the table mumbling into his folded arms.

'He is very frustrated that he cannot talk to you,' explained Aleksandr I. 'He makes a joke, he wants to know if you are English spies.'

'They would never let me be a spy. I talk too much,' I replied.

Aleksandr II picked his ear and frowned, before asking a long and detailed question. Compared to Aleksandr I, he was tiny, with deep-set suspicious eyes and a thin mouth. In the sweltering June heat, he too was wearing an Adidas top, and sliders.

'He wants to know where you stayed in Moscow,' said Aleksandr I.

'Are you sure that's all he asked?'

'Mostly, yes.'

'The Mercure in Baumanskaya.'

'And what was the price of the hotel per day?'

'About £35?'

'In roubles, he wants to know.'

'Why?'

'He says to me he is "just interested".'

'About 2,800?'

Aleksandr II looked satisfied enough, then tapped Aleksandr I on the arm. Another long discussion ensued while Oksana settled herself at the opposite table scowling at the pair and slapping the table with her serving cloth. Aleksandr I exhaled, then smiled: 'How do you like our President Putin? This is his question. He wants to know what your impression is.'

Over the next three hours Aleksandr II managed to find out where I bought my watch; our mortgage repayments; how schools cleared snow in winter; the price of a butcher's chicken; whether village football was popular among local people; and why the English were so uptight. In return we learnt that he was a freight-train engineer from Chita. If anyone at the table worked in intelligence, it certainly wasn't us. Preferring to fade into the background and observe, I embraced the ambassadorial nature of our role; Aleksandr II had never met an English person on board the train and he was as interested in us for his own ends, as I was interested in him for mine. Satisfied, and clearly the worse for wear, he swirled the dregs of his third pint, whereupon a woman came up to the table and shook him by the shoulder. Her messy bun was wet with sweat, her face puffy and pink, as though she'd been sleeping. Shrugging off her hand, Aleksandr II dismissed her, but not before she'd slung a few insults. I didn't need to speak Russian to know abuse when I heard it. Rolling his eyes, he grumbled into his glass.

'His girlfriend is angry that he is sitting here with us and she is left alone, and he is drinking, and it is just a tragedy,' explained Aleksandr I.

'He left her alone? I didn't realise he was travelling with anyone.'

'Yes, they are two, and there is another girl in our compartment travelling on her own.'

'I feel so guilty.'

'Don't feel guilty, it's okay. He wants to stay here and talk to you. He says he will not quarrel with his girlfriend if he stays here.'

Based on the shouting from their compartment that night, this was not true.

An hour after we had ordered them, a plate of chips arrived on a saucer, drowned in oil and draped with dill. Food was not the train's high point and this was more a drinking car than a dining car, but at least there was more to eat than black bread and oily eggs. With its red fairy lights, red booths, and Eurodance on a loop, the car had the seediness of a Soho basement bar, the kind you end up in at the end of the night after exhausting efforts to find anywhere better. Anyone who actually wanted to eat had set up picnics in their compartments, the tables piled with fruit, cartons of juice, and dried omul fish wrapped in paper, a local favourite. A fishy fug hung around the corridor from the yellowing omul, which was long and narrow as though ironed into strips. After his fourth pint, Aleksandr II stumbled off for a cigarette. Smoking was banned on the train, but everyone smoked – from the passengers hanging out of windows, to cooks lighting up off the hobs. Aleksandr I pulled back the curtains and peered into the darkness.

'He jokes that I have a lot of state secrets because I work in prosecution, and he thinks I'm going to reveal it to you. He is worried that you are a spy.'

'Is he, or are you?'

'I am not worried.'

I wasn't sure whether his response was a compliment or an insult. 'Do people use the trains a lot?'

'Yes, Russian people use the trains a lot. After travelling by car, trains are the second. This is a normal train for us, without it many of us can do nothing.'

'Is this considered a comfortable train?'

'This train is trash! In my opinion this train is terrible. I hate it. I hate to travel to Kirov because this train is bad. You are crazy to use this train.'

Aleksandr II returned with an SLR camera and pointed at my notebook.

'He likes your handwriting, he thinks it is very beautiful,' said Aleksandr I. 'He asks if he can photograph it.'

Impressed by his ingenuity, I was about to respond when Aleksandr II grabbed the notebook, turned it around, and began photographing the pages as though documenting a crime scene. Far from exposing state secrets, all he would discover – if he bothered to translate the pages – were a few tedious descriptions of birch trees and some pretentious notes about how humans evolved with the landscape.

From across the car, an old man in a muscle vest approached and leant over our table. Taking my hand, he performed a lengthy monologue before kissing the back of it, then retreated to his table where he continued to stare over his cans of Stella.

'What was that about?' I asked.

'He is welcoming you,' said Aleksandr I. 'It is a way of telling you that you are welcome in Russia and welcome on the trains.'

'That's nice,' said Jem, smiling at the man.

Overcome with emotion, Aleksandr II suddenly jumped up and shook both our hands before drawing us in for hugs, smiling for the first time. He smelt of stale beer and fresh sweat, leaving a wet patch on my cheek. From over his shoulder I saw Oksana shaking her head.

Exhausted, we went back to our compartment where I dug out a bowl of instant noodles, then stood in the corridor filling it with boiling water. Each carriage was fitted with a samovar that was perfect for making tea and noodles, soaking flannels, and exchanging gossip. Jem went off to clean his teeth while I waited for the bowl to cool. Just then, the connecting door opened and the hand-kisser came through and took my hand again, a borscht stain down his front. Smiling politely, but warily, I pulled away as he reached for the second time, gripping my wrist and kissing my forearm. My instinct was to fling the boiling noodles on him, but I was hungry and didn't want to waste them. Panicked, I used my free arm to hammer on the carriage guard's door, just as the man seized me around the waist. Our guard, or *provodnik*, was a friendly chap with a lisp, incidentally also called Aleksandr – or Sasha, for short. He and I had spent the afternoon swapping coin souvenirs from different countries. I prayed that he was in his compartment. Sasha opened the door and prised the man's fingers from my wrist with a reflex that suggested this was not his first time dealing with gropers. Placing a hand on the opposite wall, Sasha pushed himself between us and pointed down the corridor. The man hovered with a pout, refusing to go; until Sasha shouted one last warning, at which point he threw up his hands and flounced off to his carriage. Grateful for the intervention, I ducked into our compartment to find the last of the English money I was carrying. Finding nothing smaller than a ten-pound note, I took it next door to Sasha.

'*Nyet, nyet, nyet*, no, no,' he said.

'Souvenir,' I said. 'Charles Dickens.'

His face lit up. 'Haaaaaa! Okay! Rouble rouble!' he said, passing me a calculator. I tapped in the exchange rate as he watched closely, his mouth wide. 'Waaaaah!'

'Souvenir,' I warned.

'Yus, yus,' he said, beaming at the note.

There was no way that he would keep 800 roubles as a souvenir, but it was his to do as he pleased with. Ten pounds was a worthwhile tip for a harassment-free five days.

That night I lay in my berth, seething. Had I sent out the wrong signal by allowing the man to kiss my hand? Could he not see I was with Jem? Did he consider it a challenge? When travelling alone I usually dressed as demurely as a Victorian maid, averting my eyes and keeping my nose in a notebook, but the nature of my work impelled me to engage, to be open and approachable. On my travels around India I'd often been harassed – which was never my fault – yet the onus always fell on women to protect ourselves, to dress down, cover up, look away, keep off the streets, go home early, stay in after dark, travel with a chaperone. No one ever told the men not to grope, not to stare, not to touch, not to follow women, and not to rape. The injustice tied my nerves in knots. This was why so few women explored the world with the freedom and abandon of men: they were far too frightened of what might happen at the hands of one of them.

It was Tuesday evening, our second on board the train, and we were now sharing with a Dutch father and son duo named Franz and Rens, who had joined us at Yekaterinburg. Out of the purple flash of an electrical storm, they had appeared in the doorway, water pooling around their boots. Rens had just finished his degree, and the two were on a six-week bonding trip, travelling by train from Amsterdam to Beijing. Franz and Rens were full of fun, and thanks to them we were now sharing traveller tales over metal mugs of Nescafé, fresh bagels, and cups of tiny, sweet strawberries we'd bought on the platform at Perm. They were serious travellers – staying only with Russian families with allotments – and were happy to share ice cream. Subsequently, after our evening of bonding, Aleksandr I had got off at Kirov, and Aleksandr II had spent most of the night arguing with his girlfriend, the rest of the night being sick, and the next four days ignoring us.

'The Trans-Siberian was never meant to be about luxury among a travelling elite intent on sipping champagne in a spectacular wilderness. It was to facilitate the resettlement of Russian peasants to Siberia. Did you know that between 1891 and 1914 over five million new immigrants sought a better future there?' asked Jem.

'Did you? Or are you just reading out loud from Rens's guidebook?'

Jem peered up from his berth. 'I might be. At least we know we're taking the appropriate peasant service instead of some fancy fake tourist trap.' He pressed open the page and read on. 'It used to be known as "track of the camel" because it wound and bypassed so many towns and ran through the middle of nowhere.'

'I don't like that term,' said Rens, retying his pony tail. 'It's only city people who say "middle of nowhere". It's so presumptive.'

'Like "lost" tribes,' said Franz, making air quotes with his fingers.

I'd never really considered what was a flippant and commonly used phrase, but now that I thought about it, 'the middle of nowhere' was loaded with disdain. Nowhere was only nowhere from the perspective of those who didn't live there. But for those who did, nowhere was home. From my berth, I had spent most of the day staring out of the window, the monotony of the countryside broken up by smatterings of villages that had names, shops, schools, communities. The phrase chimed with the same arrogance as 'lost' tribes, who were only lost insofar as the Western world hadn't yet succeeded in arriving on their shores to haggle for hand-woven rugs and rate their local brew. Assuming these tribes were sitting around all day waiting to be discovered by some Old Harrovian striding along with messy hair and malaria, was conceited at best and reckless at worst. They were evidently content in their habitation, having chosen not to venture further afield. Guiltily, I made a note not to use the phrase again.

Taking temperatures to both extremes, Siberia's heat was crippling. The air conditioning barely functioned and the windows served only to channel hot air into the compartments. Tangled in damp sheets, I spent a lot of the journey lying limply, watching leafless trees roll past like rows of unsharpened pencils. Every few hours a farmhouse or two would appear with a Lada parked outside. Scarecrows tilted in potato patches and dirt tracks wound into woods. Having picked up our location on Google Maps in Moscow, I followed the blue sphere as it bobbed across blank territory. It was as though we were crossing a hinge in the earth. By air, the notion of being in-between was constant, but by rail there were always villages, towns and seas emerging like stepping stones between destinations. Neither west, nor east, we were hurtling through the borderlands.

At dusk, halos of mist swirled above ground, orbiting forests like a magical force. Five days on board a continuous train had presented the rare opportunity to read great tomes, and in keeping with our surroundings, I'd downloaded *War and Peace*, *Crime and Punishment* and *Young Stalin* onto my Kindle, hoping to emerge in China a more refined and cultured person. But each time I began *War and Peace*, the heat and the swaying did nothing but lull me to sleep: I never made it past the list of Kuragins before dropping off.

Between Moscow and Irkutsk, the train stopped at around eighty stations, for no more than two minutes at a time, with the odd one-hour break when the toilets were bolted and anyone inside was collared and hauled out to continue their ablutions on the platform. This was usually Jem, who picked inopportune moments to clean his teeth, and was left spitting Sensodyne in between the tracks. For the rest of us, these hour-long stops presented an opportunity to break free from the tedium, to stretch our legs, and to remember that a world existed beyond the four corners of our compartment, which had begun to smell like an old laundry basket. Russian stations are handsome affairs: painted peppermint with white piping and adorned with old clock towers. Wandering from one buxom babushka to the next, I'd buy a hunk of cheese or cake, or pass the time watching large women in tiny shorts selling rows of omul fish bunched like keys and hooked through the eyes. At one such stop I rifled through the trolley of a lady too busy chatting to a friend to bother with me, and offered her 90 roubles (£1) for a pack of playing cards. She laughed in my face, nudging her friend, who also laughed in my face. Even her son, who was sitting in the bottom of the trolley, covered his eyes with disbelief that anyone would offer more than a cursory glance for what turned out to be a pack of thirty-six cards.

By Wednesday evening I'd stopped bothering to change my clothes or brush my hair, and lounged in my pyjamas in the drinking car where the air conditioning worked, and it was marginally cooler than the sun. Oksana kept bringing me plates of fried mushrooms covered in dill, patting my head and flapping her cloth at anyone who came near me; watching closely as an elderly man offered me cottage-cheese blinis, repulsed by my instant mash. She chatted in Russian, wholly unbothered that I replied in English, neither of us understanding the other, but happy in each other's company. Provodnik Sasha went to and fro presenting me with commemorative coins from the Sochi Winter Olympics and books left behind by passengers, until I'd gathered a small jumble sale of wares I could hawk. I was beginning to run out of things to offer in return, plying him with toothbrushes that Jem had collected from various hotels. The initial iciness with which the Russians greeted us had thawed, and as the miles accumulated, our shared experience of pleasures and pains spurred the natural symbiosis unique to train travel.

By Thursday afternoon I had lost all awareness of place and time, convinced it was Wednesday, comfortable in my ignorance. Two soldiers were playing cards at the next table, nursing the first bottle of vodka I'd seen since we boarded. Challenging us to a few shots, they chased each one with mouthfuls of Tropicana fruit juice, which defied the hardy Russian image I'd once feared. Swapping souvenirs, I gave them a couple of second-class Christmas stamps, and was amply rewarded with a smoke grenade. It went nicely with the gas mask Jem had stolen from our hotel in Moscow.

On Friday, we arrived in Irkutsk at dawn. Since Moscow we had passed through four time zones, yet every station's clock was set to Moscow Standard Time, and we were now jet-lagged and roaming around in a state of total disorientation.

'Mongolia doesn't look all that different from Russia,' said Jem.

'We're not in Mongolia.'

'I thought we were stopping in Ulaanbaatar?'

'We are, but not for another four days. We're in Irkutsk.'

'Where's Irkutsk?'

'Siberia. Russia.'

'We've been on the same train for five days and we're still in Russia?'

Like most tourists, we'd stopped in Irkutsk to visit Lake Baikal – the deepest, oldest and largest freshwater lake in the world. Franz and Rens had chosen to hike its longest trail, but considering the heat – which was even more vicious in the open – we were opposed to any activity more strenuous than sitting down, and chose to see the lake via the Circum-Baikal Railway, a fabulous old steam locomotive. After the first shower in five days, we had a breakfast of dumplings at the cafe over the road, then set off on foot past rows of shuttered wooden houses to take the local train to Slyudyanka from where the Circum-Baikal train departed. Passing through thirty-nine tunnels and crossing around 200 bridges, the train travelled around the oldest section of the Trans-Siberian railroad. However, we had passed no more than four tunnels and nine bridges before it broke down, conveniently overlooking a bay where we could skid down to the pebble beach and paddle in the icy water. Formed in the middle of a giant crack in the earth's crust – the Baikal rift – Lake Baikal is dubbed the 'Galápagos of Russia' by UNESCO, owing to the unique species of flora and fauna, most of which are endemic to the area. Scientists had predicted that one day the entire continent of Eurasia would split into two along the lake, and I hoped it wasn't today.

A couple of French tourists were skimming stones at the edge of the water, and never one to shy away from Anglo-French rivalry, Jem began to whip a few of his own, pleased at the way his stones bounced just a couple of times more than theirs did, before disappearing with a plop. But when the Russians stripped off and plunged in headfirst, he sat tight. Numb to the ankles, I watched the water twinkle in the light, green and blue hues bleeding into one another's paths. From time to time concentric circles emerged and expanded on the surface where freshwater seals turned somersaults. Dwarfed into insignificance, I clambered back up to where the train was beginning to exhale, pumped up and ready to go.

From across the bridge we could see the train on the platform, convinced it would leave for Ulaanbaatar without us. Staggering beneath the weight of our rucksacks, and breaking into short, pitiful sprints, we made it to the station with five minutes to spare and stumbled up the steps, each one blaming the other for the delay. As the train pulled out of the station, I leant back in what was a lovely, plush berth with carpets and air conditioning. We were now on board the Rossiya, the train we had expected to board in Moscow. There was something I knew I was supposed to do before we left Irkutsk. I racked my brain, then shrugged it off.

That night I awoke with a start and emptied my rucksack onto the floor. The soldiers had reminded us to get rid of the smoke grenade before crossing into Mongolia and I was now standing in my pyjamas staring at what looked like a tiny atom bomb in my grip. Wondering if I should leave it in the toilet, but knowing it would be discovered and cause a commotion, I wrenched open the window and tossed it out into the darkness, hoping for the best.

Now fully awake and curious about where we were, I eased the door ajar and slipped out into the corridor. I could hear the *provodnitsa* cackling with her pal, the Russian equivalent of Pat Butcher with an orange perm and a sneer, but everyone else was asleep. Holding back the curtain, I stilled my breath as a glow lit my face. It was 2 a.m. and the train was curving around the southernmost point of Lake Baikal, which shone like a spill of mercury. The sun had set hours earlier and I couldn't understand where the light was coming from. A strip of red sky lay against a sliver of silver lake as though fire danced on the water. I wanted to capture the moment and keep it alive, touching my head to the glass to bring it closer. Until now I had taken the train for granted, dismissing it as just another long-distance service to endure. But I saw now that this train carved up the earth, shining a light into its darkest corners. It unlocked the land and threw open the skies, revealing forests tall and fearful, the night gold and bright.

★

'Well, that was a total waste of time,' said Jem, banging the door and kicking off his shoes.

'Did you get the tickets?'

'No, they were sold out.'

'Then where have you been for the last hour?'

No one comes to Ulaanbaatar for a city break. Every summer the Mongol Rally lures petrolheads, students and adventurers who come careering in by jalopy, bringing tales of foreign police, bribes and breakdowns, while others arrive on the train, hostage to timetables that prevent exploration of the countryside. It was into the latter category that we fell, hoping to make the most of a two-day stopover. Our hotel was behind the opera house on Sukhbaatar Square, so we had decided to book tickets for *Swan Lake* with the help of our concierge, who had promised to take Jem there first thing, as soon as he finished his night shift. Jem had set his alarm, creeping out before breakfast, and he now looked thoroughly annoyed.

'Did he manage to help you?' I asked.

'I had to wait an hour for him to shower and change before he finally took me to the opera house, where they told us they'd sold out of tickets ages ago. He then said we didn't have to go to the opera and could do something else.'

'Like what?'

'No, we, as in he and I.'

'No!'

'I told him that I'd wanted two tickets to go to the opera with you, my fiancée, and he suddenly turned all cold and mean, and said: "That woman is your wife? Is she Indian? I've been to India, it's dirty, the people are dirty." He then walked me back to the hotel and said he had the day off, and asked if I wanted to go for breakfast.'

'Poor guy. He thought he had a date all lined up, and you broke his heart!'

Mongolia grew more intriguing by the minute. Until now, I'd expected steppes, gers, and men who looked like Genghis Khan; yet here was a city of skyscrapers, towering cranes and cruising concierges. Gold, copper and coal mining had spurred economic overdrive to the extent that new offices, condos and hotels appeared almost overnight. Here was Singapore in its infancy. Ulaanbaatar was apparently surrounded by mountains, none of which we could see through the yellowy cloud of smog blotting out the sky. Disappointed, we set off in search of anything ancient, finding a couple of scrappy Buddhist monasteries, subdued during Soviet rule. It took us a couple of hours in the National Museum of Mongolian History, looking at armour, costumes and jewellery, to gain any sense of the city's old culture, which had collapsed under the might of eleven KFCs and an IMAX. The rest of the afternoon was spent in shopping malls, trying on cashmere, and watching young Mongolians flirt and buy shoes. While the country's past was hard to fathom, its future was patently clear.

The following morning at breakfast we got chatting to Steve and Caroline from Cumbria, who had just returned from a weekend at a nomadic homestay and were aghast that we hadn't ventured further afield.

'You can't say you've been to Mongolia if you've not been riding on the steppe,' said Steve, his cheeks browned by windburn. He had on a tight Rip Curl surf top, and wore his sunglasses on the back of his head.

'How did you find out about your homestay?' I asked.

'Google.'

I didn't doubt that our opinion of Mongolia was cemented by a skewed first impression, but observing the evolution of the capital was more fascinating to me than riding horses. That afternoon, before the final leg to Beijing, we stopped at a restaurant called Modern Nomads, a popular chain where the staff dressed in warrior costumes. Sipping from a broth blobbed with fat, I looked around at the other diners drinking Johnnie Walker and watching bad music videos. Perhaps I had tasted only one slice of Mongolian life, but my experience was as genuine to me as Steve and Caroline's was to them. In a year, even six months, neither truth would be valid: here, in the city, hotels would multiply, bars would open, business would thrive, pollution would choke, and the population would explode. Meanwhile on the steppe, climate change would dominate, temperatures would rise, grass would dry up, livestock would die, and herders would migrate to the city. If we ever returned, this Mongolia would no longer exist, and another one would be waiting.

A slim man wearing a black T-shirt appeared in our doorway, looked in, then returned to the neighbouring compartment. 'Their bed looks loads more attractive without that blanket on it. Get it off.'

'You get it off,' said a second voice.

'Give me a hand at least.'

'This is amazing,' said the second voice. 'It's like moving from a maximum security prison to a low-level one. I'm actually allowed to operate my own fan and open my own window.'

'I wouldn't though, unless you want half the desert in here.'

'And look! Hang on, where's the toilet?'

'You're looking for a rabbit in a hat, mate, it's not there.'

'It's just a sink. If only it didn't smell like a Victorian sewer.'

Ed and Alex were two brothers travelling to Beijing. As a Christmas tradition, they treated each other to experiences instead of presents, and one had bought the other a trip on the Trans-Mongolian.

Having gradually upgraded along the route, Jem and I were now in first class for the final night, in a private compartment with red-velvet berths. This was also a Chinese train – which was infinitely nicer than the Russian ones. Pulling open the door that led to our shared bathroom, however, I immediately slammed it shut as the stench of urine soured our compartment.

'Shame we didn't keep that smoke grenade,' said Jem.

Ed appeared at the door again. 'You don't want to open that too much. I'm a bit worried about why it smells of piss when there's no actual toilet in there. Rest assured I won't be washing my hands in that sink.'

After leaving Ulaanbaatar we'd travelled through parched grassland where double-humped camels knelt by gers, smoke funnelling from the tops of the tents: round and white, the gers looked like giant cupcakes with candles. While the others got chatting, I sat by the window, looking out, waiting for the symmetry of sand dunes whipped into peaks by the wind, but they never came. The Gobi Desert here is flat and rocky, mottled by sad tufts of grass. Taking the train is the best way to cross any desert. Jeeps cause whiplash, and no one really wants to ride a camel for more than ten minutes. At least by train, you can speed across the whole expanse and be satisfied not to have missed anything, while escaping boredom, sunburn and saddle-sores. I was still marvelling at the notion that this desert would soon spill into China, when Ed appeared again, holding out a packet.

'Have some cheese.'

'Thanks,' said Jem, 'would you like a Kinder Bueno?'

'It's not prison, mate, you don't have to swap anything. Having said that, I'd give you five fags if you've got a cold beer on you? All I've got is a bottle of vodka and a satsuma ... to make the vodka taste, well, less so.'

Alex came in caressing a bottle of Sauvignon Blanc. 'This, is my baby,' he said. 'This cost me a fortune on the black market, and I'm going to put it in the fridge in the dining car and crack it open at the border.'

So far, customs and border crossings hadn't been a problem. During passport checks I'd increasingly been scrutinised as my miserable face became less and less recognisable beneath the accumulation of dirt and sweat. The sniffer spaniels had shown more interest in my instant noodles, panting at my lunch instead of looking for contraband and stowaways hiding beneath my berth. Otherwise we'd smiled, obliged demands, and listened for the thrilling scuffle of genuine criminals being hauled off the train. The five-hour crossing from Mongolia into China was almost as legendary as the train itself, and Jem had downloaded five episodes of *Game of Thrones* to see us through it. China and Mongolia use different rail gauges: Mongolia's broad gauge is 85 millimetres wider than China's standard gauge, a hangover from the Soviet era, and one that Mongolia refuses to cure. In a real-life version of *Game of Thrones*, Mongolian authorities considered the obstacle a necessity in hobbling the economic rise of its powerful neighbour – and one-time overlord. China was already the main recipient of Mongolia's exports, and threatened by its rise – and fearing dependency – Mongolia had resorted to an age-old tactic of statistical railway-building to scupper China's dominance. This meant that both passenger and freight trains had to wait on the border until the undercarriages – bogies – could be changed, a laborious process whereby the carriages were jacked up by hydraulic lifts, and the entire chassis slid out and a new one pulled into place. But China also played the game to its advantage: in 2002 the Dalai Lama had visited Mongolia and China had thrown a tantrum by blocking trains at the border for two days.

Curious about what the Chinese dining car had to offer, Ed, Alex, Jem and I sat down at a booth. Now that we were in first class, local people were conspicuously absent, the seats taken up by English people drinking from cans. The Chinese staff made no effort to hide their revulsion as passengers knelt up on seats, spilt food, and mimicked Chinese accents, sharing their most hostile experiences at the hands of foreigners. It was at times like these that I was embarrassed by my countrymen, who waited until they were abroad to show their worst. Lasting no more than five minutes, we extricated ourselves from the car and went back to enjoy the luxury of our compartment, but not before Alex had lovingly laid his wine to rest in the fridge.

'People keep looking at me,' said Jem, 'do you think they think I'm Mongolian?'

'I think it's because they've never seen anyone wearing pink swimming shorts and loafers in public.'

'I haven't been this high in ages … not since Dublin.' Ed was craning his neck out of the window and trying to film the engineers changing our chassis, blocking my camera with his elbow. It was around midnight and we were now in a shed just outside Erlian, around ten feet off the ground. So seamless was the movement that none of us had realised we were levitating until we looked down upon hard hats bobbing below. We had been suspended here for more than two hours, unable to get down to use the loo, and Alex was pacing around in a frenzy.

'No wonder that sink stinks. If we're not on the move soon, I'm going in.'

A horn rang out as a second train rolled into the station. 'Keep your horn for your wife, you dirty bastard,' yelled Ed. 'Wait, hang on, that's our dining car!'

'Fuck, it is as well,' said Alex, moving to the window.

A few hours earlier, the train had, for no clear reason, uncoupled from the dining car, and the four of us had watched as it rolled away up the tracks and into the distance. Convinced it would come back again, Alex had pawed at the circular window, whimpering with disbelief as his bottle of wine rolled away with it. Now, it had reappeared as if to taunt him, attached to another train. He cupped his hands around his mouth and hollered to where a couple were waving at us from their compartment.

'Can you check the fridge for a bottle of Sauvignon Blanc?'

The woman waved and laughed.

'No … no, seriously. It's in your fridge.'

Wrapped in our blankets, Jem and I went back to watching *Game of Thrones* as the train was slammed and jolted for the next hour. Suffering from cabin fever, Alex and Ed had made friends with a drunk Dutch schoolteacher named Max, and were now killing time by making phone calls to Max's wife in Leiden and pretending he'd been arrested on the border for possession of drugs.

Shunted out of the shed, the train eventually rolled across the border into Erlian where we were allowed to get down and wander around on the platform or stock up on Chinese vodka, noodles, juice and lychees at the station shop. Moonlit and quiet, it was a warm night, with a waltz playing over hidden speakers. Crouching on a wall, I watched passengers milling around in the dark, smoking and stretching, as I absorbed the enormity of what we had achieved. Over the previous eleven days the Trans-Mongolian had shown me that there were no real beginnings or endings, borders or boundaries. I'd watched lakes grow into seas, mountains rise then recede, deserts expand then shrink. Passengers had come and gone with a gradation of features that sharpened and darkened from one end of the line to the other. For days, the train's trajectory across space and wilderness had plagued me with a feeling of displacement, the state of being in between. But now, I had a greater sense of place than ever before, bearing witness to the truth that the world was small, close and connected.

Waking to the sound of Ed asking Alex why he had missed calls from a Dutch number, I sat up and shuffled to the window just in time to catch a glimpse of the Great Wall, a fine grey thread worming around the mountainside. Running a gauntlet of cliffs, the train had renewed vigour, thundering across bridges and gearing up as it rode the home stretch to Beijing. Snaking around rock faces, we bored into tunnels, round and black like surprised mouths swallowing us whole. Orchards huddled on the slopes, slipping down into the valleys, and muddy green rivers meandered around fishermen in bamboo hats. Women waved from the doorways of rhomboid houses, the roofs turned up like hems on dainty skirts. But the softness of the scene soon began to fade, and the harshness of steel and concrete loomed against a sickly-looking sky: billboards lined up, wires swung low, and buildings rushed towards the track as if to catch a glimpse of our arrival. Rolling into the station, the train came to a standstill, and we stepped onto the platform to where China was waiting.

3

From Hutongs to Hanoi

Unsure whether to scream, cry, laugh or put a stop to the ordeal, I held my breath and tensed as a pair of meaty palms slapped my buttocks. Pinching the base of my back, dry, rough fingers worked their way up to my neck as though playing piano scales on my spine. On the advice of my friend Jamie, who lived in Beijing, we were now lying in a row at Tang Massage in the city's Dongcheng district, trying to unwind after the journey. Having browsed through the list of treatments on offer – which included massages to soothe ovaries, boost fertility and cure insomnia – I had opted for a simple neck and back massage and was handed a pair of pink pyjamas, while Jamie and Jem were given blue ones. Each masseur or masseuse had a number so that clients could request the same one each time, and Jamie had fist-bumped his masseur like an old pal.

'Do they not use oil for their massages?' I asked, gathering my pyjamas as they trailed along the ground.

'No. It's all fluidless,' Jamie replied, shuffling into place. 'Well, depending on what kind of massage you want.'

Jamie was a friend from journalism school who had left a job at *NME* and moved to Beijing where he had embraced the expat lifestyle and forged a career writing about the Chinese experience, in between sitting in Australian-themed bars watching football. Over the previous two years his research had led to his being imprisoned in an internet-addiction clinic; strapping on a pair of lactating fake breasts at a class for men

43

to understand childbirth; and visiting an acupuncture clinic for crippled cats and dogs – including a French bulldog named King Kong that had successfully regained control of his bladder after suffering a herniated disc. Cock-a-hoop from the previous week's interview with the dissident artist Ai Weiwei, Jamie had met us at the station, hands stuffed in his pockets, bag strapped across his chest, looking thoroughly out of place. Tall and lanky with wispy blond hair like a young Sting, Jamie was easy to spot in a city where tall, lanky Sting lookalikes were rare. As such, his journalism was not the only business in operation: the novelty of Jamie's aesthetics had opened up the world of Chinese dating apps, and judging by the buoyancy in his step, he'd completed Tinder in Beijing, and was now working his way through the suburbs.

Our three masseurs came back into the room and I watched their feet moving around under the table, listening with mild embarrassment as Jem and Jamie were thumped and pummelled in a blur of pleasure and pain. The two were meeting for the first time, forced into bonding over the shared experience of hearing each other's involuntary grunts and groans.

'I wish there was a beer under here with a straw poking through,' said Jamie, who was lying to my right. 'Or a person holding it for me, but not making eye contact or anything so it's not awkward.'

'Do you come here often?' I asked.

'Christ, what a line: is that how she got you, Jeremy? Once a week probably.'

'Sorry, it's not very relaxing if I'm talking,' I replied.

'No, I like being talked to. Otherwise I only have this guy to chat to in my amazing Chinese, and I don't think he's really into football.'

'What's his name?'

'No idea. I just know him as '14': 14's awesome.'

While the three of us chatted, 14 and his friends were carrying on their own conversation above our heads, turning the whole affair into a mutually beneficial one. Soon, the feeling of having my pyjamas rubbed into my skin turned from chafing to burning, and I yelped in pain.

'If it hurts, just say "aaaaaaaaaaaaaaaaaaaa-ow",' said Jamie, 'that means "ow". That's one of the first things I learnt when I got here.'

Beijing was the first city in which I had felt lost. Smoking, sprawling, crawling, built up, and bound by ring roads and tangles of motorway, Beijing was like a city of cities. Thick with fumes, the air tasted of oil and exhausts, reaching into my throat and coating my tongue. A Dickensian smog obscured buildings, crept over walls and swirled around lamp posts. Despite snippets of English on road signs, it was futile to guess the correct intonation and impossible to explain anything to taxi drivers, who made a habit of avoiding foreigners; assuming – often correctly – that they didn't speak Chinese, drivers of empty taxis would wave away desperate passengers, knowing that their journey would be spent in frustration, driving round in circles, reversing down dead ends, and arguing with ever-increasing volume. The key was to keep the address written on paper in Chinese or to show them a photograph of the destination and nearby landmarks. Ordering food was a hit-and-miss affair. I wanted to eat where local people ate, but that meant staring longingly at their plates, pointing and doodling pencil sketches of chickens and pigs for the staff to understand what we wanted. Being rendered impotent by language was humbling. Almost everywhere I'd travelled in the world, everyone from street kids to elderly rickshaw drivers could speak enough English to hold a decent and entertaining conversation that usually covered Premier League football teams, Bollywood movies, and various English friends they had in Manchester. Shamed by the imperialist arrogance with which the English still expected the rest of the world to speak their tongue, I could see that most Chinese had no need or desire to speak English, and were perfectly fine without it. That morning, we'd set out on foot to find the Forbidden City, and returned two hours later having managed to get no further than buying bubble tea and a cardigan from Zara.

After our massage, Jamie wanted to take us for a Sichuan hot-pot dinner – where the staff spun fresh noodles into skipping ropes – and began the task of hailing a cab. Lingering at the side of the road, we watched in disbelief as more than eleven empty taxis drove past, swerving to avoid him as he walked into moving traffic, silhouetted by the glare of angry headlamps. Drivers pounded their horns and slammed their brakes; bikes wobbled around him. With determination etched across his face, Jamie leant through open windows like a gigolo, his jaw muscle flinching as each taxi drove on. Intent on proving to his visitors that two years in China hadn't been a total waste of time, he finally yanked open a door and got in, belting up and signalling for us to do the same, ignoring the driver's protests. Once you were in, there was little they could do but take you to your destination. Jumping in to avoid being run over, we sat quietly in the back as the driver ranted, and Jamie sighed with relief.

Ashamed by our poor attempt to negotiate Beijing, I conceded that a guided tour would be the fastest way to learn about the city – which went against my every instinct. On a good day, guided tours were hell on earth: I hated being part of a conspicuous crowd, unable to move at my own pace, and would invariably drop off along the way to rummage through a market or sniff around a cul-de-sac. Tour groups to my mind comprise people who lack the initiative to discover a new place, relying on parroted information that may or may not be true. These are the same people who take cruises, happy to be herded on and off a boat, then bussed around like schoolchildren, reassured by the knowledge that wherever they go is pre-paid and safe for consumption. However, casting an eye around the streets of Beijing did nothing to reveal the layers of stories and cultural oddities. Everything from the colours of gates, heights of buildings and markings on doors, was loaded with historical significance that only a scholar could explain. On an unusually clear morning, we met Jamie by the ancient Drum and Bell

Towers to take a walking tour of the *hutongs* – the network of alleyways that made up some of the city's oldest neighbourhoods.

Our guide for the day was a Dane named Lars Ulrik Thom of 'Beijing Postcards', a two-man company that had started by selling old photographs and postcards to galleries that they'd dug up in flea markets, then expanded into giving lectures and walking tours, constructing as clear an image of history as possible through archival research and interviews with the *hutongs'* elderly residents. Lars had spread out a map of the old city on the ground and was standing in the middle of it when we arrived, a number of local Chinese lining the edges making notes, a fat, smiley baby in a pushchair looking on. A series of narrow, mainly residential streets, the *hutongs* were understood to have taken their name from the Mongol word for a street that led to a water well, but Lars was convinced that the name described the width required to ensure that fires couldn't spread along the alley. At no point more than ten-people wide, some tapered so dramatically that only one bike could fit through at a time.

After the Mongols were displaced from power, the capital was moved from Nanjing to Beijing and the city was built from scratch, with strict rules in place for how the *hutongs* were to be constructed: everything in the inner city was laid in straight lines and no one could build or decorate anything bigger or more colourful than the Forbidden City – which explained the *hutongs'* grey palette, a deliberate choice to indicate their subordination. Unless associated with the emperor, nobody could lay golden tiles on their roofs, and gates were typically painted black, green or red. After 1949, and the communist takeover, everything was re-painted red.

Pausing outside an old military home, Lars pointed to the stones that varied in size depending on the rank and status of the officer. Square stones were meant to resemble bookcases to show that the officer had passed the imperial examinations. The particular home outside which we were now standing had no gate, owing to its conversion into a public toilet. In preparation for the 2008 Olympics, the Chinese government had initiated a complete overhaul of the city, constructing, deconstructing and reconstructing in an attempt to beautify Beijing, and had decided that there should be a public toilet every 800 metres – which explained the ubiquity of the reeking buildings. The *hutongs* were no longer purely residential, crammed with craft shops, vegetable sellers, roast ducks hanging by their necks, and artisanal coffee shops that refused to serve milk or sugar. Every few hundred yards we found old bikes or single chairs apparently tossed into the middle of the lane, but on closer inspection they had been chained to the ground like Turner Prize submissions. It was a way for residents to stake a claim to parking spaces and ensure that no one took their spot. Cars that were successfully parked had large cardboard panels laid against each wheel, an attempt by owners to prevent local dogs from cocking their legs against them.

Like the rest of the city, the *hutongs* were under threat from a new wave of demolition as the government repositioned Beijing as a hyper-modern centre for finance and technology – with little regard for those it displaced. In an attempt to return the *hutongs* to their original shape, restaurants, bars and the fronts of small businesses were bricked up or knocked down overnight, with owners arriving to work in the morning only to discover the demise of their livelihood. Most victims of the cleansing were Chinese migrant workers who lived hand to mouth, setting up unlicensed holes in the wall to serve food and sell their wares. Their targeting was more sinister than simply collateral damage: to manage Beijing's overcrowding, the authorities were carefully sweeping out migrants whose tiny businesses did little to enhance the economy. Much of the change was welcomed by the city's residents, but as the malls went up and the walls came down, Beijing's history, grit and charm lay in ruins.

'Are you sure you don't mean Nanjing?' asked Jamie.
'No, Nanning, definitely Nanning.'
'Spell it.'

'N-A-N-N-I-N-G.'

'Oh, okay, so definitely Nanning then. I've never heard of it.'

Nanning was right at the bottom of China, about the same distance from Beijing as Hong Kong, but since travelling on the Trans-Mongolian, these distances paled in comparison. What was a mere twenty-three hours? It wasn't even a full day. After a week in Beijing, we asked Jamie to book our tickets to Nanning at a local agency, which was easier than queuing at the station. Unconvinced that we knew where we were going, he had almost sent us to Nanjing. He then took off to Shanghai, where he was reporting on a surge in sham marriages among gays and lesbians appeasing conservative family members; he was annoyed that his editor wanted photos, which went against the entire concept of the story. From Nanning, we would then cross over the border to Hanoi. These two journeys alone sent me spinning into a blur of happiness as I instantly fell back into step with the comfortable, familial way that Asians travel together. On our thirtieth train journey, from Beijing to Nanning, we sat in the dining car watching an elderly man eating a plate of steaming beef, pausing only to swig from a small bottle of whisky as though it was water. Opposite him sat his friend with puffy, deep-set eyes and grey hair, working his way through fried pork and beans, stopping to take bites from a cured sausage the size of his arm. The floor around them resembled the bottom of a hamster cage, covered in the shells of sunflower seeds that crunched under the wheels of a trolley piled with sausages on sticks. Fish heads and chewed bones lay strewn across tables in an unabashed declaration of a dinner enjoyed. At our own table, Jem swiped his plate with a finger, his cheeks flecked with chilli and oil.

There was a shared joy and deep satisfaction in these mealtimes, a contrast with the gloom of European dining cars, where single diners sat at separate tables, each nursing a bottle of Pinot Noir in a state of ennui. On the way back to our compartment, we passed people gathered at the hot-water tank, filling bowls of instant noodles and flasks of jasmine tea.

Passengers sat in the aisles watching loud soap operas on gold iPhones, shelling peanuts and throwing them on the floor. Open carriages displayed rows of cracked grey heels, T-shirts on hangers, and tightly wrapped babies in quilts. Some passengers smoked in the gangways or stood fully lathered by the sinks, shaving before bedtime. While I wandered around, Jem had made friends with a geology graduate nicknamed Xué, which appropriately translated as 'studious'. Xué was travelling home to Nanning for the first time in six months, and was sharing our hard-sleeper compartment along with two grandmas and a pretty girl who spent most of the twenty-three-hour journey watching an epic drama on a crystal-covered iPad. While the grannies made loud phone calls, broke wind and ate mantou buns, Xué sat in between us watching *Game of Thrones*. None of us used earphones, and yet the combined noise did nothing to upset the harmony of our temporary communal living. The next morning, Xué accompanied us to breakfast, ordering soft *mei fun* noodles with black cabbage and peanuts, and chatting to us about his job prospects as rain lashed at the windows.

'I've been away from home for too long. It will be good to go home to my mother.'

'Do you have brothers and sisters?' I asked, forgetting that Xué was part of the generation affected by the one-child policy.

'No.'

'What does it feel like being an only child?'

'You don't really think about that. For all my classmates, it is the same. They are all only children as well, so I don't feel any different. I don't feel like I'm missing anything.'

Straight away I realised the stupidity of my question. Of course Xué felt no different. Having no siblings was as normal to him as having a brother was normal to me. I'd never considered what life might have been like as an only child or with more brothers and sisters.

'At the moment there is a huge problem with jobs,' said Xué. 'Everyone is leaving the countryside to get jobs in the city. On the farms they earn maybe 10,000 yen per year, in the city they can earn up to 60,000 yen, so they are abandoning their farms and it's a big problem for the government. They are trying to build better schools and more hospitals in the countryside to encourage people to stay, but I don't think it will be easy. There are too many people looking for jobs. Sometimes the government is right and having less people will control the problem.'

When we arrived in Nanning, Xué walked with us across town to help collect our onward train tickets to Hanoi from a local travel office, which we would never have found without him. He'd then brought us back to the station, located the platform, and wished us luck, telling us that his mother would be wondering where he was. These random acts of kindness always reaffirmed my faith in humanity. For Xué, there was nothing to gain but a telling-off from his mother, yet he'd given up an hour of his time having not been home for six months. Maybe he wanted us to have a positive impression of Chinese hospitality, or perhaps the answer was simply that he had enjoyed our company and wanted to help, but I will never know.

In the same way that some travellers are drawn to collecting postcards, coins, stamps or beer bottles from other countries, I am obsessed with fast-food outlets, particularly KFC and McDonald's, which always feature appropriated versions of classic items – like India's Chicken Maharaja Mac, and France's Le Croque McDo. On finding one I'd never seen before, we wandered into Dico's, a fried-chicken chain. Slapping an English-language laminated menu under my nose, the server waited patiently as I ordered a couple of double-decker burger combos. As much as the West had influenced Chinese tastes and fashions, they remained resolutely Chinese: looking around the restaurant, I saw teenagers wearing fat trainers, eating fast food and reading their phones, but they sipped soy milk instead of Coke, and crunched shrimp sticks instead of chips.

The overnight journey to Hanoi was spent sleeping, pulling bags off the train at the border, sleeping, pulling bags off the train at the other side of the border, then watching a young woman sob as she was taken into a back room, then led away in handcuffs. She'd been sharing our compartment – shoving her pink plastic suitcase under my berth – and now I was desperate to know what she'd hidden inside. The idea of wilfully committing any kind of crime in Southeast Asia never failed to baffle me. Security officials in this part of the world had the kind of demeanour that made me want to cry when they so much as appeared in the doorway. They didn't come across as the sort to offer tea and sympathy to a spindly student in yellow flip-flops. As our train pulled out of the station, I looked over at her now-empty berth, the blankets bunched where she'd left them, a few long hairs on the pillow. She'd lifted clean out of our story, and we out of hers. Flipping off the light, I stared at her berth in the darkness, wondering if someone was waiting for her in Hanoi, and hoping she'd be okay.

Bangkok has the worst traffic in the world – at least that's what I'd thought until I'd visited Delhi and decided that Delhi had the worst traffic in the world. But now that we were here, I could see that Hanoi actually had the worst traffic in the world. Almost a source of national pride, it was so bad that hotels offered guests instructions on how to cross the road, none of which worked. We had been standing at the side of the road for more than seventeen minutes, trying to work out how and where to cross in what had turned into a real-life version of Frogger. Vietnam's capital was home to more than five million motorbikes, most of which appeared to be swarming down this street, carrying crates, poultry and families of four. Inching back onto the pavement, we waited as another torrent of mopeds, motor scooters, bikes and Vespas came flooding around the corner, the women wearing reversed jackets and what looked like oven gloves to protect them from the sun. Trapped between parked scooters, and scooters trying to park, we were about to step off the pavement when a black Yamaha transporting a giant plasma screen came hurtling towards us and we leapt back. The traffic lights turned from red to green and back again, as what we'd thought was a one-way system had rapidly developed into a two-way, then three-way system, as new lanes of traffic emerged and began to flow against the tide.

To ease congestion and pollution, the department of transportation had announced plans to ban all motorbikes and scooters by 2030, but there was no way the city's residents would survive without them as few could afford a car. Waiting for a lull, we hovered around for another ten minutes before deciding it would be faster and safer to hail a taxi to the other side of the road; but taxis knew better than to interrupt the flow of two-wheelers that dominated the roads like skinnier, more colourful versions of Hells Angels, and had kept away. Mustering up the faith of Moses, we stepped forward and hoped the bikes would part. Walking steadily around wheels and headlamps, we saw that the riders wanted to avoid us as much as we wanted to avoid them, twisting away as we approached. As we reached the other side, we jumped off the road just in time for a scooter to come careering down the pavement and into a fellow pedestrian.

Every traveller we had met along the way had used Hanoi as a base from which to explore Halong Bay, before working their way down to Saigon. But as we strolled around Hoan Kiem Lake, the morning sky not fully awake, we had no desire to be anywhere else. Yogis stretched at the water's edge as we sat beneath a tree eating fried egg and pork *bánh mì* baguettes and watching a group of old women doing t'ai chi. The slowness and precision of their movements was at odds with the pace at which the rest of the city moved around them. Happily unhurried, they lifted their limbs with careful control, their whole being present in each moment. As a people we'd become obsessed with speed, checking our watches, glancing at the clock, running for the Tube, inventing bullet trains, faster internet and instant coffee, yet where was the extra time we were saving? And what were we doing with it? If speed was improving our lives, then why were the days busier, longer and harder, our minds overburdened and tired? Over the previous weeks, the slowness of train travel had replenished my own mind, allowing me to pause and pick apart my thoughts – which it turned out were gratifyingly few.

Leaving my job, my home and my possessions had quietened the noise in my head. My immediate concerns were where to eat and where to sleep. The less I carried, the less I worried.

Jem and I spent the next few days strolling Hanoi's tree-lined boulevards, eating big bowls of pho, and sitting in rooftop cafes, drinking dark percolated coffee with condensed milk, as tiny birds beat their wings in wooden cages. One afternoon we paid a visit to Ho Chi Minh's mausoleum, not realising that he received guests only until 11 a.m. Housed in a starkly Soviet marble monument, the late leader was embalmed in a glass coffin – which it turned out had gone completely against his own wishes to be cremated and to have his ashes placed in three urns buried upon unmarked hilltops in the north, south and centre of Vietnam. In 1989 the Vietnamese government admitted to fiddling with his will and falsifying the date of his death to make sure it did not coincide with Vietnam's National Day and turn it into one of mourning. After finding out we'd arrived too late to see the inside of the building, we'd staggered around the grounds, cursing the humidity, and reassuring ourselves that Uncle Ho had never intended to be seen in that state.

Sad to leave Hanoi, but eager to see the rest of Vietnam, we arrived at the central station ready to board the Reunification Express, which runs from Hanoi to Saigon. Like the Trans-Mongolian, no single train bears this name, but the route is still commonly known as such. Completed by French colonists in 1936, the line was severed in 1954 when Vietnam was divided into north and south. Throughout the Vietnam War the railway was battered and bruised by American bombs, but resurrected itself and resumed a regular service after the country's reunification in 1976. We were travelling at peak season and an extra service numbered SE17 – the Limited Express – had been put on to cope with the increased demand. Approaching the train, I eyed the hem of rust and struggled to decide what colour the outside used to be. Nervous to put my foot on the steps in case they broke off and fell into the tracks, I climbed into the carriage as it creaked beneath my weight. 'Limited' was an understatement: the inside of the compartment looked like the aftermath of a fire. Paint flaked off the walls like dead skin, covering the berths with yellow dandruff. Rat-grey tufts sprouted from the edge of the air conditioner, which was held together by four pieces of tape – two of which were flapping off, the body of a bluebottle attached. Black mould stained the ceiling, and the smell of decay leaked from under the sinks where a pipe had broken and was bubbling down the carriage. Ankle-deep water sloshed along the side, swept up by a guard whose shirt was stuck to his back.

Whenever I read about these kinds of trains on blogs, they were described as having comfortable compartments with vendors bringing food to the seat, and were usually accompanied by twee photographs showing tied-back curtains, pink plastic flowers, and bald middle-aged men holding aloft their beers. No one else seemed to travel in these mobile skips, and while appalled, I was inwardly thrilled when faced with journeys like these. It was a test of wills, to see what stuff I was really made of, and how long I could go without contracting tetanus. Keeping my rucksack at the foot of my berth, I moved to the window as the carriage began to shake, assuming we were on the move, only to discover the quaking was the result of four brothers and sisters under the age of six, tearing up and down the corridor in vests, pants and bare feet. A Danish couple was sharing our compartment, reading in their berths, and getting ever more annoyed by our attempts to make conversation – eventually turning over to face the wall.

Over the PA system, an anguished woman began singing like a sonic weapon as we rolled out of the station through a downpour of warm tropical rain, the kind that obscured and drenched everything in the three minutes while it lasted. The city's red lights blurred at the window, as water wormed down the glass. For the first hour, the train ran parallel to the highway with nothing more than a single wooden fence separating us from couples on scooters, and trucks flashing past in the opposite direction. After running neck and neck with lorry drivers chewing cigarettes, glancing sideways into our compartment, the train wrenched away from the road, delving into the guts of the city. Presumably resigned to the dire state of the compartment, whoever was in charge of the railway's soft furnishings had attached a pair of incongruous gold curtains in the hope that they would distract from everything else. Holding them back, I sat at the window watching as the train panted in the darkness past run-down houses lit by hurricane lamps, and strung with children's laundry. Night trains indulged a special kind of voyeurism, and I sat in the dark as the others slept, spying on inner-city families winding down for the night: fathers washing dishes and mothers unpinning their hair. But soon the shops were shuttered, the lamps blown out, and nothing but blackness met my gaze. As the city fell away, I let go of the curtain and crawled into my berth, the train thundering on through the night.

A groan came from the berth above, followed by the sound of a pillow being punched. The Danes were not having a good time. Mandolin music began to whine from the PA system that was just outside our door, along with the same woman who was still in mourning or pain – or both. Dawn was about to break, and this was not at all conducive to a relaxing journey. The Vietnamese siblings were charging down the carriage playing knock-and-run. Whether I liked it or not, I had to concede that the day had already started and I threw off my blankets. Rolling back the door, I met the red-eyed gaze of the children's father who was standing in resignation, smoking out of the window. With a sympathetic nod in his direction, I realised that what was an isolated experience for me, was his daily existence. He nodded in return with an expression that was part apology, part envy, part suicidal, as his children clattered past for the third time, the smallest covered in the dank water from the night before.

Sharing a metal mug of hot chocolate and a packet of sugary biscuits, Jem and I sat by the window enjoying the warmth of the sun as it winked through the trees. Thick, waxy leaves flapped at the sides of the carriage, rustling into the windows, opening up to reveal fat fists of green bananas. Skinny palm trees leant to the side and buffalo wallowed in lotus-filled waters, white birds prancing boldly on their backs. The Danish couple disembarked at Hué, neither of them saying a word as they packed up their things and left. It takes such a valiant effort not to talk to fellow passengers when travelling in such close proximity that I couldn't help but admire their determination to remain as unfriendly as possible. Between Hué and Da Nang, the jungle crept up the hill and wrapped itself around our train, shadows and sunlight strobing through the carriage. This was the most beautiful stretch of the journey, and I was pleased the Danes had missed it. Leaning from the doorway, I watched the front of the train curling in and out of tunnels and boring into cliffs, when suddenly the South China Sea opened up below in a magnificent haze of blue. From Lang Co Bay, a finger of creamy sand ran along the edge of the water, tracing the foam all the way to Da Nang where we were due to break the journey. Stopping just long enough for us to drag our bags across the track, the train shuddered, then continued down the coast and on to Saigon.

4

The Death Railway

Cambodia had no trains. For the first time since we had left London, we came to an abrupt halt. After a couple of nights in Hoi An, buying tailored silk and eating *cao lau*, we had re-boarded the Reunification Express at Da Nang and carried on down the country, sitting upright on wooden benches for seventeen hours. The Vietnamese had watched us as closely as they watched TV, and I suspected they'd placed bets on which one of us would be the first to have a mental breakdown. Aside from being cheaper, the ordinary hard-seat carriages had no benefit other than to offer better opportunities for photography from the open windows, but this half of the journey was nowhere near as scenic as the first, and it was mostly dark.

Having taken for granted that every country would have some form of train travel, we were now hovering at the edge of a yawning gap in Asia's railway network, unsure how to make the leap from Saigon to Siem Reap. Built for the purpose of trading rice, but blighted by a dark history, Cambodia's 380 miles of tracks were first laid while under French rule. Between 1930 and 1942, the first line was constructed linking Phnom Penh to Bangkok in the north, and in the 1960s a second line connected Phnom Penh to Sihanoukville in the south. A third line between Phnom Penh and Saigon had been planned, which would have connected Vietnam and Thailand, but it was never built. The two lines had been used to ferry freight and a few passengers, but after Pol Pot captured Phnom Penh in 1975, the trains played accomplice to his genocidal regime, enabling the evacuation and relocation to the countryside of hundreds of thousands of Cambodians forced into hard labour that led to their starvation and eventual massacre. Even into the late 1990s, Khmer Rouge guerrillas saw the trains as ripe for ambush and attack, kidnappings and murders. After years of civil war and damage from exploding land mines, the railways fell into a state of disrepair. Trains regularly derailed, owing to neglect by the Cambodian government, and eventually they faded out of operation. However, not long after we visited, the line from Phnom Penh to Sihanoukville was resurrected and a regular service put on for passengers.

Bridging the crossing by a series of buses, we arrived at Poipet and joined the queue of backpackers on visa runs. Hinging the two countries together, the place was a strip of no-man's-land swarming with scammers, hustlers, conmen and touts. Surrounded by slums and markets, Poipet was marked out by a corridor of casinos, each more garish than the next, with a string of names like Holiday Palace, Grand Diamond City, and Star Paradise, as glorious and aspirational as their establishments were not. Gambling is illegal in Thailand and the casinos provide a legal outlet for Thais to pour in and lose their money at craps and roulette, and for Cambodians to find employment. Trudging up the strip past the scammers, hustlers and touts – the conmen had bee-lined for the Europeans – we crossed over the friendship bridge to Thailand, had our passports stamped, then squeezed into a tuk-tuk that took us up the road to Aranyaprathet station, a pretty wooden building with picket fencing and an assortment of preened and potted bushes.

Boarding a train at its origin brought with it a position of privilege. While it was fun to hop on and off along a route, I always felt like I was arriving in the middle of a story, wondering what I'd missed, and who had warmed my seat. Now, as Jem and I sat in the carriage, balancing two boxes of fresh *pad kra pao* on our knees, I was ready for the story to begin. The train had basic wooden interiors with padded seats, and the walls featured adverts for shower gel and ketchup. Metal shutters were pushed down into the window frames allowing a breeze to carry in the aroma of stir-fried basil from the ramshackle restaurant by the station. Looking around and sizing up our travelling companions, I saw a crop of carefully tended hair moving in my line of vision, and I strained to look over the top of the seats to where an elderly Indian man was sitting next to a young Thai woman carrying a bag of bottles and cans. Like most Indians who spotted one another on holiday, there was instant curiosity, followed by immediate hostility, and Mr Walia took one look at me peering from my seat, before ignoring me completely and continuing his conversation with the passenger opposite him.

'You're really seventy?' remarked a quiet male voice, which sounded American.

'I know,' he boomed. 'Look at my passport, you'd hardly believe it, would you?'

Mr Walia had styled his hair into a Bollywood bouffant, and dyed it an interesting shade of maroon, a hem of white around his forehead. I could believe he was seventy.

'I tell you, our bodies are like sewers,' said Mr Walia, shaking a finger. 'Detoxify, drink beet juice, and don't have chemo!'

A young boy leapt onto the train clutching a chicken leg and a bag of sticky rice, and looked around for a place to sit. Spying an opportunity to move within earshot of Mr Walia, I offered the boy my seat, and sat with my back to the conversation, sinking low against the berth. A hoot rang out, followed by a comical ding-ding, and the train began its journey to Bangkok. Over the rumble of the wheels, I realised Mr Walia had gone quiet, and was forced to look elsewhere for amusement – which didn't take long after a mother pulled out an industrial-sized nail cutter, yanked her son's leg across her lap, and began clipping his toenails. Usually heartened by the way in which Asians refuse to distinguish between home and public transport – turning berths into dining tables and saris into cradles – I was fascinated and repulsed in equal measure by the shards pinging around the seats. Applying make-up and combing hair in public were just about tolerable, but beautification that resulted in the depositing of human debris was a step too far. No one cared though, most passengers staring out of the windows at the herons picking their way through waterlogged fields. It was a humid but grey day, the sogginess of the ground and air merging into one as we rattled our way west. Rain soon hit the sides of the train, drumming the roof as passengers scrabbled to pull up the shutters. Swapping to the other side of the carriage, I shifted along to the window and leant out, enjoying the warmth of the summer rain and the dull smell of wet soil.

In my new seat, I was now diagonally opposite Mr Walia's interlocutor, a waif of a man with sunken cheeks, wearing a checked shirt and a vintage army cap. He had curled himself into the furthest corner of his seat and was gripping the window ledge like a lost child.

'I'm always willing to try different things,' he said, his eyes darting across wild grass that was almost as high as the train.

'The best thing is you take care of yourself. You live a good life on the outside, and your body will be healthy on the inside. Chemotherapy is just chemicals again. It is chemicals that destroy your body in the first place!'

'What would you suggest I try?'

Interested to hear the extent of Mr Walia's oncology expertise, I leant forward. Seeing my face, he declared he had a headache and closed his eyes, as the woman began rubbing his temples. The American pulled out a jar of tiger balm from his knapsack and offered it to Mr Walia, who opened one eye and looked at it as though he had just been gifted a turd in a box.

'We're herbalists,' he said, as the woman produced a similar-sized tub of balm. 'We've tried them all, and we make our own. You won't find anything like this on the market.' The woman, who turned out to be Mr Walia's wife and business partner, unscrewed the lid and explained that the balm contained honey, turmeric and pepper, and began rubbing it along his legs, which apparently were the source of his headache. 'But I can sell you whatever you need. I assure you, it can fix any ailment.'

A wonderful aspect of travelling by train is the transactional relationship between passengers who feed off one another, picking up tips, offering advice, guarding each other's belongings, and generating a trust that is unique to railway travel. But this trust is not to be abused. Like a masonic handshake, these on-board interactions are understood to be for the benefit of all concerned. Mr Walia was a traitor to the cause. If the cure for cancer lay among the contents of my spice rack, I'd willingly have massaged his legs myself.

Having heard enough, I moved back to where Jem was sitting with his legs crossed, now chewing chunks of sticky rice and sweet pork that he'd bought from a woman with a bucket and a limp. In spite of his Malaysian background, Jem's supremely white-centric, Surrey upbringing had played a key role in cementing his stiffness and politesse. Whereas most people left their comforts at home, it was a joy to watch him relaxing into his true comfort zone as he found affinity, rather than strangeness, in his surroundings. Until now, the longest train journey he'd ever endured was between King's Cross and York, yet he was more than happy to pass hour after hour on trains where the likelihood of derailment was far higher than that of arrival, and where there was no more entertainment than that which was sourced on board.

Our train was already delayed. New track had recently been laid, and the train had been slowed down to give the sleepers time to settle, which also gave us time to take in the sight of burning potato fields and apple-green rivers dotted with the heads of kids bobbing up to the neck. The train clanked along as we hung over the window ledges watching local train stations sail by. With names like Khokmakok and Bandongbang, they looked like private cottages surrounded by potted palms and landscaped gardens. Each station was painted red and white, featured life-sized portraits of the king, and was hung with a large gold bell that bonged three times as we departed.

A couple of hours later, a curve of white moon appeared in the corner of the sky, waiting for the sun to take leave. The last light fell on pink lotuses floating in the dirt, and a chill crept along the floor of the carriage. More than eight hours after we had set off, the train picked up pace and began to canter into the city, which greeted us with the stench of open sewers, rotten bananas and fish. Flyovers twisted overhead, and the orange glare from lamp posts swept through the train like a searchlight. Billboards warned not to buy Buddha heads, next to adverts for Canon – *Delighting You Always!* Mr Walia was now awake, combing his hair and ranting about private hospitals. Sliding his comb back into his breast pocket, he stretched out a hand to his wife who reached into the carrier bag and cracked open a can of Black Panther extra premium stout that she passed across to him. Feeling sorry for her, Jem struck up a conversation and asked her how we could continue from Bangkok to Kuala Lumpur.

'It's better you take the train to Batawat,' she said, her toes scrunching in silver sandals as the wind intensified, blowing dust through the shutters.

'Batawat?'

'Yes, from Bangkok Hua Lamphong station you take the train to Batawat on this side,' she said, gesturing to the left. 'This other side is very beautiful, but it is not safe.'

There were two train lines that could take us down the country to Malaysia: one was a straightforward route down the west coast, the other a jungle route down the east coast that was infinitely more beautiful, but a hotspot for separatist violence – which made it oddly alluring. A few months earlier, Thai rebels had bombed a section of track between Yala and Sungai Kolok, which was the exact route on which we would travel, but I conceded that as much as I would have liked to gather stories of adventure, I wanted to live to tell them. Thanking Mrs Walia, we gathered our bags as the train slowed into Bangkok Hua Lamphong. Outside the station, we flagged down a tuk-tuk and swung off into the traffic just in time to see Mr Walia getting into a taxi, his wife standing on the kerb with their bags.

Khao San Road was every grubby tale about Thailand packed into one street. Reeking of sticky cocktails and desperation, it was a magnet for gap-year students, stag parties, and sexless creeps in their fifties looking for massage parlours, hostels, cheap eats, cheap clothing and cheap beer. You could pick up everything on Khao San Road, from tie-dye T-shirts and skewered scorpions, to henna tattoos and herpes. Having spent my own gap year teaching English at a high school in Cannes, I'd bypassed this particular rite of passage and first travelled to Bangkok in my late twenties to visit my friend Jane. We'd spent two hedonistic weeks reading books and playing Scrabble, and had even stayed up past midnight one night, much to the confusion of everyone around us who swiftly gave up trying to offer us drugs, get into our knickers or sell us Full Moon party buckets, concluding we were lesbians or nuns in training. Determined to avoid the debauchery of a Friday night on Khao San Road, I took Jem to a comparatively sedate bar nearby that served the same delicious chicken massaman curry as I remembered, and watched as he absorbed the bedlam. Until now, Jem had never picked up a backpack, let alone owned one, and his holidays had usually involved family trips to the same resort in Antigua. Keen to see Bangkok in all its fabled glory, he finished his curry, and the two of us walked around the centre of town watching skinny posh boys dribble after tanned girls with braids.

Perched on a plastic stool, I sipped an iced coffee and observed the scene around a hawker setting up a push-cart of fried bamboo worms, crickets and grasshoppers, their bodies glistening beneath the light of his hurricane lamp. Gathering with curiosity, his customers comprised Western tourists taking selfies, goading one another into machismo. Across the road, a line of waiters wearing white cycling shorts and headbands strutted among the tables, blowing kisses to their regulars. All around, the Thais were performing, putting on accents, batting their false lashes and playing to the crowd. In the ten years since I'd last visited, the area had changed for the worse. Free wi-fi was so widely available now that the internet cafes had vanished and been replaced by more bars selling cheap cocktails. Wanting to stay at the heart of the action, Jem had insisted we book into a hostel a few streets away from Khao San Road; we arrived to find the staff sitting on the floor watching Liam Neeson films on a loop. Making our way up to bed as our neighbours were on their way out, we wrestled open the door, breaking the lock in the process.

'You know that hostel is only a few letters away from hovel?'

'Ha, bloody ha,' said Jem, grimacing as the door swung open. 'It's not that bad.'

Bundling the sheets off the bed, I spread out our sleeping-bag liners and lay on my back, stretching my arms so as to reach both sides of the wall, which were splattered red.

'Okay, it's quite bad,' Jem called from the bathroom, where a family of cockroaches had gathered around the drain as though attending a funeral. Hoping to wash them back to where they'd come from, Jem picked up the shower hose and found the head was missing, a pair of feelers waving from the open pipe.

'I think that's where they came from.'

Now convinced that if he left up the lid a python would swim up the toilet, Jem placed his washbag on top, and attempted to close the window to shut out the shrieks and screams, and what sounded like alternate gun shots. I crawled into bed, trying not to touch too much and waiting for him to realise that the window wasn't even open. Jem put his hands over his ears as the lights from a nearby bar flashed across our ceiling.

'How the hell are we supposed to sleep through this?'

'It's Bangkok. You don't sleep at night. You stay out until the morning then sleep through the day.'

'Okay, we can stay at the Peninsula next time.'

Staring up in the dark, we lay side by side in the silent realisation that we'd finally reached that point in life when the thought of slippers and Netflix was more exciting than a drunken night out.

Considering her choice of husband, we'd had little reason to trust Mrs Walia's judgement, but went ahead and booked tickets from Bangkok to Batawat – or 'Butterworth' as the ticket vendor had corrected me, laughing at my writing and showing it to his colleague, who had laughed and shown it to everyone in the office. Looking down at the tickets, I saw that Train 35 was known as a 'Special Express', and was immediately suspicious about what made it so special. As vague and noncommittal a term as 'Limited Express', it had the potential to be the best ride of our lives, but also the worst.

'Perhaps it's like special fried rice, full of exciting things you weren't expecting,' I said, trying to look on the bright side.

'Or full of leftover bits that nobody wanted.'

Still annoyed by the previous night's stay, Jem was in no mood for pleasantries. With no television of our own, we'd lain awake listening to the staff watch *Taken*, followed by *Taken 2*, falling asleep before they'd started *Taken 3*. After a roadside breakfast of roast duck and a pineapple smoothie, we'd walked up Khao San Road to visit Wat Chana Songkhram temple, skirting around the posh boys who were now sitting in the gutter, their Oxford shirts damp with moonshine and vomit. The July heat had already reached intolerable levels by the time we'd taken an air-conditioned taxi to the station, after discovering they were cheaper and faster than tuk-tuks, and didn't involve swallowing mouthfuls of filth and fumes.

Happily, we had no reason to worry about the train to Butterworth. The Special Express trains were speedy, long-distance services that provided only first- and second-class air-conditioned sleeper berths – the top tier of Thai railways. Boarding just before 3 p.m., we found ourselves sitting next to Joe, who was hugging a satchel to his chest, and looking from the floor to the ceiling fan as it whirred hot air around the carriage. At the age of sixty-five, Joe was about to take his first-ever train journey. Having just retired, he had decided to treat himself to a week visiting old friends in Bangkok, and had flown up from Penang, booking his return journey on the train. Fishing a tiny Pentax from his breast pocket, Joe slid over to the window and put one hand to the glass, his eyes following the billboards, rusty rooftops and washing lines, as they slid past in a kaleidoscope of metal, cloth and colour. As a child growing up in Borneo, Joe had cycled to and from school, taking buses between cities, buying his own car when he could finally afford one. Somehow train travel had passed him by. Watching Joe take pleasure in the unremarkable way the bunks pulled down or the lights switched off, I was reminded of why my passion for train travel deepened every time I boarded a train. No matter how many journeys I took, or how awful the train, each one brought an element of surprise or wonder, usually to be found in the least expected places and people.

In just under an hour the train had shaken loose the city and relaxed into the countryside. Lakes of flooded paddy were marked out by footpaths and bendy palms that crossed at the waist like hastily scribbled kisses. A haze of mountains sat on the horizon, nudging the underbelly of the clouds, summer storms greying their tops. As the afternoon blurred into evening, unread books lay face down on sleeping chests, and I crept out of the carriage to thaw out in the vestibule. There was no happy medium with Asian air-conditioning: it was either broken or cranked up to fridge-cold, imploring passengers to layer on jumpers and socks. Standing on the hinge of the two carriages as they slid around, clashing against each other, I peered through the rubber edges, basking in the heat that rushed through. Soft light fired the paddy, turning the lakes to liquid caramel, the palms silhouetted like black windmills. The view moved with me, offering itself up and allowing me to draw in as much as I needed, for as long as I wanted, before I stepped away, sated.

Our entire trip pivoted on punctuality, which contradicted the ease with which travellers usually drifted from one place to the next, driven by the weather, the prospect of sex, or dwindling funds. Were it not for the rigidity of our train bookings – most of which were popular long-distance routes – we too would have lain around in cafes, playing chess, watching the sun rise then watching it set. However, time was only of the essence until we caught the train. Once on board, it ceased to matter. We couldn't slow down a journey any more than we could speed it up; delays were inevitable, and our arrival was at the mercy of others. From this point on, mealtimes defined our existence, bringing structure to the languor of our days. Now, judging by the smell of fried fish and lemongrass drifting up the carriage, it was already time for dinner, so I roused Jem from his slumber, and asked Joe to keep an eye on our bags while we went to investigate what was on offer.

A Malaysian student sat sideways in a booth playing Selena Gomez on his phone, while waiters in silk waistcoats carried trays of stir-fried sea bass, and pork in oyster sauce. For the price of a Big Mac, the dining car offered set menus with mains of fried meat and fish, soup, side dishes of duck red curry and chicken green curry, with pineapple for pudding. There were alternatives for vegetarians, and 'non-spicy' menus for foreigners, along with bowls of steaming jasmine rice. Alcohol was banned on board, but, as is common on all good trains, the activity still centred on the dining car, where passengers played cards, smoked roll-ups out of the windows, and made friends over cups of tea and Milo. Unlike on European trains – where dining alone is like the modern-day equivalent of having leprosy – lone passengers looked content in their solitude. There was no need for an accompanying phone, book or bottle of wine for them to be visibly at ease as the countryside beat on past the window, the smell of burnt fields carried in on the wind. Wiping up the last bit of red curry with a sweetly sticky glob of rice, I watched the sky turn sepia, the night still warm and alert after dark.

For the first time in a long while I felt at home. The concept of home was fluid for someone like me. As the child of two doctors whose training had required them to move all over England, I had lived in eight cities, attended six schools, and never stayed anywhere for longer than three years. Putting down roots, then pulling them up again, I was deeply envious of the stability and identity that came from living in one place. It was only in my twenties that I became grateful for how this peripatetic lifestyle had cultivated my ability to make friends, embrace change, and relish travel. More recently though, as race and identity had become hot topics of discussion, I was regularly branded a pretender by both my country of birth and my country of origin, and I had started to consider where I most felt at home. Our flat in London was currently someone else's: strangers were sleeping in our bed, watching our TV, cooking with our pans, and looking in our mirrors where our faces used to be. In a few months' time they'd be gone, and we'd return to a flat that smelt of someone else's food and laundry, our letters piled high by the door.

By 10 p.m. we had far outstayed our welcome and wandered back to the carriage to where our seats had been unlocked and converted into berths, folded up and pulled down to create one small and one enormous berth that could easily sleep two. Slotting our bags into the smaller, overhead berth, we crawled into the bottom one together, spreading out blankets and making a den. Joe had already climbed up to bed, and waved from his berth, having changed into a pair of striped pyjamas.

The following morning, I woke to a scream and a bowl of chicken congee hovering beneath my nose. It was barely 6 a.m. and we'd forgotten that, while enthralled by the dining car and its menu, we'd ordered breakfast to our berths. Sitting up with one eye open, I took the bowl from a bony brown hand, the steam from the broth seeping up my nose. The hand appeared again, holding two plastic cups of freshly squeezed orange juice followed by a couple of straws. Now grateful for the intrusion, we ate in silence, watching as farms and villages embraced the new day. While the rest of the carriage was curtained off, we moved into the dining car, enjoying the stillness of the morning. No one else was awake and we relished the opportunity to imagine for a short period that we were the only ones on board. With a cup of milky coffee, Jem opened up his copy of *The Railway Man* by Eric Lomax, and I took out my copy of *Prisoner of Japan* by Sir Harold Atcherley.

A week before leaving London, I had sat in the living room of Sir Harold, a ninety-seven-year-old delight, who lived on

Sussex Square, overlooking Hyde Park. Tall and alert, with translucent skin, Sir Harold had spent a morning with me discussing his time as a Japanese prisoner of war. In April 1943 he was one of 7,000 members of F Force, transported in successive trains from Changi in Singapore to Banpong in Thailand to construct the Burma–Thai railway – better known now as the 'Death Railway'. Hoping a rail link between the two countries would facilitate their invasion of India, the Japanese had seized upon the ready-made workforce of Allied prisoners who languished in Changi prison, deemed too sick and unfit to work elsewhere. Under the guise of moving them north to 'health camps', where there were supposedly greater food supplies and an opportunity to recuperate, the Japanese subjected the men to forced labour. After arriving in Banpong, the prisoners spent the next four weeks being marched for more than 200 miles to Kanchanaburi, where they were put to work building the railway. Driven by wire whips, bamboo rods and beatings, the British, Dutch, Australian and American prisoners, along with conscripted nationals from Burma, Malaya and Thailand, toiled for up to eighteen hours a day, eating nothing more than 250 mg of rice and a handful of beans. Stricken by cholera, beriberi, dysentery, dengue and pneumonia, and suffering tropical ulcers that often led to fatal amputations, the men built 257 miles of railway track in fourteen months – 372 including branch lines and sidings – with one death for every sleeper laid.

With disbelief, I had listened to how the cheerful nonagenarian had survived the horrors that killed an estimated 12,300 prisoners of war and 90,000 Asian labourers. By the time Sir Harold was transported back to Changi in December the same year, more than 3,000 members of F Force had died, and another 3,000 were hospitalised, leaving just over a hundred men deemed fit for work, Sir Harold included. He was sent to build a runway for Japanese kamikaze pilots.

'Not many people know, but that runway now lies directly under the present Changi airport,' said Sir Harold, rubbing the top of his walking stick. 'Those pilots were almost madder than brave – or both. There were two squadrons there, and when they took off to attack, the chances were that they wouldn't come back.'

Sir Harold remained at Changi until the end of the war, describing the period as 'not too bad', 'sort of a nine-to-five job – although we still didn't have much to eat'.

For his memoir, Sir Harold had pieced together his war diary from 1942–45, with a glaring gap during the eight months he was working on the railway. Under the cruel eye of his Japanese guards he was unable to keep up his diary, but surreptitiously scribbled on scraps, which are now preserved at the Imperial War Museum, London. Declaring that he couldn't remember anything at all of this period, Sir Harold had gently batted away my questions. Although disappointed that he couldn't offer any more information, I had left with a copy of his book, determined to retrace his tracks as best as I could from Singapore to Kanchanaburi, and to visit the remnants of the railway that still carries passenger trains between Nong Pla Duk and Nam Tok, crossing the bridge on the River Kwai. Our current descent from Thailand to Malaysia and Singapore was really an extravagant piece of research to help us retrace Sir Harold's journey from Singapore up to Kanchanaburi.

At the Malaysian border town of Padang Besar, the train was stripped down to two carriages and passengers disembarked for immigration and customs checks, which presented an opportunity to stroll around and look for coffee and amusement. Scouring the menu at the upstairs cafe, I found Joe looking less perky than the previous day, wearing a light dusting of stubble, dark circles under his eyes – the sign of a night-train novice. I asked him how he'd found the Special Express, and he screwed his eyes shut and shook his head.

'Oh, it's special, it's really something,' he replied. 'I don't know why I waited so long to do it. But I'm going to keep on doing it now.'

'No more planes?'

'Well, that depends. But I'm surely going to bring my wife next time, I want her to see everything again with me,' Joe said, waving his Pentax. 'I took so many photographs to show her.'

Together we re-boarded the train to Butterworth, none of us knowing that we were some of the last people who would ever get to enjoy this service. Less than six months later it ceased to exist, terminating at Padang Besar from where a connection on a high-speed electric train covered the final stretch to Butterworth.

Although it sounded like a hamlet in the Lake District, Butterworth was an industrial town and a major transportation hub from where we caught the high-speed train to Kuala Lumpur, followed by a drawn-out day service to Johor Bahru. So cold that it was impossible to sit in our seats, we spent the seven-hour journey lounging in the dining car eating hot *nasi goreng* as palm-oil plantations swept by, barely an inch of sunlight passing through their closely packed fronds. Wondering what kind of creatures lurked in the thickets, we got chatting to Christopher, a Tamil Malaysian who had worked in the palm-oil industry for more than forty years. He was sitting on his own eating toast with *kaya*, nodding with approval at our plates of fried rice and eggs.

'Rats,' he said, making a pair of pointy ears with his gold-ringed fingers.

'Is that all? No snakes?'

'Sometimes cobras, but mainly rats. Rats are the biggest problem, or should I say, were the biggest problem. They eat the fruit from which the oil is produced. At one time we even introduced snakes to kill the rats, but then the workers were bitten so we had to come up with a different method.'

'Rat poison didn't work?'

'No, chemicals are too toxic for fruit production.'

'What did you use then?'

'Owls,' said Christopher, making two circles around his eyes. 'Barn owls to be precise. It's a more natural way of managing the problem.'

'I don't think we really use palm oil,' said Jem, looking at me. 'I've never cooked with it.'

Christopher burst out laughing. 'Do you drink Coke? Eat KitKats? Wear lipstick?'

'Well, not me personally,' said Jem.

'Almost everything you consume has palm oil in it: detergents, make-up, chocolate, ice cream.'

Behind Indonesia, Malaysia was the second-largest producer of palm oil, and the country was under fire for vast deforestation and the destruction of ecosystems in its quest to keep up with foreign demand for the product.

'How sustainable is Malaysia's palm-oil production?' I asked.

'It isn't.' Christopher rubbed his thumb and forefinger together. 'Money is important. Like every country, Malaysia wants to be the big player in the market. Who cares about the environment when you're making so much money and living in a palace.'

Christopher got off before us, and we spent the last hour staring into the depths of the jungle, wilting with exhaustion as the successive journeys began to take their toll. Unable to travel all the way into Singapore, where the main station had ceased operation, we boarded a five-minute shuttle service at Johor Bahru that took us across the causeway to Singapore Woodlands, where the journey finally ended under the twinkle and shine of the city.

There wasn't an awful lot to do in Singapore, a starchy, characterless city with the superficial appeal of Dubai, and the same brutal levels of heat. Everything was convenient, efficient and sterile, and after three days of roaming around nice hotels, eating chicken rice, and complaining about the heat, we were ready to get back on the train. The grand old heritage station at Tanjong Pagar was no longer in use, so we began the return journey by crossing back over the causeway to Johor Bahru, where I was reminded of a story Sir Harold had told me. When I'd visited, he and his wife Sally had been preparing for the arrival of Mikio Kinoshita, an engineer with the Imperial Army who oversaw workers on the Death Railway. The two had never met before, but Sir Harold had watched a documentary in which the remorseful Kinoshita had expressed a desire to meet any former British POWs, and immediately invited him and his granddaughter to London.

'We invited him because I believe very much that you cannot go on hating people,' said Sir Harold. 'If you do, it only damages you, not them. Even more than that, it is really ghastly to refer to a nation or a religion or a group of people – whether they're journalists or politicians or bankers or what you will – and hating "them". It's nonsense, because I should think equal proportions of good, indifferent and lousy people exist in any group, any country, anywhere you like. Anyway,' he continued, 'there were a few days where we were being freed, as it were, or rather dumped in Changi, and becoming very impatient to get away, and the Japs were becoming prisoners. They were being marched off Singapore Island in masses over the causeway into Johor Bahru, and I remember one of our soldiers shouting out to his mates – there was a group of them just watching the Japs – and he said: "Look at those poor buggers ... now it's their turn." And that to me sums up the whole thing. There were plenty of good Japanese and I could go into that longer, but generalising is something I cannot, cannot abide.' And with that, I knew immediately how Sir Harold had survived the ordeal. He hadn't allowed the torment to affect him on a personal level, and had refused to let his own anger and frustration get the better of him.

At Johor Bahru we boarded the same ice-cold train to Kuala Lumpur, and I looked out across the jungle with fresh eyes, trying to imagine what was in the minds of Sir Harold and the other 659 on board his train, as they travelled up the country. Aware only that they were in for a week's train journey, the men had no clue as to where they were being moved, assuming that the destination was Chiang Mai. However, a few days before departure, a rumour went around that it was in fact northern Malaya. Having gone from reading Flaubert, Austen and Hemingway, and applying boric acid to his blistered feet,

Sir Harold was loaded onto a train believing that the reason for the move was a shortage of food on Singapore Island, and that where they were going would have a plentiful supply, along with gramophones, blankets and mosquito nets. Throughout our successive journeys back to Bangkok, I sat up with endless cups of Milo, oblivious to the once-enchanting scenery, reading Sir Harold's memoir, which detailed a train ride to the depths of hell where most of the men would die:

> Conditions on rail journey, Singapore to Siam. Five days and nights, allowed to get out of train for 30 minutes twice a day. No latrine arrangements, we had to urinate and crap out of the wagon door, being held by others as we did so. Most had dysentery and were very weak so that many who could not get up simply defecated where they lay and conditions in wagons were soon revolting. Little or no sleep at night, very hot by day in all-metal box wagons, too many in each to allow all to lie down at the same time. Appalling stench. Occasional food buying at stations; eggs, papayas.

A critical segment of the Death Railway had been under repair for more than a month, and unsure if the train to Nam Tok was even running, we came careering in by tuk-tuk to Bangkok Thonburi station at first light, determined not to miss out on tickets, but fearing the worst. Made up of three windows and a few benches under a corrugated roof, the station was empty. Online information suggested the service was due to start that morning, but in practical terms that meant nothing. The shutters were down on the windows, and we hovered around anxiously. We were just over forty trains into the journey, and after having travelled a sizeable distance around the world, I didn't dare even consider the disappointment of not being able to take the train: it was akin to turning up at the Louvre to find the *Mona Lisa* on loan. Over the road, a woman was scraping a heavy iron wok, squirting various bottles of *nam pla* fish sauce and oil into the base, ripping and flinging in handfuls of coriander and beansprouts. A fantastic smell drifted across to where we stood, and we both knew that we were about to have our second breakfast in the space of an hour. A good rule of thumb while travelling is to eat when food is available, because you never know when you might have the opportunity again. In Thailand, this was a ridiculous and dangerous rule to live by. It was impossible to walk more than a few metres without finding a squat, muscly lady with her sleeves rolled up, frying noodles or flipping crêpes. Even on a patch of pavement the size of a postage stamp, if it was possible to light a flame, there would be a vendor grilling satay. As a result, Jem and I had gone the opposite direction of most travellers, and over the previous few weeks, had bloated to the point that we now struggled to fit into our clothes. Still, the weight gain was nothing that a raging bout of diarrhoea couldn't fix.

The train was running. Like a rusted old Portakabin on wheels, it rolled in a little before 8 a.m. to applause, causing great fuss on the platform as young Thai families milled around, shouting, clattering on and off the train, bagging seats and rounding up missing children. Held together by rust and hope, the whole thing would have flaked to the ground from a sneeze. The carriage had an unusual layout with a long bench running around the sides and a huge empty space in the middle. Marching down the carriage and banging shut all the windows, the conductor jumped out and raised a green flag as we gathered at the now-closed windows, pulling them all open. Moving off, I sat back overwhelmed with relief and sick excitement as the train ploughed through the city, its horn blaring non-stop. Neither feeling lasted long as we broke down after an hour and sat halted on the tracks, surrounded by dried fields and complaining children. With the wind rushing in through the windows, we'd failed to comprehend the intensity of the heat that was now raging through the carriage, along with an army of mosquitoes taking up residence on vulnerable patches of flesh. In these situations, there was always a self-appointed leader who hung out of the doors, peering up the track, and offering a number of confident explanations about the breakdown, none of which was ever correct. Ton, a father of two little girls in matching orange dresses, assumed the role and jumped onto the tracks while everyone else watched from the windows. Pleased with his audience, Ton returned a few minutes later, shaking his head and waving his hands as a crowd gathered round to hear his news.

'Problem on the tracks,' he said, which was fairly obvious to everyone on board. 'Staying here for one hour.' Even before the collective sighs of annoyance, the train jerked and began moving towards the next station.

Leaves and jungle inched closer to the track until the greenery began to climb into the train, twigs and flowers snapping off through the windows and scattering around the carriage as passengers shrieked and ducked away from the glass. It shouldn't have taken more than three hours from Bangkok to Kanchanaburi, but we broke down three more times, finally stopping in the middle of the jungle where creepers with pink flowers dripped down towards the tracks. A couple of hawkers started to work their way up the carriage, one selling fishcakes and noodles, the other dragging an ice bucket stacked with cans of Nescafé. It was a good time for a lunch break, and most other passengers had pulled out their bags of biscuits and fruit, offering their goodies to one another. A Dutch family swapped a few of their bananas for a couple of my Snickers bars and between us we were managing to forge a pretty decent meal.

'It's so lovely,' said the mother. 'We have a word in Dutch, *gezellig*, which means that there are no boundaries and that everyone is sharing and getting along with everyone else.'

'Is there an English equivalent?'

'No, it's a word that describes an atmosphere or feeling … like we are a train family.'

No one had ever summarised the nature of train travel in such a simple and wonderful way, and as the train clanked and jolted on its way, I kept repeating the word to myself, *gezellig* …

★

Sweat trickled down my neck and the backs of my knees, as I bent over, struggling to find my breath. Welts had risen on both legs, my ankles were bitten and bleeding. We'd drained both water bottles, and as we stood at the top of the clearing, licking our lips and panting, we could see Burma to the west of the mountains, thunder clouds milling above.

Every morning just before dawn, a handful of prisoners would gather here before beginning their work, looking down onto the Khwae Noi Valley, which was now thick with bamboo, but then a cheerless woodheap. Unable to walk any further, we slipped and stumbled back down towards Hellfire Pass. We had come to visit the Hellfire Pass Memorial Museum, which sits in the middle of the jungle, above the most deadly stretch of railway, so named owing to the hellish sight of emaciated workers toiling at night by firelight. Carved out by hand, using picks, shovels, hammers, and sticks of gelignite lit by cigarettes, the Konyu rock cutting along the mountainside measured 600 metres long and 25 metres deep at its highest point. Wide enough for the train to travel through, the pass was lined with remnants of wooden sleepers, spikes and rails, paving the way along the old trail. Clambering up the rocky pathway, we reached the top and looked down onto the pass. It was from this vantage point that Japanese guards had thrown rocks onto the prisoners starving and slaving below. Abusing and torturing the very workers that they needed to do the job seemed so counter-intuitive to their long-term goal. There was little point in trying to rationalise what had happened, yet I was desperate to understand. Reading books and watching documentaries conveyed some idea of the weight of what had taken place around us, but treading through the teak and bamboo jungle, hearing the crack of twigs break the silence, made it real. Smothered in insect bites and bleeding, I needed to see and feel to be able to begin to understand the mental strength and physical endurance required to survive in what Sir Harold called 'the most indescribable ghastly jungle, geographically speaking, an appalling 250 miles', where he and others had had to tie string from their big toes to their calves in order to hold up their injured feet and walk.

We should have missed the last train back to Bangkok, but understanding how Thai railways worked – or didn't work – we'd tried our luck and arrived at Nam Tok to find the train delayed and the platform full of passengers. Nam Tok marked the end of the functioning line, the remains of the track tapering off forlornly into the bushes, the sleepers overgrown with grass. Now, Jem and I stood in the open doorway as the train slowed towards the Wampo Viaduct and inched onto the wooden trestles as though unsure they could take the weight. Thumping down, the train squeaked and wailed, and I held my breath, convinced it would break the bridge and tumble down the slopes into the river. Just over a year later, the line was completely rebuilt, with continuous welded heavier rails fixed to concrete sleepers, so the train could travel faster and was almost always then on schedule. But to me, the charm lay in its shabbiness. The braver passengers swung out of the door, their T-shirts flapping in the wind as they snatched at wet leaves dangling within arm's reach. Sliding wide around the jungle, the river was a milky brown, muddied by rains but beautiful, restaurants and houses bobbing by its banks where trees peered over one another into the water. Scanning the caves and sheer cliffs as the train twisted towards Tham Krasae bridge, I was increasingly in awe of the challenges the workers had faced, and sat back preparing for the approach to the bridge on the River Kwai – which I'd discovered wasn't actually the River Kwai at all, but the Mae Khlung. When writing *The Bridge on the River Kwai*, the French author, Pierre Boulle, had made a lazy error, attributing the railway track to the wrong river. When fans of the book and David Lean's film of the same name had turned up looking for the bridge, the Thais made a quick decision to rename the river the Kwai Yae, meaning 'big Kwai', which appeased the tourists.

A few miles past Tham Krasae bridge, we broke down. Within fifteen minutes of our rolling to a standstill, the smell of hot butter billowed through the carriage and I looked out of the window to where an opportunistic hawker had wheeled over her cart and begun to fry fresh *khanom buang* – crêpes filled with egg and sweet orange shrimp. More than two hours passed and the conductors showed little sign of concern, chatting over a bag of gooseberries covered in chilli and sugar, offering them round. Wandering out onto the tracks, I looked up at the engine's empty cabin and found the drivers squatting in the grass, smoking. I'd now given up on seeing the bridge before sunset. Indigo shards had already begun to splinter the sky, and even if we'd got moving that moment, darkness would have settled before we arrived. While waiting for the train to move, I noticed a monk in burgundy robes who hadn't so much as raised an eyebrow, let alone his temper. I realised that I could sigh, pace the carriage and swear – and we would still be here – or I could use the time to read, enjoy the warm rain, and try some crêpes and gooseberries. The railway was a memorial in motion; to complain about delays was the height of impertinence while sitting upon wooden sleepers laid by those who had died doing so.

Just as spending the night on board was looking like a distinct possibility, the train was shunted back to Tham Krasae and a new engine attached, which saw us on our way. An hour later we had made it to the river, but before we crossed, the train came to a standstill, passengers hanging from the windows. A long horn blast heralded our arrival and we inched forward, then thudded onto the bridge. Like a grande dame, the train made the two-minute crossing amid the flash of cameras from tourists who had gathered on the bridge to witness the event. A dusk sky reflected off the river where a floating village of thatched restaurants swayed drunkenly around, strung with golden lights. Uplighters threw shadows like spectres onto the sides of the train, wrapping long black fingers around the roof. From the other side of the bridge, I took one last look over my shoulder, and settled in for the ride back to Bangkok. Under the dim lights of the carriage, I thumbed through my notebook and began to read what Sir Harold had told me about his final days, once he'd been transported from Kanchanaburi back to Changi, and the immediate aftermath of the atomic bomb:

> The Japs assumed of course that the bomb was a massive earthquake – which it could have been – and when we got the radio back on again, we heard what in fact it was. What I found fascinating was that the bomb enabled Emperor Hirohito to call it a day. Japan was bloody starving, which the British are so ignorant about – well, ignorant about most of the world outside Britain because they're not taught any history of anything else – but very few people know that there was an attempted coup by Japan's middle-level army officers who refused and didn't want to give up. The emperor had to send a member of his family down to give a personal order to the commander of Southeast Asia to pack it up. I felt for years that there was a hell of a moral question about the atom bombs, and I think there always will be in people's minds, but I'm biased, because that saved my life.

5

Bombs and Bullet Trains

Tetsushi Yonezawa took his mother's hand and boarded the Hiroden streetcar. It was just after 8 a.m., at the peak of summer, and the car was rammed with more than two hundred people on their Monday morning commute. No seats were available, so eleven-year-old Tetsushi wormed his way into the middle of the car, stifled by the heat from sweating bodies chattering and greeting one another. They would soon arrive at his grandmother's home in Funairi. Fifteen minutes later, the streetcar was rolling past the Fukuya department store, when the skies tore open, turning brighter than a thousand suns. Glass shattered, buildings blew upwards, and the smell of blood came fast. The summer morning turned black as night. Dust and ash darkened Hiroshima's skies, and the sound of screams and wailing filled the silence that followed the bomb. All around him, the city burned and bled, but Tetsushi and his mother remained unhurt; the sturdiness of the steel streetcar had withstood the blast.

Now eighty-one years old, Tetsushi wiped the orange juice from his mouth, and peered from under velvety lids.

'For me, Japanese trains are a symbol of strength.'

When the atomic bomb struck Hiroshima on 6 August 1945, the city was all but flattened; the skeletons of a few buildings stayed standing, along with a number of camphor trees, but the trains were up and running almost immediately. Sensing the need to flee, Tetsushi and his mother ran through the sticky, dirty, black rain that had begun to fall across the city, as it smoked and hissed. Arriving at Yaguchi station, they found three trains on the tracks and more than a thousand people picking their way through dead and writhing bodies.

'The first train was going north to Miyoshi,' Tetsushi recalled. 'Everyone was trying to get on this train, but the weak were trampled. People with bones poking out were clinging to the rooftops and hanging from the sides. Parents forced their children through windows. I remember a woman with a triangular shard of glass in her back, like a shark's fin, and blood running down her legs. Her skin had blistered and peeled off, like gloves hanging from the ends of the nails. Even those about to die crawled into the train to escape the city. Everyone had to get on.'

Tetsushi leant forward and cupped a liver-spotted hand under one eye. 'There was a grandma opposite me, her right eyeball was hanging out of the socket and she was trying to hold it in her hand.' He paused and wiped his mouth again.

'At 3.30 p.m. the train moved and we arrived at Shiwaguchi station at 5.30 p.m. If I had stayed in Hiroshima, I would have died. These trains saved my life.'

Japan's railways are synonymous with Shinkansen, the bullet trains that put the rest of the world's railways to shame. To the Japanese, however, the railways embody the resilience of their nation. The Hiroden streetcar began to run soon after the uranium bomb hit Hiroshima, and even today, two bombed cars continue to sail up and down the city's streets. We were in Hiroshima for the seventieth anniversary of the dropping of the A-bomb, and to meet Tetsushi, who was determined to keep alive the story of the *pika-don* (*pika* meaning flash, and *don* meaning tremendous sound). Year after year, he travels by train from his home in Kyoto to talk to schoolchildren and tour groups about the day the 'Little Boy' bomb fell from the *Enola Gay* and all but annihilated Hiroshima, changing Japan's fate for ever. Tetsushi was frightened that the memory and enormity of what happened would die with him and the few remaining bomb survivors, known as *hibakusha*, most of whom were nearing their nineties. However, as Jem and I squeezed through the crowds awaiting the memorial ceremony, it was clear that the memory was embedded not only in the psyche of the city, but in the thousands who had flocked from around the world. Representatives from a hundred nations had gathered in the Hiroshima Peace Memorial Park, along with the families of survivors, and local schoolchildren handing out colourful paper cranes in memory of Sadako Sasaki – a little girl who had died from leukaemia more than ten years after the bomb. On hearing the legend that whoever folded a thousand paper cranes would be granted a wish, Sadako had passed her time in hospital folding as many cranes as she could before she eventually died at the age of twelve, having made more than 1,600. After her death, her parents gave a number of the cranes to her classmates and teachers, keeping some for themselves and placing the rest in her casket. A statue of Sadako now stands in the centre of the park, covered with colourful origami birds left by visitors.

For a memorial ceremony, the atmosphere was ripe with unease. Prime Minister Shinzo Abe was on the verge of introducing legislation that would commit a pacifist Japan to transporting the nuclear weapons of foreign forces, and protesters had packed in to heckle his hypocrisy. At 8.15 a.m. a peace bell marked the moment the bomb fell. The air was heavy with humidity, and as the crowds hushed, the sound of cicadas shook from the trees like a million tiny maracas. I glanced up at the blankness of the sky: a plane passed overhead and I shuddered, knowing that someone somewhere on that day had looked up at the sky, seen a plane, oblivious to the horrors that were seconds away. A flutter of doves broke the silence and a cheer rippled across the crowds. Three days earlier, we had walked through the Hellfire Pass and witnessed the remnants of Japanese evil; yet here I was mourning for Japanese souls. The human capacity to hurt one another was so great and unstoppable that we were doomed forever to make the same mistakes. Hiroshima had risen from the ashes and bloomed into a green, thriving city filled with bars, cafes, and kids wearing Nike, but the memory smouldered beneath our soles.

★

Equipped with a two-week Japan Rail Pass, we had arrived in Osaka at 2 a.m. the previous day and had barely a few hours to nap in a capsule hotel before taking the Sakura Shinkansen to Hiroshima in time for the ceremony. These futuristic pods, each one reachable by a step ladder, were barely long enough to fit a single mattress, and no wider than an arm span. I usually relished curling up in confined spaces, but climbing into the capsule had felt like going to bed in a mortuary refrigeration unit, with bodies lying side by side, stacked one on top of the other. It was my first time in the country, and I was primed to embrace all the consumerist trappings of modern Japan: I'd made giddy plans to roam around cat cafes and robot restaurants, but the sombreness of Hiroshima had dulled my desire to eat *matcha* cake with a Siamese kitten on my lap – at least for now. Every country has a history of war, but Japan's had caught me off guard. The inhumanity of the bombs had burnt a hole in the Japanese soul.

Flicking through my notes, I reread the last line of Tetsushi's testimony. Although the trains had saved his life, irony saw to it that they had also created a unique – albeit wildly unlucky – concentration of survivors known as *nijū hibakusha* or 'double-bomb' survivors. In their desperation to escape Hiroshima and find their way home to loved ones, an estimated 300 people had boarded two different trains to Nagasaki, among them a twenty-nine-year-old named Tsutomu Yamaguchi. Determined to reunite with his wife and five-month-old son, Tsutomu's survival was all the more remarkable given that he was the only victim to have been standing within the ground zero zones of both atomic bombs, which killed more than 210,000 people. In 2009, he was officially recognised as the first double-bomb survivor, but died a year later from stomach cancer, aged ninety-three. We were now on our way to meet his daughter, Toshiko Yamasaki, who, like Tetsushi, was worried that her father's story would be lost if she didn't continue her role as an oral historian.

The Kodama Super Express slid out of Hiroshima station, humming with acceleration. Accustomed to the jerks and thuds of most departures, I was bemused to look up from my notebook and see the platform sailing past, yet feel nothing but a clean surge. For the first time in my life I was able to write a sentence on a moving train that didn't skate across the page. As a student, my father had travelled around Japan and told me the Shinkansen were so smooth you could place a coin on its side and it wouldn't fall over. Fishing through chewing-gum wrappers, receipts, and dead flowers I'd intended to press, I found one of Sasha's Sochi Olympics commemorative coins at the bottom of my satchel, and stood it on the table in front of me. With a twist and a whoosh the train entered a tunnel while the coin stayed upright. Another Shinkansen shot past making our train tilt for a moment before it steadied and continued at pace. The coin clattered over and I clamped a hand on top, wincing at the sound. Other than a whistle of wind, the carriage and its passengers were silent.

Easing up the slats on the window, I peered out and watched the evening sun weave in and out of the high-rises, a molten spill on the horizon. Peppered with shrapnel, Tsutomu Yamaguchi had boarded the train at Koi station, now known as Nishi–Hiroshima, and travelled this route to Nagasaki as the city burned behind him. He had left Hiroshima on 7 August, the day after the first bomb, and arrived the following afternoon in Nagasaki, the day before the second bomb. As we passed Kokura station, I caught sight of an orange R, neon-lit above the Hotel Relief, and wondered if the hotel was so named as a result of the city's relief at being spared the second atomic bomb. The intended recipient of the world's first deployed plutonium-based bomb, the city of Kokura, had had the good fortune of being covered by a thick grey cloud on the morning that the B-29 bomber, known as *Bock's Car*, was circling overhead looking for the arms factory below. Unable to see the target, the pilot had given up and diverted south to hit Nagasaki's Mitsubishi factory, the back-up target.

Owing to their spectacular speeds – which topped 200 mph – bullet trains had rendered overnight train journeys in Japan almost obsolete, but the rail pass gave us the freedom to dart around the country on a whim. Having read that the city of Hakata was famous for its *tonkotsu* ramen – one of our favourite dishes – Jem had insisted we make a diversion en route to Nagasaki, and in just under an hour from Hiroshima we pulled into Hakata station, having travelled 170 miles for a bowl of pork bone broth noodles. During rush hour on the Tube, it took me the same time to commute from London Bridge to Bayswater. It was well worth the detour, and with our bellies full, sleep in our eyes, and sweet pork in our teeth, we settled onto the 885 Kamome Limited Express to Nagasaki, drifting in and out of sleep as the train skimmed the edges of the Ariake Sea.

Over the previous week, I had scoured newspaper cuttings, trawled the Hiroshima museum, and stared at footage of the bombs and their aftermath, but still a glass wall stood in the way of my ability to comprehend the implausibility of surviving not just one, but two atomic bombs. Now, greying with elegance, Tsutomu's daughter, sixty-seven-year-old Toshiko Yamasaki, sat before me wearing angular brown glasses and a rose-pink smile that matched the colour of her cheeks. Even though her father was no longer alive, Toshiko was the keeper of his story, and I needed to hear her testimony to know the whole. Below us, trains pulled in and out of Nagasaki station. Thousands had gathered for the second memorial ceremony at dawn, leaving most latecomers with nothing to see other than the tops of heads and a slew of angry banners: the heat and hostility had convinced us to abandon the crush and meet in air-conditioned peace at the station's restaurant. That we were sitting at the very spot where her father had arrived home gave poignancy to our meeting.

'As a child, I didn't know about war, and I didn't know about the atomic bombing,' Toshiko said. 'There was no peace education and the only thing I knew was that there were two atomic bombings in Hiroshima and Nagasaki. My father didn't talk about his experience until I was much older.'

While working as a naval engineer for Mitsubishi, Tsutomu Yamaguchi had been transferred from Nagasaki to Hiroshima on a three-month contract, and was due to return home on 7 August. On the morning of the bombing, Tsutomu left his dormitory with two other colleagues, but on the way to work he realised he had forgotten something and turned back. Taking a detour through the potato fields he noticed how quiet and peaceful it was, with no one but a lady carrying a parasol to protect her from the sun. Then, the sound of a bomber passed overhead and both Tsutomu and the lady looked up as two white parachutes fell softly from the sky. In a golden flash, a ball of fire rolled upwards. Thrown into a ditch, Tsutomu remembered little of the immediate aftermath, but crawled to take rest beneath a tree as black rain began to fall.

Toshiko smiled. 'Rather than go home, my father walked to work. He was a very honest man – company first! He reunited with his colleagues and the three of them tried to find their way back to their dormitory. In Hiroshima there were five rivers, but the bridges were all destroyed and they had to take a small boat to go back to the dormitory.'

At 7 a.m. the next day, the three began the long walk to Koi station. Rumour had it that the next train to Nagasaki would leave at noon and there would be no train again for another month. With every bridge in Hiroshima burnt, Tsutomu was forced to cross rivers using charred bodies as human rafts.

'Usually, it took one hour to walk to Koi, but it took five hours, and when they arrived at Koi there was a long queue, everybody had heard about the departing train and they were all trying to catch it. My father was able to find a seat at the window side, from where he saw a broken water pipe spouting water. He was so thirsty, but he knew that if he stood up he would lose his seat.' Toshiko sipped her coffee and wiped a shimmer of sweat from her hairline. 'He had a high fever, bad injuries to his arm, and he lost consciousness, falling asleep. The conductor recognised him even though he was so burnt, and tried to offer him *onigiri* – rice balls. I always thought it remarkable that even in this situation there was such a good, generous person. It took my father almost twenty-four hours to travel and he arrived home at noon the next day at this very station.'

Toshiko gestured for me to walk with her through the station, past the Seattle's Best Coffee shop, to the platforms. 'When my father arrived, he went straight to a clinic that was on his way to his parents' house. The doctor was a friend of the family and he peeled off the dead skin and cleaned the muscle. He wrapped my father from top to toe with white bandages, and when my grandmother came home from the air-raid shelter she found him sitting by the Buddhist altar, praying. She and other family members had heard about the new type of bomb in Hiroshima, and the damage, and they thought he might have died. They were already talking about going to Hiroshima to collect his bones. My grandmother asked him: "Do you have legs?" You see, in Japanese culture, ghosts do not have legs. The next day my father went to Mitsubishi to tell his boss what had happened. His colleagues didn't recognise him and his boss didn't believe what he was saying. "One bomb could not destroy the whole city. You must be crazy," he told him. And at that very moment, at 11.02 a.m., my father saw another flash of light and he hid under the desk. His bandages blew off and his injuries were covered in dust. Once again, my father had to flee, and ran outside the building and up the hillside behind the company. From that hill, he saw the mushroom cloud rise above the Urakami area, and it was on fire.'

Tsutomu Yamaguchi shied away from speaking about his experience as a double-bomb survivor in order to protect his family from irrational criticism, and in turn, they were reluctant for him to become a peace activist out of fear that Americans would see him looking outwardly healthy, and declare that nuclear weapons couldn't be all that bad if he had survived both. However, Tsutomu had lost hearing in his left ear, his gallbladder was removed and he had a perpetually low white blood cell count. Every summer his hair fell out and his old burns festered. A few years before his death, while on a rare visit to the Hiroshima

Peace Memorial Park, he had a chance encounter with a pair of American tourists from Hawaii who learnt that he had survived both bombs, and apologised on behalf of their country. From that point on he decided to tell his story publicly. Tsutomu spent his final years giving lectures, talking to schoolchildren, even applying for his first passport at the age of ninety to travel to the UN in New York to make a direct appeal for the ban of nuclear weapons.

Thinking back to Sir Harold Atcherley's remark that the bomb had saved his life, and the lives of more than 200,000 Allied prisoners, I asked Toshiko how she felt about the idea that the bomb had ended the war. She was standing next to a local train, staring at the nose. 'My father lived until ninety-three, but all my family suffered the effects of the bomb. My mother had cancer, my brother died from cancer, and I have a low white blood cell count. The bomb was not just one person's story, it became the story of so many afterwards, for generations. That is not right. The nuclear bomb was inhumane, killing indiscriminately. My father used to say that it was no way for people to die with dignity. In the past, I hesitated to tell my father's story, but now I strongly feel it's important to tell the story to the next generation.'

The JR Seaside Liner rumbled up a hill with the rhythm of a proper train. Sunlight flooded the carriage through wall-sized windows and passengers gazed at the waters of Omura Bay, pleased with its sparkles, murmuring and pointing at the mountains, and photographing each other with fingers flicked out in victory signs. During previous journeys, I'd had nothing but portholes to peer out of in the sad hope of glimpsing some scenery. Towns, woodland and paddy fields had rushed by in a blur. Compared with Shinkansen, the Seaside Liner shambled along allowing me to absorb the world beyond the windows. After a breakfast of miso soup, pickles and rice, we had left Nagasaki, passing yellowing paddy and life-sized Monopoly houses, the edges of roofs curled like piped icing. Leaving the gloom of the city behind, this journey oozed energy and life. In just under half an hour the train wove through valleys flanked by trees that appeared like gigantic broccoli florets, tumbling down the hillside in bundles of green. Slipping in and out of tunnels, we overlooked the water's edge, the wheels drumming the tracks, and eventually pulled into Huis Ten Bosch station, ready to indulge in an altogether different side of Japan.

At 2.55 p.m. everyone was asleep. Behind the reception desk sat a young woman with delicate features. She wore a cream jacket, a neckerchief, and a look of satisfaction. To her left, a velociraptor leant forward sporting a bow tie and a bellhop's hat at a jaunty angle. Its wrists hung limply, its mouth agape. Unsure who to approach, I noticed a sign by the woman that read 'only Japanese', and stepped up to the velociraptor. I waved and it stared past.

'Maybe it's voice-activated,' Jem suggested.

'I'd like to check in, please,' I said.

Nothing.

'I have a reservation,' I said, feeling suddenly ridiculous.

'Speak slowly, maybe it can't understand English accents.'

'As opposed to what? I can't speak any slower.'

'Just try again. Or maybe push one of those red buttons on the pad.'

'Oh, for god's sake, I WANT TO CHECK IN!' I hollered, shaking my passport in front of two glazed eyes.

A door flew open to the right and a harassed man in a black T-shirt looked out.

'Check-in opens at 3 p.m.,' he mumbled, closing the door.

Marketed as the world's first robot hotel, the Henn na Hotel had opened two weeks earlier to much excitement. Newspapers reported talking dinosaurs, robotic porters, and a foot-high concierge that could order taxis, so we had arrived to see what all the fuss was about. Expecting an army of R2D2s beeping around pulling suitcases, and androids opening doors, I was disappointed to see no more than the receptionist and the dinosaur – unless the vending machine counted as a member of staff. At precisely 3 p.m., the velociraptor jerked to life.

'Welcome to the Henn na Hotel. If you want to check in, please press one,' it announced, in an American accent. 'Please say your name in full.'

'Monisha Rajesh.'

'Thank you for your business,' it replied. 'Your name and the room's card, on top of the fill in the phone number. Please put us to the bottom of the post. Please press to proceed.'

Flummoxed by this instruction, I pressed the red button and began to tap my name into the computer screen, when the door opened again.

'Excuse me,' said a camp voice. 'Please give me your passports.' It was the man in the black T-shirt.

'Wow, they're so lifelike,' Jem whispered.

The experience was beginning to feel like an embarrassing party trick that wasn't going to plan. It transpired that the dinosaur was unable to process British passports, so we hovered around until the humanoid checked us in, and appeared for a third time with a key card. Too poor to stay in the premium wing, we carried our own bags, as electronic 'porters' were reserved for guests in those rooms only. Arriving at our door, I scanned my key card and paused as a camera snapped a photograph of my sceptical face. From then on, I was able to use facial recognition to enter our room. It was a nifty security measure and one that also negated the need to traipse back and forth to reception to reactivate defunct cards. Jem pushed open the door and turned to me with a grim expression.

'Minimalist,' he muttered.

Hotel literature usually contains the kind of jargon no normal person uses in conversation, and so far on our travels I had tried a massage that claimed to 'restore polarity', dined in a ground-floor restaurant described as an 'elevated amenity', and washed with a 'moisture infusion facial bar' – otherwise known as soap. Yet to stay in a 'well-appointed' room that had 'stunned' me, taken my breath or made my 'jaw drop', I was most wary of 'minimalist' – a cunning term for a room in which I was destined for boredom. Staff would insist it was designed for the benefit of the guest to take full advantage of the hotel's amenities. It was anathema to me why anyone would book a room hoping to feel compelled to leave. Hotels are for reliving the student experience in luxury: where else can you wear a dressing gown all day, eat and drink in bed, have plenty of afternoon sex, and know that someone else will replace the toilet roll? The room was minimalist. Painted a shade of Scandinavian bland, the walls were bare and begged for us to spend the afternoon elsewhere; two single beds ensured that afternoon sex – if any – was highly unlikely. The floors were tiled and looked cold, and the only electronic items were a kettle and a cute little toy with a tulip-shaped head, sitting on the bedside table. Dressed in a pink dress and yellow shoes, Chu-ri-chan was an in-room concierge with a set of laminated instructions that would prompt her to switch on lights, offer weather forecasts, tell the time, and provide a wake-up call – all in Japanese. Launching himself onto the sofa, where his head and feet hung off each end, Jem tossed me the instructions, which read as follows:

How to well communication.
Please talk in front of the chu-ri-chan as much as possible!
If reply or reaction are no so good, please talk near the chu-ri-chan.
If become unable to know what you talking, please call again 'chu-ri-chan'.
If you want to stop talking or wakeup timer function, please hand over in front of the forehead for heart mark on your right hand side.

Shuffling up to the toy, I leant towards her. 'Chu-ri-chan?'
She remained smiling.
'Chu-ri-chan?'
'Maybe her batteries are dead,' Jem suggested, trying and failing to get comfortable.

'CHU-RI-CHAN!' I screamed where her ear should have been, as Jem rolled off the sofa in giggles.

'*Nandeshouka?*' came the reply. Asking 'What is it?', Chu-ri-chan's voice had the cloying sweetness of a tiny child.

'*Akari-tsukete!*' I commanded, reading the phonetics off the sheet.

Nothing.

'*Ak-a-ri-tsu-ke-te!*'

We both glanced up.

'Did she just put the lights on?' Jem asked.

'Yup.'

'Great. Can you ask her where the TV is?'

Within ten minutes the novelty of Chu-ri-chan had worn off, and Jem was now standing on the balcony watching teenagers careering down the grounds on a zip wire. Adjacent to the hotel was Huis Ten Bosch theme park. Nothing in Japan came as a surprise, but for no apparent reason the park was built as a replica of the Netherlands – a Dutch Disneyland of sorts – and provided a way for Japanese families to take their kids to Europe without actually travelling there. The proximity of the park also explained why the Henn na resembled a glorified Premier Inn: it was where families stayed when they visited the park, needing nothing more fancy than a place to sleep, shower and have breakfast before setting off for a day of zip wires, barging on canals, and chasing children through tulip beds. After a few minutes' standing below the screaming teens, Jem decided that the zip wire was not for him and instead we wandered around the park with ice creams and hot chocolate waffles, dodging hordes of schoolgirls wearing backpacks, and lovers linking fingers. It was an incredible little kingdom with a games zone featuring old Sega, Nintendo and Atari consoles. For a place designed for children, there was something strangely romantic about theme parks, whether it was the fairy lights and fireworks or the illusion of permanent happiness, and we strolled back hand in hand to the Henn na, clutching a bag of hot teriyaki beef, as toddlers slept in pushchairs and the illuminations sprayed magic in the sky.

Worn out, we watched the lights from the balcony before turning in. Fishing my cleanest pyjamas out of my rucksack, I headed towards the bathroom. 'There aren't any light switches.'

'There must be.'

'Where are they?'

'I don't know, by the door?'

'Where do you think I've been looking?'

'Maybe they're on the bedside table.' Jem rolled across his bed to have a look. 'No, can't see anything. Just use the torch on my phone.'

'Oh, come on, there must be lights around here somewhere,' I insisted, patting the wall to the bathroom.

'Maybe we have to use that toy to put them on.'

'You've got to be kidding me. Where's the sheet?'

Jem passed me the instructions, and I read out the command. '*Akari-tsukete!*'

Nothing.

'*Akari-tsukete!*'

The lights in the room went off.

'For god's sake. Tell her to switch them off and they'll probably come back on.'

'*Akari-keshite!*' I called. '*AKARI-KE-SHI-TE!*'

After a third attempt, I flung the card on the floor. 'Forget this, I'd rather go in the dark.'

Taking it in turns to clean teeth, we felt our way around the room and slid into our single beds.

'This hotel is ridiculous,' Jem grumbled in the darkness.

'I know, I can't believe so many journos wrote glowing guff about this place.'

'You lot will do anything for a freebie.'

'Don't tar me with the same brush. Anyway, goodnight.'

'*NANDESHOUKA!*' came a voice from the table.

'Oh, my god. That thing's come on.'

'*NANDESHOUKA!*' Chu-ri-chan chirped again.

'I thought you turned it off?'

'There is no off button. It's supposed to switch off on its own. Stop talking,' I hissed. 'It's responding to the sound of your voice!'

'You stop talking.'

'*NANDESHOUKA!*'

'I'm going to dropkick that thing off the balcony in a minute.'

A spotlight went on above my head.

'Did you just turn that light on?' Jem asked.

'No.'

'Why has it come on then?'

'I don't know!'

Feeling around for the instructions, I squinted at the page and tried a number of commands to no avail. Giving up, I tossed them back onto the floor and yanked the duvet over my head to block out the spotlight in my eyes.

'This is the worst hotel,' Jem groaned into his pillow before we eventually drifted off to the sound of Chu-ri-chan chattering into the night.

The Huis Ten Bosch Limited Express was an unremarkable service that cut through the countryside in a couple of hours, arriving in Hakata at lunchtime. With just over an hour to spare before our connection to Osaka, we now had an opportunity to browse the local *ekiben*. A hybrid of *eki*, meaning station, and *bento*, meaning packed lunch, *ekiben* are unique to each region of Japan, enabling vendors to showcase their specialities using local, seasonal ingredients – and to compete with rival stations. Sold through train windows by hawkers on the platform, the first *ekiben* are thought to have originated in 1885 at Utsunomiya station; a simple pair of *onigiri* rolled in sesame seeds and flavoured with pickles. As the train network threaded its way through the country, a niche cuisine had cropped up along its lines, inspiring a cult following.

It's not unusual for food obsessives to hop aboard the Shinkansen and travel around Japan on a quest for limited-edition *ekiben* that often become collectors' items. Fitted into round, octagonal and rectangular bamboo boxes, partitioned Styrofoam or hermetically sealed cardboard, each creation is a work of art: mounds of green-tea rice are moulded into flowers, edamame peas arranged in lines, and grated radish scattered like snow. To buy *ekiben* is to treat yourself to a gift: wrapped in delicate paper and trimmed with bows, the boxes open up like Christmas presents, revealing whorls of noodles, dots of wasabi and slivers of eel liver. The dynamism behind Japanese train food certainly put British efforts to shame: what is a soggy Cornish pasty compared with these masterpieces, each one a miniature Kandinsky? Spoilt for choice by the variety of models on display, I walked back and forth inspecting the flashes of neon, curls of prawn and dumplings snuggled together, eventually selecting a lacquered box of beef on rice with a silky half-boiled egg. Drawn to the local speciality, Jem chose the *karashi mentai bento* – rice with tubes of sheathed spicy cod roe, and cubes of cold, brightly coloured pickles.

Pleased with our purchases, we arrived on the platform twenty minutes before the Sakura Shinkansen was due. Our final destination was Kyoto, but the direct services from Hakata were not valid with our rail passes. In a cruel irony, the fastest Shinkansen, the Nozomi – meaning 'hope' – was not available to us, and we were relegated to the relatively slower train, which arrived an entire two minutes later. Part of the N700 series, the Sakura Shinkansen comprised six carriages, three reserved and three non-reserved. Marked out on the platform edge was a pair of blue feet indicating where the door would open, and where the queue should begin; and passengers had already formed a line, reading newspapers and tapping phones, with one lady squatting on a foldaway tripod seat, picking at a bento box. Counting them up, I was confident we'd get on. With just twelve minutes until departure, the Sakura Shinkansen slid up with the stealth of a creep at a bar, and a woman stepped out carrying a bin bag. She stood next to the door holding it open as passengers exited the train, and bowed as each one deposited their litter. So used to the carpet of crisps and cans of Carling on British trains, I couldn't imagine anyone collecting their own rubbish, let alone being grateful for someone else's.

When the last passenger had disembarked, our line filed through the door, filling the rows one by one. No one broke rank and tried to bag a window seat, clamber across fellow passengers or hold up everyone by shoving bags overhead. They slipped into seats and swiped their phones in silence. It looked so easy, and yet I knew it would never work anywhere else in the world. Most people are simply too selfish to be sensible. From the window, I glanced up at the clock ten seconds before departure and watched the dial turn the moment the train set off. Beside us was a teenage girl with long auburn hair, wearing a pair of Beats by Dre. She scrolled through her music with her thumb, the nail of which was painted with a minuscule vase of red flowers. Humming to itself, the train leant into a corner and passengers opened up laptops and books, the homely, umami smell of cooked food filling the carriage. Unpacking our boxes, we poked at the seeds, sauces, nuggets, shreds, rice and pickles, as the girl pulled out a paper bag and bit into a Teriyaki McBurger, leaving pink lipstick on the bun.

Jem, who had been staring out of the window, turned to me and whispered: 'Is it weird that I'm secretly hoping there might be an earthquake while we're here?'

'Yes, it's very weird.'

'Do you not wonder what it would be like?'

'No more than I've wondered what it's like to die in a plane crash.'

'I don't mean a massive, swaying one, like those videos on YouTube where the filing cabinets fling out and the whole room looks like jelly, but a little one.'

'I can't believe we're actually having this conversation. We're on one of the fastest trains in the world and you're hoping for an earthquake that would probably kill us in an instant.'

'But it wouldn't.' He held up a magazine article. 'It says here that there's a mechanism in place where tremors are detected almost instantly and then counter measures trigger automatic braking that can stop a train at 187 miles per hour within 300 metres. Isn't that amazing?'

It was amazing. And the trope that Japan was decades ahead of every other country was wrong. No one could ever emulate the way the Japanese designed, lived, ate or travelled. Everything was conceived with ingenuity and precision to make life easier and more enjoyable for everyone. Not only did public toilets have heated seats, they had buttons that played music or white noise for added privacy, and baby harnesses on the backs of doors so mothers could use the loo in peace. Packets of chopsticks contained toothpicks, taxi doors opened automatically, mirrors didn't fog in the middle, shop doorways housed plastic bags for wet umbrellas, takeaway ice cream came with a chunk of dry ice to keep it cool, and hot dogs were served with a joint packet of mustard and ketchup that squeezed out in parallel lines. Japanese trains were unlike any other in Asia. Used to yelling, delays, hawkers, muck and mayhem, I couldn't fathom how this single nation had mastered utopian travel: dubbed the 'seven-minute miracle', sanitation teams at Tokyo station took just under seven minutes to clean the Shinkansen from end to end, wiping tray tables and windows, scrubbing toilets, emptying rubbish and turning seats around before the next batch of passengers boarded; and the average Shinkansen delay was fifty-four seconds. At home, a Tesco carrier bag being caught on the overhead wires was enough to bring our train network to a standstill. So punctual are Japan's services that railway companies issue train-delay certificates – known as *chien shomeisho* – for any journey delayed by as little as five minutes, so passengers can prove to employers or schools that the tardiness is no fault of their own. But despite the speeds, punctuality and perfect queues, something was lacking, and I realised that it was because of the yelling, delays, hawkers, muck and mayhem that I lived for train travel. From within my bubble, I thrived on the commotion around me, drawing comfort from all that went wrong.

After lunch, most passengers were napping. Some read and others were working when the conductor entered the carriage.

He removed his hat and bowed deeply. I smiled as he passed and watched him working his way up the aisle checking tickets. Once he reached the top of the carriage he turned round and bowed again before leaving. No one looked up and I felt bad for him. But in that one small action I realised that Japan's trains didn't need to be falling apart or filled with noise to be endowed with a character and soul of their own.

From Shin-Osaka station, a fifteen-minute Hikari brought us to Kyoto. After the Nozomi, the Hikari was the second-fastest service on the Tokaido Shinkansen line, followed by the Kodama, which stopped at almost all stations. Just the sound of the trains' names was enough to make me want to ride them all: 'Hikari' means 'light'; 'Kodama' means 'echo'; 'Sakura' means 'cherry blossom'; and 'Kagayaki' translates as 'glitter'. Even without knowing the meanings, I loved the gentleness of 'Midori', the softness of 'Asagiri' and the aptly titled 'Joy trains', of which the 'Aso Boy!' sounded fantastic. A limited express service that took families up to the Aso caldera to see the volcano, the four-carriage train looked as though it were designed by Paul Smith, and was kitted out with rainbow-striped fabric seats. Complete with a supervised playroom, a wooden-ball pit, a picture-book collection, and a cafe with a child-height counter, the Aso Boy! was every child's dream on wheels.

With just under a week left, we had a couple of days to drift in Kyoto. For unknown, and probably ridiculous reasons, I never felt I had truly experienced a country until I had traipsed through a temple or two, or at least dragged my feet around a museum. A pencil museum was enough to legitimise my visit. And in the absence of religious sites, anything old and crumbling would do. Perhaps I needed to understand the past before connecting with the present, and Kyoto was one of the few cities to embody Japan's ancient cultures. Surrounded by smoke and rubble, the country's old capital had escaped the wartime bombings and endured as a city of stillness and beauty. While half the city soared on the wings of consumerist modernism, the other half was frozen into a time capsule of cobbled streets, traditional ryokan inns, and geisha tea ceremonies. Now, for the first time since we had arrived, Kyoto's shrines, temples and maple trees whispered to us to slow down and breathe.

On a pair of un-traditional electric bikes, we rode along the riverside to Shinto shrines, and hid in the shade of reddening leaves, watching families gather at the *temizuya* – the water pavilion where visitors cleansed before entering the shrine. Keiji, a night manager at the nearby Ritz-Carlton, Kyoto, saw us both lurking and called us over to explain the ritual. Ever nervous of offending in places of worship, I was grateful for the inclusion and watched as he picked up the long wooden ladle.

'With your right hand, dip the ladle in the water and use it to wash your left hand. Then change hands, and wash the right hand.'

Keiji then sipped a little water from his palm, gargled and spat it out, before draining the remaining water and placing the ladle face down for the next user. Beckoning us to join him, Keiji lead us to the Torii gate, the marking between the secular and the holy ground. He pointed out a large case of rice in a cabinet to the left, and a load of premium-quality sake to the right, both placed as offerings. Guiding us through the right of the gate, he explained that worshippers never walk through the middle of the entrance as it's reserved for deities. Following Keiji over tiny wooden bridges that hooped over streams, we wandered around shrubs and flowers so dainty I felt like Gulliver on the island of Lilliput. Fresh spring water ran through the temple, so pure it was possible to cup a hand beneath the flow, as Keiji explained that in the absence of rules and religious texts, Shintos hold nothing but nature in reverence. It was the first time a religion had ever held appeal.

That night we stayed at a ryokan and dined on the banks of the Hozu river. Like a scene from a medieval battle, fires raged in the darkness, lighting up the water from long wooden boats bobbing around. In the tradition of *ukai* – an ancient method of fishing – trained cormorants on leashes pierced the water's surface, bringing back fish in their beaks, while tourists clapped and filmed videos. Sipping ice-cold sake, I examined the first of eight courses laid out on a black tray, too scared to disturb the display. A porcelain spoon was piled with what appeared to be shavings of fried onion, but on closer inspection, the shavings had eyes and revealed themselves to be dried shrimp. A fresh fig gleamed pink, and a cube of cucumber wobbled in a block of jam. Willing to try most things, I withered at the sight of the second tray from where a grilled fish glared and bared its teeth next to a pile of prawn tempura.

'You can have my fish if you like,' Jem offered generously.

'I'm okay thanks.'

'Are you ... going to have all your tempura?'

'Nice try. Just leave the bits you don't like.'

'What on earth is this?' Jem picked up what looked like a piece of old ear.

'Not sure,' I replied, checking the menu. 'Sliced abalone?'

He pulled a face as though chewing cardboard.

'It's expensive stuff! It grows a millimetre a year or something.'

'I don't care, it's vile,' he whispered.

'What's under the grilled cheese? Seared scallop?'

'Can't tell.'

'I hope it's not eel.'

'Eel's okay.'

'No, it's not. Ever since that ad on telly with the black eels thrashing around in the sink, I've never been able to stomach the idea of them.'

'Christ, it's a baked sea urchin. Aren't they poisonous?'

'Shush, just eat the pickles and nori.'

'How is everything?' our waiter asked, palm up.

'Delicious.'

'Lovely! Thank you.'

He bowed and walked off, just as Jem hid a bit of chewed abalone under his tray.

Wincing and swallowing our way through the meal, we smiled weakly at one another – prodding at fungus, sipping at hot, salty broth, and nodding at the waiter.

'You're the one who wanted the traditional meal,' Jem reminded me.

To my mind, there is no point in leaving home if the intention is to take home with you. To recoil from anything new and unnerving is to do a disservice to your hosts, but more so to yourself. Being willing to try another person's way of living is the first step towards developing a spirit of empathy. But I couldn't pretend to feel something I didn't, and sometimes I had to concede defeat and accept the truth that there are times when only a fat cheeseburger will fill the void.

'I know, and I'm glad we tried it. Anyway, what's next?'

Jem traced the courses with a finger. 'Steamed egg custard with pike conger eel.'

'Call me Lady BaBa ... *not* Lady Gaga.'

Swept up into an enormous crescent moon encircling her head, Hanako BaBa's hair gleamed in the afternoon light. More than five inches high, it was so black it appeared blue – with the exception of one white stray wiggling at her hairline that her beautician had missed. Kneeling on the tatami mat – made from rice straw – her white-socked feet folded together, Lady BaBa gestured for Jem and me to move closer towards her. Earlier that morning I had spotted her in her doorway, adjusting the signs outside the Kaikaro teahouse and she, in turn, had spied me staring from across the street. Flashing an impish smile, she had raised a hand in greeting. The geisha underworld is renowned for its secrecy, and having glimpsed only a couple of geishas skittering around the cobbles of Kyoto, I was taken aback to see her in all her regalia, hovering around like a tout. Chatting to me in perfect English – which wasn't common in Japan – Lady BaBa had invited us in to look around her teahouse, and had now sat us down to discuss Japan's ancient profession of female entertainers.

The previous evening, the fabulously named Thunderbird Express had swept us into Kanazawa, a historic castle city known for its gold-leaf production, geishas, and gardens filled with bridges and koi. Like Kyoto, Kanazawa had escaped the wartime bombings, leaving its ninja temple and old samurai and *chaya* (tea) districts largely intact. Whereas Kyoto had sometimes appeared too perfect and stage-managed, Kanazawa's unassuming neighbourhoods bore no airs or graces. Japanese tourists wandered its paved streets, twirling parasols, pushing French bulldogs in buggies, and licking gold-leaf ice cream – or they sat at sushi bars engrossed in Japanese baseball. Smelling of grilled fish, and lined by latticed doors, the blind alleys in Higashi district had been designed to trap invaders, and evidently still served their purpose as we had got lost, got into a fight, and now found ourselves upstairs in one of the old *chayas*, kneeling on the floor with Lady BaBa.

'This house is a heritage site for Kanazawa city,' said Lady BaBa. 'When the foreigner visit to Japan each one of them want to know, what is a geisha, what is a teahouse? The geisha and the teahouse is very secret and mysterious, but it's really nice culture so I decided to open the door of my teahouse to the foreigner, and the traveller, like this. Mmm, yes.'

In keeping with tradition, evening entertainment at Kaikaro teahouse was restricted to members and referred guests, but during the day it was open to the public to take tea and talk to Lady BaBa. Dating from 1820, the teahouse was smooth with red lacquer and covered with gold-trimmed tatami mats.

'When we have clients, the lovely geisha – ah, I use the word *geiko*, it is the same thing – the lovely *geikos* come to this room. We serve the sake to guests, then they play *shamisen*, like a Japanese guitar, and they sing a song and dance. Guests enjoy a really beautiful performance. But I have the limit of the time. It's just ninety minutes.'

'Why is that?' I asked, my knees beginning to ache.

'Ah, long, long time ago we couldn't buy watch and clock, it was very rare, very expensive, so we measure the time with a stick of incense. One stick of incense takes forty-five minutes to burn. Two sticks take ninety minutes. It is very traditional time.'

'And that's all the *geikos* do?'

'It is common for guests to go to the restaurant for dinner first, and then they come to the teahouse. Teahouse is like the second stage of the occasion. But I have a chef here who makes *kaiseki*, a very traditional food. It has regularly thirteen or fourteen dishes including fish and beef and rice and miso soup and dessert. Then after, some say to me, "Lady BaBa I don't want to go to outside from main entrance." Some clients have important meetings here with their guests, famous musician and movie star, they don't like gossip or paparazzi, so I have a secret stairway in my house. I always have to keep the secret and privacy of guest. Guests trust my business and they continue to use this teahouse and guests introduce new member to me. My business is based on mutual trust. So, I go to the main entrance and get their shoes and take them to the secret stairway.'

Unsure why secrecy was such a pressing issue if all the clients did was enjoy dinner and a music performance, I shifted on my now-dead legs, determined not to look uncomfortable. Lady BaBa meanwhile had not moved for more than an hour. Fascinated by her make-up, I wondered whether the whitening was a way to suggest high status – an unhealthy, racist fixation in most Asian countries.

'Are there traditional ways to do make-up?' I asked.

'My face is a little bit white, but some *geikos* they make their make-up very white. It is very, very traditional. Long time ago we don't have good light, so if the face is very white, it is very beautiful, and you can see it in the dark. Still now they make it very white in the evening, like a Japanese doll.'

'How long does it take you to get dressed?'

'In my case, it takes me three minutes to put on my kimono, but it takes forty minutes – including make-up maybe one hour – and many *geikos* use a wig.'

'Is that your own hair?'

'This is my hair. I go to beauty salon every morning at 8 a.m. Today they remove the pins and do brushing and shampoo and colour so it takes one hour. Tomorrow morning, just to fix, it takes fifteen minutes. I love this style, like a mushroom,' Lady BaBa giggled, 'it is very rare, in fact, only me.'

Formerly an air hostess, Lady BaBa had become the owner of the teahouse eighteen years earlier. Bored by her career, and with a hospitality background, she took it over, studying the history and dialect of Kanazawa. 'Kanazawa city has no school for training for *geiko*. *Geiko* here have to take lessons one by one. One morning is *shamisen*, tomorrow is dance, tomorrow is the drum.'

'How long does it take?'

'Depends on the *geiko*, depends on the girl. If a girl had training from five years old, she can become a *geiko* very quickly, maybe six months, maybe seven months. But if you go to university and then decide to become a *geiko*, it takes maybe one year or two years, but the *geiko* have to become very, very popular to be successful.'

'What makes somebody good at their job?'

'Actually, the performance is really important, but the best one is personality. Our geishas have a lot of topic of conversation, they have to do a lot of study, and keep tradition and technique, but personality and hospitality is important. Cute, beautiful, and performance is important too.'

Over the previous two weeks I had observed a country so advanced in almost every way, that I couldn't understand why young Japanese women would want to forge a career being beautiful and cute for men.

'Is the art of being a geisha dying out?

'So, now Kanazawa city has only forty-two *geikos*, and this area, Hirashi, has only twelve *geikos*. But long time ago it had 150 *geikos*, getting to small number now. Training is very hard. So, if they cannot become popular and famous, they cannot make money.'

'Do you worry about safety?'

'How to say in English ... it's like a members' club. And I have a strong connection with the police, so if I have some accident, the police come soon, very quickly. And foreigners are not trusted clients, so if they want to use this teahouse they have to apply through travel agent.'

'How much does it cost?'

'Ah, the cost depends on the guest. Our fee includes dinner. Two weeks ago, from Brazil we had two guests, and three *geikos*, and with dinner and a drink it cost maybe three ... three and five zeros.'

'300,000 yen? That's about £2,000,' Jem calculated.

It was an extraordinary sum to earn for singing, dancing and being pretty, and I fought the urge to ask if geishas performed any extra services. 'What's the strangest thing anybody has asked you during one of your sessions?'

'Ah, yes. So, everybody get confused about geishas' work, sometimes gentlemen ask to me, "Do you have sexual service? Do you have personal service?" Yeah.'

'Geishas don't do that?'

'No. Actually long, long time ago, maybe, maybe they had, but now we don't have sexual service.'

'Same in Kyoto?'

'Yes, of course. Around sixty years ago, Japanese government passed a law. After that law, how to say, nobody is allowed.'

'Do you have a lot of married men coming as clients?'

'Up to fifteen years ago, the gentlemen have wife and daughter at home. Now, foreigner coming, husband coming, girlfriend coming. Our guests have important meetings for business so if you are owner, and you have important client, the client enjoy a beautiful performance in this house, then the business is successful. Do you understand? Our fee is very high, it is very expensive. The foreigners say: "Yes you must have sexual service, or why you have secret staircase?"'

'Which foreigners ask you that?'

'America and England!' Lady BaBa pulled a meek face and batted her winged eyelashes. 'England is: "Excuse me, I have personal question ...", American is very, very casual.'

'What's your retirement age?'

'Ah, we don't have retirement age. Young *geikos* in Kanazawa, youngest is twenty-three years old, oldest is eighty-three this year. She plays the *shamisen* and her voice is really beautiful, and lots of my guests want her. She knows lots of history and so her conversation is really wonderful. She is very famous. We don't have retirement age, but if I can't sit down like this' – she gestured to her knees – 'I have to stop the business because our eyeline is always eyeline of guests. Eyeline is always same.'

'Do you have children?'

'Yes, I am married with one daughter. I am teahouse owner now so I have a mission, I have to connect this teahouse to the next generation. I always ask to my daughter: "Can you become a *geiko*? And after the *geiko* can you become owner like me?" But she said "I'm so sorry, Mum, I want to live in England." And she wants to marry with English.'

'Does she live in England now?'

'No! She is just ten years old. So, her mind will change, I think so. I have to find a stepdaughter to take this house. Every house is always run by a woman. Gentleman can never run this teahouse. Never.'

Glancing at my watch, I saw that we had kept Lady BaBa for more than two incense sticks, and was aware that a group of Americans were waiting outside in their socks. Thanking her for giving up her time, I stood up and hobbled across the matting in search of the secret staircase. Far from being a traditional teahouse, Kaikaro had moved with the times, and the shrewd Lady BaBa had harnessed quite the money-spinner, selling tradition to tourists. Booked up by a travel agent for more than 200 days the following year, it was no wonder that a naughty smile played on Lady BaBa's pink and pencilled lips. Taking the secret staircase, Jem and I passed a glass case with items for sale, including gold-leaf face cream, green tea powder, and miniature models of Lady BaBa herself, complete with kimono, mushroom hair, and carrying a tiny red handbag.

'She must be absolutely loaded,' I said. 'Imagine being booked up for 200 days when she charges around two grand for dinner and dancing.'

'Moni, she's had her own merchandise made up.'

As we descended the stairs, a voice sang out from the meeting room.

'Call me Lady BaBa … *not* Lady Gaga.'

Formed from two twists of red wood, shaped like drums, the Tsuzumi-mon loomed above our heads. Lit from below, it shone against the night sky as visitors scattered around its shadows murmuring in awe. Neither a temple, nor a shrine, the *torii* gate towered like a sentry guarding the entrance to Kanazawa station, Japan's most beautiful railway station. Sitting cross-legged on the warm ground, away from the crowds, I stared up at the gate. *Torii* represented the crossing from the secular to the sacred, but which side was which? Did visitors step from the station into the sanctity of the city, or did we enter a sacred space when embarking on a journey? On all my travels, no station had embodied transience as literally as Kanazawa's. Behind me, a fountain gushed and splashed the pavement, and I saw that in the middle was a digital clock spraying up the local time in coordinated white jets, followed by the word 'WELCOME'. Spirituality escaped me at the best of times, but on this late summer night, I felt the gentleness of Japanese warmth and homeliness. So often depicted as alien and otherworldly, Japan had quietly worked its way into the waves of my hair and pores of my skin. It was a rare but familiar feeling, the feeling of having fallen deeply in love.

The Hokuriku Shinkansen line had recently been extended to connect Kanazawa with Tokyo, and we were now on board the Hakutaka 566 heading to the capital city. At Toyama, a lady boarded carrying a number of bags, a baby and a little boy. Her thin summer dress stuck to her legs and she swept long strands of damp hair off her face, while hoisting the baby onto her hip. Packed with passengers, the train moved off as the lady balanced herself in the aisle, the little boy clutching her knees. Nudging Jem, who was nose-deep in a book, I stood up and offered the lady our seats. Breaking into a smile and bowing, the lady accepted, nodding and smiling every time she caught my eye, while Jem and I stood in the aisle reading chunks of his book together. In 2000 a former British Airways stewardess named Lucie Blackman had gone missing in Tokyo, and the book was an account by the journalist Richard Lloyd Parry, who had covered the case. A harrowing reportage, *People Who Eat Darkness* had shone a light into a dark corner of Japan, including the world of hostessing in the seedy clubs of Tokyo's Roppongi district. As the author himself put it, the role encompassed 'a spectrum of sleaziness and elegance, cheapness and expense, openness and exclusivity' all of which boiled down to little more than myriad ways to package paid sex.

As we read on in horror and revulsion, billboards and buildings closed in, pylons straddling the tracks. Wires sagged and apartments grew high, signalling our arrival into Tokyo. White trains slammed past in the opposite direction, and a series of pretty bing-bongs played through the speakers followed by nothing we could understand. Pulling on my rucksack, I felt a tug at my sleeve and turned round to find the little boy holding out one of his mother's shopping bags – an exquisite cellophane bag with pink writing.

'*Arigatou gozaimasu,*' (thank you) said his mother, the baby on her lap smiling through a thread of drool.

'Oh, no, that's okay,' I said, embarrassed.

With both hands the lady placed the bag in my hands and bowed her head twice, pushing the bag until I accepted it.

'*Arigatou,* you are … very kind.'

She stayed in her seat until everyone else had got off the train, and the three of them – baby included – waved from behind the tiny round window as we walked off with two chocolate puddings tied in bows.

★

'*Mr Kazu sent premium fantasy ... my stockings ... lip them ... lip...
my ... stockings! Yes, prease. Lip them.*'

'*What?*'

'*Lip them. HEY! LIP MY STOCKINGS!*'

'*Hey? Lip them, lip them, what?*'

'*Lip them, like this.*'

With his laptop open on his chest, Jem was slumped against
the pillow in a silk dressing gown watching Bill Murray trying
to disentangle himself from a hysterical Japanese woman urging
him to rip her stockings. He narrowed his eyes at the screen,
licking the last of his chocolate pudding with a finger.

'This woman is able to pronounce the "r" in "Mr Harris", and
"premium fantasy", but we're supposed to believe that she can't
pronounce "rip"? Really?' He slapped the lid shut. 'I can't watch
this bilge any more.'

I'd first watched *Lost in Translation* when it was released at
the cinema. Having never been to Japan, I was bewitched by
Sofia Coppola's soft-focus illusion, imagining myself one day
caught up on the Shibuya Crossing wearing a similarly vacant
expression to Scarlett Johansson, buying ironic Hello Kitty
T-shirts, and singing karaoke. But in as little as two weeks in
Japan, I now saw the film as xenophobic. Jem sat up and re-tied
his gown, plucking a white peach from the fruit bowl. It was so
big it looked like a melon.

'Why are we supposed to feel sorry for this awful girl? She's
staying in a fabulous hotel while her husband is at work. She's
got one of the world's most enigmatic cities just outside the
window, but spends the day lying in bed in her pants, and staring
at the wall as though she's in a prison cell. And when she does
finally mobilise herself, the only person she shows any interest
in getting to know is another American. Of course, the shower
cubicle is too small for him, and he's about a foot higher than
everyone else in the lift – which is such bollocks as some of the
men we've seen are as hefty as samurais. No wonder Americans
who've never left the shores of their own country think the rest
of the world is odd. I mean, I can't believe she takes her shoe off

in a restaurant and shows him her manky black toe in front of the *teppanyaki* chefs, and they're made out to be weird for being straight-faced and unimpressed.'

His rant over, Jem joined me on the balcony from where we watched Tokyo in silence as it flashed and soared, dwarfing us, shoulder-to-shoulder in our gowns. I had waited more than thirty years to travel to Japan, expecting the capital city to entrance and evade me, but as neon lights travelled up and trickled down the sides of skyscrapers, brake lights glowed below and bats swooped in the darkness, I took comfort in the newness and uncertainty. Big cities heaved with potential: for the next two days there would be doors to open, streets to cross, corners to turn, alleys to discover, people to brush past, smoke to inhale, *sashimi* to taste, buttons to press, clothes to try, metros to ride, cats to stroke, eyebrows to raise, and ramen to burn my tongue. But at this moment, the unknown was all I needed.

6

No Vacancy

If there was one mode of transport guaranteed to disorientate and anger me, it was a night flight. Having departed Tokyo at around half past five on Thursday evening, I spent the first couple of hours mindlessly sipping one tomato juice after another and watching a string of old *South Park* episodes. Then, as the lights and blinds went down, my blood pressure went up: I twisted in my seat, folded pillows in half, pulled a static-filled blanket over my head, lifted armrests, put them down again, whacked my knees, hated the passenger in front, enraged the one behind, regretted the tomato juice, and squirmed in misery for just under nine hours – falling asleep twenty minutes before landing in Vancouver. To add insult to injury, we had crossed the International Date Line, landing on Thursday morning at ten o'clock, convincing me the past nine hours had occurred in a time warp, and leaving a hideous eleven hours before it was acceptable to go to bed. While determined to stay overland for as much of our journey as possible, I knew that there was no way to travel to Canada without flying – though the Chinese already had wheels in motion to realise the seemingly impossible. Loath to believe anything peddled by the state-run *China Daily*, I had read an article claiming that they had the technology in place to build a 125-mile-long undersea tunnel that would enable passenger trains to run from China to North America. Beginning in the northeast of the country, the track would wind up and along Siberia, crossing beneath the Bering Strait to reach Alaska in just over two days. Now, with my rumpled clothes, dry skin, and eyes that had turned a conjunctivitis pink, I would have done the journey by horse and cart if it meant I could have slept.

With Asia well behind us, the plan for the next five weeks was to cross the length of Canada, then hop over the border to New York and cover as much ground around the United States as possible, using a one-month Amtrak pass, before looping back up to Vancouver. Our next train departed from Vancouver Pacific Station at half past eight that evening, which was far too soon to be leaving the city, but *The Canadian* ran only three times a week and there was no alternative but to travel that night if we were to make our connections; missing even one train would have a domino effect on our entire trip. A train that I had coveted since I was a child, *The Canadian* connected Vancouver in the west to Toronto in the east, taking three days and four nights to complete 2,775 miles. Running through the Rocky Mountains, Jasper National Park, Kamloops, Edmonton, Saskatoon, Winnipeg, Sioux Lookout, and Ontario's lakes, the train provided the most efficient way to absorb the vastness of the world's second-largest country in one sitting. It was also effortless. Canadians don't take trains, they drive monster trucks from one province to the next, but that requires concentration on the road, and the need to stay awake. With this in mind, it now dawned on me why long-distance train travel held such great appeal. No other mode of transport combined my two favourite pastimes: travelling the world and lying in bed. Propped up with pillows, holding a morning cup of tea, I could lean against the window and watch as villages, towns, cities, states and countries swept past, safe in the knowledge that I was going places, while also going nowhere. And if I stopped for an episode of *Game of Thrones* and a Twix it didn't make us late, and the world kept whipping by. The Mughal and Roman emperors had it all figured out: why move when you could rule empires and command armies from the comfort of a silk recliner?

Now, with bags on our backs and no place to go, we took a taxi into the city for a breakfast of maple syrup. What it accompanied was of little concern, but being in Canada for the first time, we had to eat maple syrup – with maybe a bit of Bryan Adams playing in the background. No hotel would allow us to check in before 3 p.m., for only half a day, but just as we were on the precipice of vagrancy, scouring the city map for parks and benches to sleep on, the joy of social media enabled me to track down old friends from my time teaching in Cannes, Sarah and Scott, who lived in a cute little flat with a view of the mountains on one side and the ocean on the other. Expecting a baby any day, Sarah wasn't expecting two adults to turn up and stare longingly at her sofa. Nor was her cat Eric. But in keeping with all clichés, Canadians are wonderful, welcoming people – as are their cats – and Sarah took us in for the afternoon, Eric sharing his sunny spot on the sofa with Jem. As he slept, Sarah and I discussed our itinerary, much to her amusement. After one night on *The Canadian* we were scheduled to disembark and take a round-trip detour up northwest British Columbia, through Jasper, Smithers, Prince George and Prince Rupert – which sounded more like a reunion of Old Etonians than a rail route.

'Wow, that's way out in the wilderness,' Sarah said, frowning and rubbing her belly. 'Most Canadians have never been anywhere like that. That's far.'

I knew better than to question her. Canada has as many residents as the state of California – four people per square kilometre – so when a Canadian tells you that where you're going is in the wilderness, you'd better believe it.

Snaking like a line of silver Dualit toasters from the 1950s, *The Canadian* flashed in the late evening light. This metallic bruiser, which dwarfed our British trains, needed boarding with a stepladder. Straight from the movies, attendants wearing blazers and shiny shoes registered each passenger, driving beeping buggies piled with luggage and grandmas down the platform to their cabins. Travelling in sleeper-plus class, we had a private cabin and quickly inspected our new surroundings, opening drawers, checking taps and peering into the loo. Satisfied with the compact compartment, we had barely shaken out our things and freshened up for dinner when the train began to pull away from the station, and the city slid by against a pink-striped sky.

Being on board was reminiscent of the first day back at school, with new faces passing our door, nervous smiles, and that irresistible urge to judge everyone by their bags and clothes. Fittingly, a bell soon beckoned us to dinner and we worked our way up the carriages, the train swaying as it gathered pace. The aroma of roast meat and fresh rolls warmed my soul as we entered the dining car to find everyone already seated, sharing wine and stories, a comfortable babble drowning out the thump of the train. There were no spare seats, so Jem and I sat alone, like the new kids arriving late to find everyone has already made friends – which was exactly what had happened. To reinforce our pariah status, the attendant cleared away the other two place settings, leaving us with nothing but a single rose for company. Over a dinner of grilled lamb, and a bottle of burgundy, I began to grow uncomfortable when Jem voiced my fears: 'Do you feel like people are staring at us?'

For a good portion of the evening I had noticed heads turning in our direction but had thought nothing of it until it was clear we were being talked about.

'We're the youngest people here by about thirty years.'

'So, it's not me being paranoid then,' Jem replied, running a finger around the edge of his plate and licking the gravy.

'Don't lick your plate and people won't stare.'

'No one can see.'

'Perhaps not, but please don't do that in public.'

'Maybe it's because we look homeless.'

'We are homeless.'

'Can we finish up and go back to the cabin?'

Nothing was more appealing than lounging in my pyjamas and socks with Jem and a glass of wine. Corking our bottle, we moved past the other tables, nodding and smiling, but I could feel the frost in the atmosphere. Instead of going straight to bed, we went in search of the glass-domed panorama car, where we found two passengers sitting in the dark. An elderly version of Alan Partridge was at the front, wearing a hand-knitted scarf and a red cardigan, holding an empty glass. Seeing people travelling alone always upset Jem, who tapped Clive on the shoulder and offered to share our bottle. Clive was from Wisbech. He and his wife Susan – who for some unknown reason was sitting four rows behind him – were celebrating their fortieth wedding anniversary: the train trip was a gift from their four children.

'Congratulations,' Jem said. 'That's quite an achievement.'

'Are you married?' Clive asked. His breath smelt of cheese and onion crisps.

'No, we just got engaged this year, so we'll be getting married next summer hopefully.'

'Oh right, well, congratulations.'

'Thanks, it's been great fun so far.'

'Wait until you're married.'

Jem's brow creased.

'Are you two on holiday then?' Clive nodded in my direction.

'No, Moni's writing a book. We're travelling around the world by train.'

'Right … so how are you paying for that?'

In the darkness, the silence was suffocating.

'I'm a writer. That's my job.'

Clive looked at me as though I'd said I had syphilis. 'Well that's a nice job you've got. And what about you?'

Jem sat up as I put a warning hand on his knee. 'I left my job to travel with Moni, it's something we wanted to do together before we got married.'

'Good luck to you both.' Clive stared ahead at the beam from the train's headlamps carving through the forests of pine.

'Anyway, I think we might hit the sack,' I said, 'we've just flown in from Japan and we're quite jet-lagged.'

'See you at breakfast,' said Clive.

I sincerely hoped we didn't. As we passed Susan, I now understood that sitting four rows away from her husband was the only way to stay married to him for forty years.

During dinner, our cabin attendant, André, had done a turndown: the armchairs had been folded away and replaced by a set of pull-down bunk beds wearing moleskin duvet covers. Sitting cross-legged on the floor, we finished the wine over a game of rummy then got ready for bed, Jem clambering up while I ducked into the bottom bunk. Footsteps passed up the corridor, followed by boozy chortles as our fellow passengers eventually retired for the night amid the sound of flushing loos and banging cupboards, until there was nothing but the dum-dum, dum-dum of the train. From the darkness, a distinct smell crept into my nostrils: the smell of burning.

'Can you smell that?' I asked.

'The burning?'

'That can't be a good thing.'

'I was hoping if I ignored it, it would go away.'

'Or engulf us in flames and kill us in our beds?'

Jem climbed down to investigate while I sat up in bed trying to look helpful but reluctant to throw off my duvet. Peering out of the door, Jem stepped out, returning with André who looked apologetic.

'Don't worry nothing's on fire,' he said. 'Sometimes the train hits a skunk, and the smell can carry through into the air systems. It should go soon.'

Relieved, but also depressed that remnants of skunk were probably smeared across the front of the train, we thanked André who slunk out, wishing us goodnight. It was close to 1 a.m. Willing the rocking to send me to sleep, I was now possessed by jet lag and the more I yearned for sleep, the more it eluded me. An hour ticked by, then two, as I lay awake staring into the darkness. A sigh from above suggested Jem was also awake.

'Still up?'

'Mmmm.'

'Come join me then.'

Jem swung down and snuggled under the duvet next to me before I shifted to the end of the bed and tucked back the curtains, curious to see where we were. The train's lights

Boarding the first of eighty trains

Russian women sell omul fish on the platform at Perm

Remnants of the Death Railway at the Hellfire Pass Museum, Kanchanaburi, Thailand

A guard waves off the train at Nam Thok station, Thailand

Monisha willing the broken-down train to get moving

Tetsushi Yonezawa in Hiroshima, Japan

Toshiko Yamasaki at Nagasaki train station, Japan

A velociraptor at the welcome desk of the Henn na hotel, Huis Ten Bosch, Japan

The view from on board *The Canadian*, en route to Jasper

Making notes on the *Sunset Limited* to Los Angeles

A child plays the piano at the Steelworks Kindergarten, Chongjin, North Korea

Missiles, fighter jets and tanks in the Steelworks Kindergarten playground, North Korea

Passengers are hurried into a carriage on the Pyongyang Metro system

Pyongyang train station on a beautiful sunny morning

One of China's numerous ghost cities

The Great Wall of China at Badaling

skimmed the foreground, illuminating rocks and shrubs at the edge of the tracks, but the sky was dancing with stars: millions of white clusters winked and glowed, with the odd shooting star flashing and fading into the blackness. Lying on our backs, we gazed up at the sky as it followed the course of the train. Silent but for the sound of our breathing, the cabin had turned into our private planetarium, and there we lay until dawn when we finally fell asleep.

Destination Canada adverts had nothing on the morning view from the train. Deep in Rockies territory, we scrambled to look out across a lake gleaming like a sheet of turquoise glass. Veins of snow sparkled on the mountaintops from where conifers marched down to the water's edge, wisps of cloud reflected in its stillness. Content to sit there all morning, we heard the last bell for breakfast and braced ourselves for the next encounter.

Running a finger down his clipboard, the attendant showed us to a table where a couple was already sitting, arguing over a pot of coffee. They stopped when we approached and the woman dusted her red fringe out of her eyes.

'Hi there, I'm Jeanette and this is my husband Patrick.'

'I'm Monisha, and this is Jeremy,' I replied, shuffling up to the window seat.

'A pleasure to meet you both.'

'Likewise. Where are you both from?'

'Sydney,' said Jeanette.

'Oh wow, you've travelled far.'

'We're here for my son's wedding in Toronto.'

'How lovely. You must be so excited.'

Patrick folded his arms and looked out of the window, as a tuft of his stomach hair peeked out of his shirt and tickled his plate.

'Well, my son's gay …' she said, lowering her voice and wrinkling her nose. But in these modern times you have to do certain things for your kids, don't you?'

Patrick inhaled, rubbing the stem of his glass between thumb and forefinger.

'It's a long way to go, so we thought we'd make a little holiday out of it, didn't we?' Jeanette said, looking up at Patrick who continued to stare at the view. 'My son's "partner",' she said, making air quotes with her fingers, 'is from Toronto, and as they can't legally get married in Australia, we had to come over here.'

Jem straightened his cutlery.

'Anyway,' Jeanette beamed, slicing a strawberry, 'we were just talking to your dad in the panoramic car this morning. Isn't that funny?'

It certainly was funny, considering my dad was, at that point, at home in Birmingham.

'He told us how you're all travelling together for his seventieth birthday,' she said, pointing over my shoulder to a Sri Lankan family sitting two tables away. 'That's so nice.'

'That's not my dad.'

'Oh, isn't ... isn't it?' She turned to Patrick who was pretending to read the menu. 'I just thought ...'

Conversation over, I turned towards the window to look for moose. I knew exactly what she had thought. Grateful for the scenery's splendour, I was overjoyed to see more mountains looming in the distance, mainly because they provided distraction. It took skill and energy to ignore these people, whose knees brushed ours every few moments. Sentenced to twenty minutes of awkwardness so intense I wanted to peel off my skin, Jem and I exchanged banalities about how snow stayed frozen in the sun. As we waited for sausages and fried eggs, I glanced down at my watch, reminded of sitting through many an awful play and willing along the interval. Mopping up the last of his yolk, Jem mumbled something about jet lag and we bee-lined for our cabin, leaving Jeanette and Patrick to sip their coffee. Just after 4 p.m. the train pulled into Jasper station, a green-tiled cottage with cobbled walls and chimney. At the height of the tourist season, only one motel was available that night and we trudged down Connaught Drive past picket-fenced lawns with 'no vacancy' signs hung in lace-curtained windows, hunting for our lodgings.

Downtown Jasper looked like a ski village, with SUVs parked outside restaurants named 'Evil Dave's' and 'Grandma's Place'. For lighter bites, there was Bear's Paw Bakery, and for something completely different, the Other Paw Bakery Cafe. This was the kind of town where there were more fir trees than people, elk roamed the streets, and shop counters sold bear spray deterrent next to the chewing gum. The queue for the most popular grill extended around the corner, so we picked up a bucket of chicken and sat in bed in the motel watching *Miss Congeniality* and spilling gravy on the sheets. Just before midnight we turned in and were on the verge of falling asleep when something slammed into the wall so hard I screamed and sat upright. Convinced a truck had driven into the building, we turned on the light, my chest hammering.

'What the hell was that?' Jem's face was drained by terror.

'Something just hit the wall.'

'Let me go and look,' Jem said, throwing off the duvet.

'No!' I lunged, grabbing his arm. 'Don't be stupid. Switch off the light.'

'Why?'

'Oh, my god! Have you never seen any horror film? Don't ever pull back the curtain on the window.'

My fingers were trembling as we sat in the dark, moonlight leaking through the curtains making puddles on the floor. A silhouette moved past the window, then stopped outside our door. I held my breath. 'Call reception,' I whispered. 'Ask them to send someone to have a look.'

'It's fine, it was probably just the neighbours slamming their door.'

'Do you think?'

'Yes, definitely. It just seemed loud as the rooms are so close together.'

'Okay, you're right. That must be what it was.' I took a deep breath, wanting to believe him, then lay down again, easing my head onto the pillow so as not to make a sound. No sooner had I closed my eyes than the crunch of metal slammed the wall again and we

grabbed at each other. This was it. This was how we were going
to die. A trucker was ramming his vehicle against the wall of our
room and any second now a second assailant would creep into the
room through a secret door in the bathroom and stab us to death
in our beds. That's what ground-floor motels with neon signs and
vending machines were made for – backpacker murders. Someone
was probably watching us right now through the air vents.

'Maybe this is redneck country. We're literally the only brown
people for miles and they're trying to scare us.'

'You're being ridiculous,' said Jem. 'This isn't America. This is
Canada, they're the most placid people in the world.'

As Jem sidled up to the curtains, I hid under the duvet and did
a quick Google search for 'murder in Jasper', and to my horror
discovered that a week earlier an elderly Indian couple had been
found shot dead in the local Best Western. I thrust the phone
in Jem's face. Scrabbling for the landline, he called reception to
come and have a look as I crawled onto the floor and sat against
the wall, my palms like ice.

'Hi, yes, I'm calling from room five. Yes, there's a loud slamming
noise coming from outside our window and we wondered if
you might be able to come and check it out … Yes, a huge
slamming sound. Er, no we haven't been out to look … That's
great, if you could … thanks.'

At that moment, the slam resounded for a third time.

'It's the air conditioner.'

'What?'

'It's the air-conditioning unit.' From on the floor, next to an
old and clanking unit, I realised the sound was the ventilation
system kick-starting itself. Jem looked at me for a full minute
before speaking to the receptionist who was still on the line.

'Don't worry, you don't need to come out. My fiancée was
just worried that our air-conditioning unit was going to kill us.'

'Ask if we can change rooms!'

'Ah right, yes, can we move to another room please? We can't
sleep through this all night. Right. Great.' He hung up. 'They're
fully booked and can't move us anywhere.'

Getting back into bed, I scrolled through Google again and discovered that the double murder had actually taken place in Jasper County in South Carolina. In the absence of cotton, we shoved bits of tissue in our ears, and I spent the rest of the night dreaming about fighting giant air conditioners with nothing but bear spray and a bucket of chicken.

'Ladies and gentlemen, we have been informed that there are moose coming up on the south side.' Popping up like a gang of meerkats in fleeces, passengers turned to the windows with cameras in hand and false hope in their hearts; the animals had already scarpered. Derived from the dialect of the indigenous Gitxsan people, meaning 'river of the clouds', the 'Skeena' train skirted the edge of Moose Lake, a body of teal water reflecting the sky. Most passengers went back to their crosswords and knitting, others milled around the open doorway, watching dandelion heads whip by on the wind. Lovingly known as the Rupert Rocket – or its dull official name, *Train Five* – the Skeena took two days to cover the 720 miles from Jasper to Prince Rupert on the Pacific coast, with an overnight stop at Prince George. Sarah was right: even for Canada, this was off-piste terrain. Veering west of Jasper, past the Cariboo Mountains, the train wormed its way up British Columbia along freshwater lakes filled with salmon, First Nations reservations, mountains, sawmill settlements, historical railway bridges, the Fraser River, and villages and towns named Telkwa, Kitwanga, Kwinitsa, Vanderhoof, and Longworth – where three times a week Walter the postman opened up his house for two hours so people could come and collect their post – and Penny, home to nine people and four dogs.

Although elk, moose, deer, and bears were common sights along this route, I'd given up hope of spotting grizzlies and was content to gaze at the army of Douglas firs standing to attention. For a moment, I was overcome by an urge to slap the glass and scream 'BEAR!' for the fun of riling my companions. Alas, our service managers Gill and Tracy, a double act in navy and neckerchiefs, began serving lunch, so I abandoned the plan.

With its glass dome and panoramic views, the Skeena mostly attracted tourists, but there were a few commuters and a number of indigenous people who still rode the train in what was an otherwise poorly connected region. One of those commuters was Jörg, who was sitting across from us sipping a glass of red wine. Jörg – 'as in New *York*' – was a journalist who used the train when travelling for work.

'In the east of Canada, people take the train a lot more through Toronto and Ottawa, but not so much here, because everybody wants their freedom and not to be dependent on the trains, which don't run often enough,' he said.

'Why do you use this train?' I asked.

Jörg was leaning back in his recliner with his laptop out and gestured towards his wine, as if to state the obvious.

'My friends don't understand why I don't drive from Jasper to Prince George, but I love it. I sip my wine, enjoy my salmon salad, I look outside, it's relaxing and easy – and it's beautiful.'

'Do you see a lot of grizzly bears around here?' Jem asked. 'We saw bear spray in the shops.'

'Grizzlies? They arrive in Jasper in spring, normally when they've come out of hibernation and are looking for food – especially if they've come down from a high altitude and it's still frozen up there. Also, black bears.'

'And they roam the streets?'

'Sometimes. Or you'll hear them going through your trash. But if you come face to face with one, never run. It's the worst thing you could do. You're surprised, they're surprised, but you should stay calm, talk to them so they know that you're human. As long as you respect them and leave them their space, you'll be fine.'

The idea of making small talk with a grizzly was less than appealing, and I prayed that, if we did spot one, it was through the glass of the train.

'Tray tables down, it's show time,' Tracy announced over the tannoy, as Gill brought her trolley to a stop in the aisle, placing two lunches in front of us. They looked good.

'Is this Alberta beef?' Jem asked.

Gill gave me a sideways glance. 'Suuuuuure,' she said, eyes wide, her mouth twitching at the edges, 'it can be any beef you want it to be. But as we're in BC, I'd say it's BC beef. Are you journaling?' she asked me. 'You have to do it every day, or at least before bed, because you forget the little things.'

'Just making some notes about the train.'

'Oh, you want to know about this train? She's your girl,' she replied, pointing down the carriage to Tracy. 'She knows every tree, every house, every lake, all the history. You come up after lunch and have a little talk to her.'

For the first three hours of the day, I'd been glued to the window, but the dynamics of the scenery had plateaued and it was all starting to look the same. Taking Gill up on the offer, I waited until there was a lull, then wandered down to take a seat opposite Tracy, a comfy-looking blonde wearing blue mascara and a ponytail. She had a matron's sternness, but eyes that twinkled with humour – a prerequisite for managing eighty passengers with only one colleague. Gill wore her dark hair in a bun and busied herself with her crossword while we chatted. On the north side, the usually green forests were knitted into a patchwork of red and brown where a pine-beetle infestation had destroyed the trees.

'Tree huggers wouldn't let 'em be sprayed,' Tracy explained. 'In the winter, it normally goes to minus twenty-five and it's cold enough to kill the larvae, but this year it wasn't cold enough and we ended up losing most of the pine in western Canada. Thanks to the tree huggers wanting to save 'em.'

'Why are there single white trees?'

'The white ones? They're so dead you could push 'em over.' Jumping up to grab her tannoy, Tracy announced: 'Now it's time to read the news, or take a snooze!' She sat down and pulled her neckerchief back into place. 'I got a few minutes' break now.'

I glanced around at our fellow passengers, none of whom were Canadian. 'Why is train travel so limited in Canada?'

Gill leant across the aisle. 'It takes too long. It's just so far to go. Listen, if you were to take a train from Vancouver to Winnipeg and you have, say, a two-week vacation, it's going to take you two and a half days to go one way. That's almost one week in travel. And it only leaves twice weekly, not on the days that are convenient for you. It's not going to leave on Friday at 5 p.m. because that's when you finish work. In Europe, trains are part of your life, everybody knows trains, and does trains, and needs trains. Here, you don't grow up with trains as a mode of transportation so most of the people we get are European. The commuter rail service, from Toronto to Ottawa, is different. In their four-hour run they got wi-fi, so they do work. But this train? Or *The Canadian*? They're strictly tourist trains.' She looked at Tracy who was sitting with her arms folded, a rueful smile on her face.

'Oh, I'm sorry,' said Gill, 'I just got carried away. You were talking to Tracy.' She sat back and gestured for us to continue our conversation.

'People don't even know we exist,' Tracy said. 'In our old uniform, I would be waiting with my suitcase at the bus stop and so many times people thought I was the bus driver. To be honest with you, when I started in 1981 I didn't know there was a passenger train either.'

'Why's this such a coveted route?'

'This is the most scenic in Canada. It's beautiful, and you don't lose anything with night-time travel. It's a whole different atmosphere up here.'

Gill put a conspiratorial hand next to her mouth. 'Tell her about the Highway of Tears,' she said in a stage whisper.

Tracy's eyebrows shot up. 'Oh … the Highway of Tears.'

Whatever that was, it didn't sound good.

'The Highway of Tears is the name given to a stretch of Highway 16 that runs alongside the train. There are a number of single young women – either white, or First Nations – who hitchhike between Smithers and Prince Rupert, and then they're not found again. They make bad choices to hitchhike and the wrong person picks them up, usually eighteen-wheelers, and they're never seen again. It's been going on for about twenty years.'

'Why do they hitchhike?'

'Lack of public transportation, no buses, no money, can't afford a car, need to get from A to B. If you are a young woman in northern BC and you choose to hitchhike on Highway 16 east or west out of Prince George, you might as well kiss your ass goodbye.'

Gill was nodding in the corner, her lips pursed together.

'I don't mean to sound cold or callous,' said Tracy, 'it's reality. The bus goes once a day and it's at a bad hour. It leaves Smithers at 3.45 a.m. and it gets into Prince Rupert at 8.15 a.m. and then turns around and goes back at 10.30 a.m. Like it or lump it, you take that bus or there is no bus. Even now indigenous people hop on and off this train to go to gatherings and events or there's no other way.'

Jem let out a low whistle.

Tracy laughed. 'You have to remember, you're in northern BC, it's very isolated, it's so vast. From Prince George straight across the way and up to the Yukon border, and that section from Prince George north to the border, and then Prince George west to the Pacific Ocean is the least densely populated area in all of North America. So, when people ask me why we don't have wi-fi on the train, I just tell them we're in northern BC.' She turned to the window. 'Oh ... that's my favourite house, that guy logged all his own logs,' she said.

I followed her finger to a tiny house with a swirl of smoke coming out of the chimney. The mountains and rivers had gone, and trembling aspen now lined the tracks, their round leaves shaking like tiny silver bells ringing in the breeze.

A tall engineer with a neat goatee, a waistcoat and a hat came through the carriage. Ed was from Smithers and had worked with Tracy and Gill since the mid-1990s in what was like a tightly knit family unit. Considering the Canadian penchant for road travel, I was curious about how long these trains were likely to stay in business and asked Ed, who took off his hat and held it in both hands as we spoke. I felt like I was in an episode of *Little House on the Prairie*.

'This train first ran to Prince Rupert in 1955 but it won't die out, for the simple reason that back in 1958 they signed an agreement with the federal government that it would always be here for posterity. It doesn't matter how many times they try to cut this train, it won't get cut.'

'Why doesn't it run overnight to Prince Rupert instead of stopping in Prince George? It would make such a great night train.'

'This was an overnight service, miss,' Ed said. 'We had a cook car on here, we had cooks on here, it was beautiful. I think they phased it out in 1993. The north was hurting bad, the downturn in the economy was so bad, and they got together with all the mayors and made an agreement with these communities to bring business to them. They agreed that this train would stop over in Prince George. If we put it straight through again, the ridership would shoot up. There are roomettes back there, with little private berths. It was nice. You should come up in the winter, it's so beautiful, especially over Christmas.'

'The train runs over Christmas?'

'Oh yeah,' said Gill. 'There's a lot of people on here on Christmas Day. Their kids are grown up or they live across the country or they can't come home for Christmas, or don't want to, or however that works in that particular family. There are a lot of empty-nesters, widows, widowers, they don't have family around so they want to be with people. In fact, we're really busy.'

'I have to get back to work, miss,' said Ed, doffing his hat. 'It was a pleasure to meet you.'

I wanted to curtsey in response.

We were nearing Prince George by the time we returned to our seats, and the sun had already slid down the skies and was sailing alongside the train. In all my time on the rails, it had never occurred to me that my fellow passengers might be travelling only to escape the loneliness of their own lives, or to ensure their own safety. Trains provided a ready-made, rolling community where you were free to be as involved or as aloof as you wanted. Conversation and good food were almost always within arm's reach, and even if you didn't want to be the centre of attention, the sense of belonging was innate. The white noise of other people's laughter, guitar-strumming and movies, provided a cloak of comfort, and the reassurance that as long as you stayed on board, you would never be alone.

Traveller privilege had hit its peak when British Columbia's sunshine, lakes and blue skies posed as nothing more than the backdrop to a day spent reading, but the second leg of the trip from Prince George to Prince Rupert went by in a blur of cups of tea and Cormac McCarthy. Throughout the day there were numerous delays owing to the freight trains that took precedence, thundering past for fifteen minutes at a time with more than two hundred containers marked 'China Shipping', and I began to develop last-mile itch in my desperation to reach Prince Rupert.

When we finally arrived, it was cold, dark and raining. Huddled together in a people carrier, wet bags on our laps, we were taxied through the empty streets to a lodge that functioned like a Canadian kibbutz. Housing at least fifteen people who were either weeding the yard, painting the roof or cooking in exchange for a bed, the lodge was a warm and welcoming sanctuary from the rain. The residents approached with open arms until we said we were there for only two nights at which point they went back to stirring pots of quinoa and listening to Fela Kuti. There was nothing to do in town but our laundry: dropping it off in the morning, we whiled away our time eating crab and prawns, and drinking 'cowpuccinos' on Cow Bay Road, leaving with a stack of clean pants as we retraced our route back to Jasper. Much to my delight, it was in the last hour of the journey when I was staring deep into the woods at a cabin where the Three Bears might have lived, that I saw one small black bear, bounding away from the train.

After the trauma of our first night in Jasper, we decided to splurge and stay at the Fairmont Jasper Park Lodge where the air conditioners harboured no homicidal tendencies. Toasting Jörg over a dinner of sweet bison steak and chilled honey beer, we watched elk skulk around the edge of Lac Beauvert and spotted a buck so magnificent we could have hung at least twenty coats on his antlers. Unknown to us, Jörg had put a call through to his husband, who was the head of sales at the hotel, and we were now the proud occupants of a lakeside suite and a basket of cheese and wine that we ferreted into various pockets before rejoining *The Canadian* the following afternoon. It felt good to be back on board and in one place for the next three nights. I only hoped our new set of companions were a touch friendlier than the last.

Over the course of the journey we played chess, filled in blanks in our diaries, and spent hours at the foot of the bed watching golden prairies curve and slope. The majesty of the Rockies was far behind and it was safe to say that the best of the views were back in British Columbia. Not that there was anything wrong with Saskatchewan's herds of bison and bales of hay, but the canary-yellow canola fields were much like the views from the train through Arles and Avignon, and they didn't make my heart pound as hard. Still, they provided a mellow backdrop to our on-board activities. With no wi-fi or network on our phones, we were freed from the clutches of Apple, and in the absence of emails, texts, Facebook and Twitter, my mind felt clean and uncluttered. On the penultimate day, we found ourselves at lunch with Tatiana, Ukraine's answer to Zsa Zsa Gabor. She was travelling with a good-looking man at least half her age, and swept through the carriage with an air I could only dream of, her freckled cleavage wobbling with menace at her drab, Crocs-wearing counterparts. It turned out that her toy boy was actually her son, Alexei, who leapt up as we sat down and shook hands with us both. Originally from Ukraine, Tatiana and her husband had fled the collapse of the Soviet Union and settled in Manhattan in 1991, where she and Alexei still lived. She wore purple Bulgari glasses and a gold cross that would put the pope's to shame.

'I much prefer taking trains,' she said, offering me a glass of their wine, 'especially after Malaysia Airlines.' She put down the bottle and pointed a heavily ringed finger right between my eyes. 'That was the Russians. They're crazy.'

Alexei winced, glancing around with a grin to see if anyone else was listening. He was in his mid-thirties, at least six foot, and had poured himself into an eight-year-old's T-shirt. Tickled by our journey, his mouth dropped open like a child's on Christmas morning. 'My mother would love to do what you're doing,' he lisped, taking a bite of his burger.

'My husband and I always hoped that when we retired we would spend six months in Canada and six months in Ukraine,' Tatiana said.

'Why Canada?' I asked.

'Oh, my husband was an internationally renowned physicist from Quebec,' she said, pride in her voice. 'We always wanted to take this train.' She rubbed her hands together then flung them out to the sides, her diamonds knocking the table. 'But then that never happened because I lost him.'

It felt suddenly cold, the sound of scraping forks filling the silence. Alexei nudged her with his shoulder, and she rubbed his arm and sighed.

'I'm sixty-seven,' she said. 'In Ukraine, I'd be told to retire at my age, but in New York I don't have to. I teach elementary school and they come running off the bus in the morning. They run at you, and hug you, and tell you that they love you. What else do you need in your day? I don't do it for the money. I do it to stay alive.'

Over dinner, I fell just a tiny bit in love with Alexei. Here was this grown man among retired couples, accompanying his mother so she wouldn't be lonely on a journey that she should have been taking with his father.

After pudding, we went our separate ways, Alexei and Tatiana to the panoramic car, while Jem and I sat at the back of the train, watching Ontario's lakes close in on all sides.

'I meant to tell you,' Jem said, 'I met this oddball on the Skeena while you were reading.'

'When?'

'After we went past McBride. He was sitting in that living-room carriage at the back with his feet up on the chairs, and I thought he was on his own, but it turned out he was travelling with his wife who was sitting in another carriage.'

'What is with these retirees and their personal space?'

'Well, get this. He overheard you having a go at me for asking Gill for extra pudding, and he told me that his wife is really controlling about what he eats. He said he waits for her to go to sleep and then he creeps out of bed, goes to McDonald's, and buys chips that he eats in the car before coming back up to bed.'

'That's hilarious.'

'I know.'

'Wait, is this the guy with the baseball cap and biro sticking out of his top pocket?'

'Yes, the one with the yellow jacket.'

'He and I had a weird chat in the doorway, too. He told me that you had to be mentally prepared for retirement, but only to retire when your mortgage is clear, your car paid off, and your kids booted out of the house. And that tiny lady in the knitted cardigan was his wife? They barely spoke to each other the entire trip. I assumed she was on her own.'

'Do you think we're going to be like that in thirty years' time?'

'I don't think I'd be marrying you if I did.'

Jem looked relieved. 'Anyway, it's a good thing we're doing our world trip now while we can still sit in the same carriage as each other.'

A lady with black Dame Edna glasses and a blunt brown bob came into the car with a copy of *National Geographic* under one arm, and sat on the sofa opposite Jem, who immediately struck up conversation. Karen was a retired railroader now working as a professor at the University of Manitoba. She had boarded the previous evening at Winnipeg.

'Where are you heading?' Jem asked her, offering her his bag of crisps.

'Oh, thank you,' Karen replied, taking a handful onto her lap. 'You know what goes well with chips? Wine. We should get some.'

I liked Karen immediately.

'I'm going to Nice.'

'Nice? As in ...'

'South of France? Yeah, Nice. I don't fly. It's claustrophobic. I get anxiety. I get angry. With these trains if they bump and jolt, I don't mind at all. On a plane, if it jolts, now, I don't like that.'

'Me neither,' Jem said. 'I'm fairly terrified of flying.'

'I'm in a minority now, but people really used the trains until the 1978 deregulation of the airlines when air travel became really cheap and everyone abandoned the trains. Everyone but me. I'm taking the train to Toronto, then the *Maple Leaf* to New York. From New York I'll take the *Queen Mary 2* to Southampton, then the train to London, then the Eurostar to Paris, and the train from Paris to Nice. My daughter's getting married in mid-October and I told my husband and daughters that I'd see 'em at the altar.'

Karen was my queen.

'I'm a train evangelist,' she went on, finishing Jem's crisps. 'For me the journey is my destination. On my fiftieth birthday I vowed never to fly again and I've stayed overland since. My family were railroaders, my grandfather came from Ireland to work on the trains and my dad was a civil engineer who got me a job on board. Railways were unionised from the very beginning, so it was a secure job, a well-paid job, and it was pretty prestigious. Canadian National and Canadian Pacific now only do freight trains and VIA Rail came about to handle passenger trains. You've done good getting on this train while you still can.'

'Why?'

'This route is severely under threat. No Canadian will take it because it only goes every two or three days, and you can't make plans around such irregular services. I only see young people like yourselves who save up and want to travel, or the sixty-somethings who are retired. Trains are just too expensive for most Canadians who would love to visit the Rockies and national parks.'

'I figured it was a special train as it features on the ten-dollar note,' I said.

'Oh, it was a special train, all right. Local fishermen used to provide the train with fish for dinner. The dining car was really lovely, and had tea in silver teapots and toast in silver racks with the crust cut off. And technically, if a hunter or a traveller steps out of the forest and raises an arm to flag down this train, it has to stop.'

'What? Even now?'

'Yeah, really. It has to stop for these sporadic towns. It can get delayed though. Freight trains always take priority over passenger trains as they cost more and the loss is greater if they're late. Anyway, you don't want to be talking to an old person like me, you kids probably have better things to do.'

'Why don't you join us for dinner?'

'You're probably down for a different sitting.'

'That's okay, we can ask to change it.'

'Then sure, that sounds wonderful.'

Karen arrived at dinner clutching a bottle of Canada merlot with a moose on the label. She'd changed into a black long-sleeved top and hooked in earrings. She also had on a pair of bright red glasses. Over smoky veal chops, Karen revealed herself to be an encyclopaedia of Canada's railways. 'You know, they had to build a railway to build this country,' she said. 'Each province has two cities, one on the CP line and one on the CN line. And then everything meets at Vancouver. But here's a stat for you, for every mile of track in Canada there's a dead Chinese person. They were all brought over to build the railways and then whoever was left was sent back afterwards. They weren't even allowed to have their families over here.'

Tracy had told me the same thing when the Skeena had passed Deadman's Island, describing how Chinese and First Nations workers had been killed in rock explosions, their bodies buried on a little island in the middle of the lakes. 'First

Nations' was the term commonly used to describe a number of indigenous people of the Americas, rather than 'Indian' or 'aboriginal' – insinuating their primary position as stakeholders to the land. Unfortunately, that was as far as their power went, and I'd read a number of magazines stuffed into seat pockets that pinpointed Karen's hometown of Winnipeg – better known as Murderpeg – as the hub of racially driven poverty. The illusion that every Canadian was a saint was fading fast.

'First Nations?' Karen asked, carefully trimming the fat from her veal, 'they're impoverished. It's so sad. They had their homes decimated. They've been driven off their land where they lived off farming and fishing and forced into the city where they can't do either and they've become the urban poor. Traditionally they hunted and fished but the construction of hydroelectric projects and facilities have ruined the reserves and they're now being forced into the sex trade. Back in the nineteenth century, they were taken from their parents and put into residential schools. They were forced not to speak their native languages, and the Catholic Churches sexually abused them.'

'To get rid of their Indianness?'

'Exactly. Now there are court cases calling it cultural genocide.'

Karen swirled the end of the bottle and poured it into my glass. It turned out that we were all booked onto the same train from Toronto to New York, a city I had visited but Jem had never seen.

'What's New York like?' he asked her. The train chose that moment to jolt, sending my wine onto its side, which was just cause to order another bottle.

'You know, as Canadians we've always had this inferiority complex that we're sleeping next to the big giant who does everything better than us, and so we've adopted their food, and their TV ... and really all that they're good at creating is ... shit. I've been to New York, and I just love that city, I really do. I walk around and think: "What's this doing here? It should be ours!" I haven't been to the Deep South. It doesn't frighten me, it ... sickens ... is not the right word. But it just ... shouldn't be.

I went to DC and I loved it. But I like to guard my prejudices in case they become real.'

'Speaking of prejudices, we got the feeling that a few people on the train were a little, let's say, peeved, that we're two young people among a bunch of wealthy retired people, travelling on this fancy train,' I said, a wine headache coming to settle between my eyes.

Karen broke into a huge smile. 'Of course you did. And they are. You know, my mom died a really unhappy person. She didn't get on with my dad too well, and she said: "When he dies, I'll be able to live my real life." And then she died. You should live your life with no regrets. I tell ya, I have friends now and they're acting old. I called up a friend last week and said: "You want to go to the theatre tomorrow night?" And she said: "What's the parking like around there? I hear it's difficult to park."' Karen swirled her wine, raising her glass and her voice. 'I mean, you're not going to the theatre because you're worried about parking? This happens to people. Your thinking starts to age.' She looked from me to Jem and back again. 'So, go out. Travel. I tell my three daughters to travel. Not to worry about work. We may not have a house in Florida and Texas and LA, where our neighbours come round for cocktails at five o'clock, but my girls are happy, and healthy, and my husband travels with me and we live happily. You have to live with no regrets. That's all.'

7

Hail to the Southwest Chief

'Amtrak? It's full of jakeys who've had their licences taken away from them or people too fucked up to fly.'

This, from a Scottish friend who lived in Chicago, was not what I'd expected to hear. Americans are so patriotic about their country that I couldn't understand why they wouldn't want to ride their railways just for the hell of it, when the list of train names read like a power list of Native American legends: *Southwest Chief*, *Texas Eagle*, and *Silver Star* to name a few. Nonetheless, jakeys and fuck-ups would at least provide more entertainment than a string of resentful retirees. With the exception of the Northeast Corridor, which runs diagonally from Washington DC to Boston – via Baltimore, Philadelphia and New York – few Americans used their railways, and more than half of Amtrak's total annual ticket revenue was generated along this single route.

After we'd finished dinner with Karen, I'd spent our final night on board *The Canadian* inhaling dead skunk and examining the long-distance services, trying to work out how we could test them all. For just under $700 Amtrak offered a thirty-day rail pass, which in theory should have been enough time for at least ten overnight journeys and a handful of day trips, but the company was crafty enough to limit this pass to twelve segments only, so hopping on and off long-distance trains in order to roam around obscure towns would have cut into our allowance. And not every train ran daily, which was fine if we could guarantee ourselves a good time exploring a town of 800 residents, two bars and a

Wendy's, otherwise it would leave us mooching around small-town America for forty-eight hours at a time, hoping not to get shot. Several years earlier I had, on the spur of the moment, taken the *Coast Starlight* from Los Angeles to San Francisco for a friend's Halloween party, and spent eleven hours reclining in the sunshine, sharing microwaved hotdogs with a hot guitarist from Pasadena, and watching the ocean crash on the cliffs below. For that reason, we decided to leave out what was one of the most popular trains, and plotted a route that would take us from New York to DC, then through the Deep South to Louisiana, before swinging all the way up to Los Angeles. From there we'd slice right up through the country to Chicago, then travel across the top to Seattle and step across the border back to Vancouver.

With just one day and one night in Toronto, we skipped the tourist sights and spent the best part of seven hours in 416 Snack Bar, downing a succession of whisky sours with an old friend, which was the surest way to come away in awe of a city – largely because we couldn't remember very much. What was certain: at some point in the evening everything became hilarious; the Chinese takeout was the best I'd ever eaten; the futon was the best I'd ever passed out on; Jem and I both woke convinced that Toronto was an incredible city and that we wanted to live there, sad that we had an 8 a.m. departure. Unsurprisingly, we found ourselves hungover in the Great Hall of Toronto Union station, silenced by its Beaux Arts beauty. At each end, two four-storey-high arched windows filtered the morning light, throwing celestial blue beams onto the herringbone marble floors. A chill took hold in the shadow of the limestone pillars, behind which I half expected to see Dick Tracy lookalikes spying on curly-haired blondes carrying hatboxes. While digital displays, solar-panelled stations and brand-new bullet trains had revolutionised railway travel, echoes of its classic charm lived on in stations like these, monuments to not just a form of transport, but a lifestyle.

Boarding the double-decker *Maple Leaf*, we found seats on the right side of the train from where I could catch a glimpse of Niagara Falls as we crossed the border into America. Prepped for its twelve-hour journey, the train was scrubbed with bleach and spritzed with carpet freshener, neither of which did much to suppress the undertones of old Coors Light. Its interiors looked much like an aeroplane, with forward-facing, huge reclining seats. Few passengers boarded and we pulled out of Toronto Union on time. For the first hour, the train sailed past suburbia, and drab tangles of highway, before pelting through wine country, miles of vineyards flanking the tracks. On the approach to the Niagara River, patches of spray were lit by rainbows, but little else was visible beyond the rough and tumble of rapids. After a two-hour stop for customs and immigration, the train curved through Buffalo, Syracuse and Schenectady, around lakes and tall grass, before making the final stretch along the Hudson River. And with the greatest of anticlimaxes we arrived in New York. Hoping for a full moon dancing Sinatra-style across the skyline, we sat tight as the train tunnelled deep underground, dumping us in the dungeon that was New York's Penn Station.

For a twelve-hour journey, my recollections of the scenery were unusually minimal, obscured by the overriding memory of Jem eating a six-year-old girl's lunch. After 'de-training' at immigration, we realised that the previous night's whisky had soured our brains so much that we had forgotten to pack any food for the trip, save for a bag of stale Maltesers in my fleece pocket. There was a dining car on board serving salads and cold sandwiches, but the card machines weren't working and we had no cash. Neither of us was hungry at that moment, but the realisation that we couldn't have food even if we wanted to made us ravenous on the spot. The issue wasn't helped by the smell of homemade fried chicken carrying over from the seats behind, where a mother with two children was unpacking a picnic that would have put Enid Blyton to shame: crisp golden chicken wrapped in foil, biscuits, gravy in Tupperware, corn on the cob, tomato salad, slabs of devil's food cake, and a bottle of Mountain Dew. As we peered through the gap between the seats, the little girl fixed us with a pair of round, shining eyes, before breaking into a smile. It was a wise and knowing smile, the kind that six-year-olds use to disarm stupid adults. Without taking her eyes off us, she tugged her mother's sleeve, wielding a chicken leg like a club.

'Mommy, that man wants some chicken,' she grinned.

Flushed with horror, I whipped round in my seat.

'She's right,' Jem whispered. 'That looks so delicious.'

'You *can* have some if you would *like* some,' said the lady, with a wheezy laugh.

'Oh, no, don't worry,' I said, kneeling up on my seat to apologise. 'Thank you for offering, but we've eaten already.' I don't know why I lied, I would have killed for a thigh dipped in gravy.

'Well, that's not what his face says,' said the mother, pointing and laughing at Jem who was now kneeling up on his chair. This was too much for the little girl, who was now brandishing her chicken leg with glee and waving it as though taunting a puppy. Filled with shame, I noticed that most of the passengers around us were now watching the scene unfold with interest.

'It's fine, we got a lot of food. When you travelling with two kids, you bring enough food for ten.' The lady pulled out a paper plate and handed it to Jem, who gave me a look that hovered somewhere between an apology and absolute disregard.

'Go ahead,' I said, giving in and hoping he'd offer me a bite.

On Indian trains, sharing food with fellow passengers is as normal as reading a book or taking a nap, but for some reason I felt prudish and proper, even though this lovely lady was more than happy to share her children's food with us. Although 'sharing' was the wrong word. 'Sharing' implied a two-way transaction. In this instance, we were just taking their food with nothing more than a bag of now-melting stale Maltesers to offer in return. Refusing it would now be more rude than accepting it, so Jem tucked in, as the lady fished out a plastic spoon for the gravy. Later that afternoon the card machine in the dining car was up and running, and we were able to buy a couple of rubbery bacon sandwiches that saw us through to New York.

★

Robert De Niro was sitting on the sofa wearing a baseball cap. It didn't come as a huge surprise considering he owned the hotel in which we were staying, but we had no reason to think that A-list hotel owners would actually choose to spend Friday night drinking in their own bars. No one booked lunch at Planet Hollywood expecting to find Sly and Arnie sharing a milkshake. My first thought when I saw him was of the Bananarama song, and I wondered out loud if he was waiting or talking Italian – a reference that was wasted on Jem who wasn't born when the song was released, and had no idea what I was talking about. Jem's reaction was plain, unbridled excitement. If you kept your eyes peeled in Manhattan it wasn't unusual to spot familiar faces beneath their sunglasses and hats, trying to avoid the common man, but often disguised with such comical fervour that they may as well have carried picket signs announcing their celebrity. Just that morning we had seen Jennifer Connelly and her youngest son crossing the road in Tribeca, and now Travis Bickle himself was sitting a few metres away. Given that it was his first time in the city, Jem was granted free rein to savour all the tourist trappings, and I'd spent the day rolling my eyes through Times Square while he craned his neck out of cab windows, and ate hot dogs and pretzels from a cart outside MoMA. Now, he wanted to go over to De Niro and say hello. Sensing that what was about to take place would be best observed from afar, I hovered in the doorway and watched with the same trepidation I felt when David Attenborough narrated the final moments of a young gazelle straying towards a cheetah. Deep in conversation with a man who must have been the general manager, De Niro curled a lip at the sight of Jem approaching, and put up a hand like a stop sign.

'Hey man, I'm off duty!' he snapped, as Jem performed the human equivalent of a handbrake turn and scuttled away.

Ego bruised, he pouted through dinner as I reminded him that De Niro hadn't done a decent film in at least ten years and was probably a very unhappy person, which thankfully, he bought. De Niro was still sitting in the bar when we came through after dinner, so Jem took a wide arc around him, as though avoiding a sleeping Rottweiler, and slipped into the corridor, glancing over his shoulder just in case.

In the US, taking home a doggy bag is normal, and has none of the stigma that repressed English people feel about asking to pack food that they've paid for. However, we were now faced with a minor quandary: unable to finish an entire roast chicken, we had now acquired several containers of meat and vegetables and had no space to keep it in our fridge, which was already stacked with bottles of Fiji water, chocolates and bottles of Newcastle Brown Ale – an unexpected choice of beverage for a De Niro hotel.

'Why don't we just give it to a homeless person?' Jem suggested.

At any given time, there were at least two or three homeless people on every block in New York, sleeping under boxes or foraging in bins, yet for the first time in many trips to the city, it was impossible to find anyone. As Jem and I strolled, bag in hand, down Hudson Street, past the roar of bars and restaurants thronging with aggressive, pretty people, and sexy shirtless joggers pounding the pavements at midnight, I looked at Jem in a new light: few people would voluntarily spend their one night in New York trawling the streets of Lower Manhattan looking for homeless people to feed. Spotting a subway station, we crossed the road and descended the steps to where the floor was lined with tarpaulin mattresses, plastic-bag pillows and cardboard duvets. To these residents, stations and trains weren't simply portals and a way to get to work; they offered warmth, safety and community. For most of the people down here, tonight this station was home. A tall man with unlaced boots was walking in our direction carrying a torn blanket, so I handed him the bag, suddenly unsure if he would be offended, but he took it and nodded his thanks as we cast one last look around at the unfairness of it all, and returned upstairs to where the rest of Manhattan was carrying on with its night.

★

Penn Station was the pits of the earth. Entombed beneath Madison Square Garden, the railway hub was a subterranean maze of misery. Serving more than 600,000 passengers every day, it was North America's busiest station. Lit by the sullen glow of neon lights, the station's three levels were connected by broken escalators and dirty stairs. Its metal and concrete reeked of damp and despair. Never had I encountered such a joyless vacuum of a station. Even the chairs in the waiting area seemed designed to provide the greatest discomfort: narrow with immovable metal arms preventing passengers from reclining, sleeping – or waiting. Happier on our feet, we strolled around the concourse, staring at the glaze on the sugary rounds at Dunkin' Donuts, and inhaling the smell of burnt coffee in the hope it would mask the pungency of urine.

Penn Station hadn't always looked this way. Built in the early twentieth century, it had once been as imposing and glorious as its older sister, Grand Central. But in 1963, owing to the decline in passenger numbers, the Beaux Arts station, its dome and its columns, were brought to their knees and interred. Pleased to leave it behind us, we boarded the regional train to Washington DC at around 11.30 in the morning and arrived just after 3 p.m. The journey was about as interesting as a South Western train to Surbiton, so I used the time to finish an obscure book by the great travel writer Eric Newby that I'd found in a homely old bookshop in the West Village. An obligatory trail around the White House, the Lincoln Memorial, and the Smithsonian, filled two days in the capital, before we boarded the overnight *Crescent* to New Orleans where we had arranged to meet my parents. Offering them the choice to join us anywhere along our journey, I wasn't surprised that they had chosen the Big Easy, lured by Creole cooking, jolly people and jazz.

Arriving at Washington Union Station at six o'clock in the evening, we stood before its majestic facade, this time with a big bag of food from Trader Joe's. A monument to rail travel, the sight of the station puffed me up with excitement as we geared up for our first overnight journey with Amtrak. Excitement, but excitement soaked in fear, owing to a recent derailment of a train in Philadelphia that had killed eight people and injured around 200 others, after a driver had become distracted by radio transmissions from another train and accelerated to almost twice the speed limit.

'It was an isolated incident,' Jem said, looking around for our seats.

While that might have been the case, that sort of reasoning was never enough to soothe my nerves. All it took was for us to be on that isolated train, and with the number of journeys we were undertaking, the probability rose every day.

'Google it,' he said, 'you'll probably find the last derailment before that was some time in the nineties.'

Taking his dreadful advice, I did a swift search for 'Amtrak derailments' as we unpacked our bags, and pulled up a *Washington Post* article that detailed how Amtrak had an average of thirty-one derailments per year. Thirty-one. Derailments. Per. Year. At the time the article had gone to press, there had been only nine, which meant that there were a potential twenty-two looming. Longing for the good old days when a lack of smartphones kept everyone ignorant but happy, I switched off my phone and went in search of the dining car for a half-bottle of Pinot Grigio that I drank straight from the bottle.

'It's me. Yeah, I'm on. I think I left my maps in the car. Did you find them? I think I left my maps … If you do find them, can you let me know? And did you find my comb? I lost my comb. I can't find my comb … Comb. For my hair. C-O-M-B. I think I dropped it in the car. Well, I can't remember, that was almost ten days ago. If you find my comb and my maps can you call me? You take care now.'

The passenger directly in front of me stood up and began to search the area around her seat. She looked up and saw me watching. 'I've lost my comb,' she said. 'If you see it, could you let me know?' My first thought was that if I found the comb I would stab her with it. Wriggling an arm out of my sleeper sheet, I peered at my watch and saw that it was almost 3 a.m. and we had just departed Charlotte, where the woman had boarded. I'd spent almost two hours trying to sleep in the blast of the air conditioning, before layering on socks, sweaters and scarves in an effort to get warm, which, when travelling with a backpack, meant wearing most of its contents. I now understood why our fellow passengers had turned up with carrier bags of duvets and pillows. Exhausted from attempting to fall asleep, I had eventually fallen asleep, then woken to the sound of a woman making a phone call while the rest of the carriage struggled to sleep with eye masks, noise-cancelling headphones and alcohol. In England, it was easy to make tutting noises, give a loaded sigh or shift a couple of times with annoyance before the message was conveyed, but passive-aggression didn't work in these parts as I soon discovered.

'Bitch, you sit yo'ass down, people tryin' to sleep!'

Unsure where the voice came from, I stifled a giggle inside my sheet as the woman muttered to herself, but continued to look around on the floor and rummage through her bags. In as little as nine hours on board, I was beginning to understand why few Americans used the long-distance services: at night, the trains were as uncomfortable and cold as aeroplanes, with interrogation-style lighting, and consistent provocations from the kind of people I was too scared to look at, let alone admonish. But for many Americans, they had no other choice but to board a train at quarter to three in the morning, or board no train at all.

In the glare of morning light, I awoke to see Jem smiling at me or, more precisely, at the line of drool down my chin. Drenched in sweat, I peeled off my layers and saw that we were pulling in to Atlanta. Overnight we had travelled through Virginia, the Carolinas, and half of Georgia, but most importantly we hadn't derailed in the dark, and I was reassured and more relaxed, ready for one of those obtrusive American breakfasts that stood proud, like an homage to type 2 diabetes: pancakes stacked like tower blocks, straddled by bacon, and zigzagged with maple syrup. One wonderful aspect about the Amtrak dining cars was how they presented a sense of occasion. Coming through with dinner tickets, the attendant allotted each passenger with a time for their sitting, and assigned us to communal tables at random – much like speed-dating on wheels.

A friendly buzz greeted us as we arrived for breakfast. Pots of filter coffee spluttered and glugged, the car warmed by frying eggs and sausage patties. From the opposite end the attendant beckoned us towards a table where two women in matching fleeces were already seated, one wearing an eye mask with frills on her head, and 'DREAM' embroidered in pink. Both were playing Candy Crush on their phones. Tiffany and Michelle were from Baltimore, travelling down to 'Norleans' for the weekend.

'I don't do flying,' said Michelle.

'And because she don't do flying, I have to accompany her,' said Tiffany, with an exaggerated eye roll. 'I don't mind flying. You from London?' she asked.

'We are, yes, we're spending a few days in New Orleans with my parents.'

'Your parents live in Norleans?'

'No, they've flown out to meet us.'

'So, you just here on vacation?'

'Sort of.'

'That's cool,' Tiffany said, pouring out water for the table.

'I'm curious,' Jem said. 'How much has New Orleans changed since the hurricane? Has it completely recovered or are there parts that are still in a mess?'

'Oh, that's a big question,' said Michelle, pushing up her eye mask. 'Depends who you asking for. For a lot of black people, they worse than ever. White people? They doin' fine.'

At the next table sat a pedicab driver named Jonah, picking at a bowl of miserable-looking fruit. I could see he was dying to join the conversation.

'It's true, some people really prospered through the crisis,' he said, pushing aside the berries. 'For example, there was this one restaurant that bought up all the fillet steak from one provider, and for two months it became the only place in town doing steak, and the queue was round the corner – the mayor was eating there once a week.'

'While others had lost their homes?'

'Right. You wouldn't believe it now, but at one time the Ritz-Carlton used to be the only fancy hotel in town, and now there are at least fourteen others.' Jonah sipped his coffee as Tiffany and Michelle watched him intently. 'All the grads who came to help, and who wanted to make a difference, ended up staying. And now local people can't afford to live there. It's been gentrified.'

'Gentrification?' said Michelle. 'Oh, I like that word. Turfing people out of their homes. That's what that is. It's the same thing happening where we are in Baltimore.'

Jonah signalled for more coffee. 'A lot of the black culture disappeared with the hurricane. It was so bad. Black culture is where New Orleans gets its soul. I mean, Creole cooking? That was ration food. Black culture percolates upwards there and gives everyone the benchmark of how to live – instead of everywhere else in the country where everybody looks upwards to the upper classes for the example. People in the Lower Ninth, they were hit the hardest and had to find a life elsewhere. Around 100,000 of the black community left.'

'What's happened to them since?' I asked.

'A lot of people didn't come back. For the ones who were relocated to places like Colorado, where the standard of living is so high, they have better jobs, a better lifestyle, and I mean, you're not going to give that up for sentimentality.'

Michelle sat up. 'But then on the other hand? The government just flew people out of there, without tellin' 'em where they goin'. They take off? They're on board? And then they announce: "This plane is bound for … wherever', and then they drop 'em off and no one's there to greet 'em. And they're, like, "Bye!"' She waved a hand in my face.

'So, what happened to them?'

'I have a girl who's part of the NGO that I work with, and she and her family have just received permanent housing,' Tiffany said. 'Ten years later.'

Michelle put an elbow on the table and pointed at me. 'And you know what they callin' people? Refugees. Yeah, that's right, they're American, and they callin' 'em re-fu-gees. In their own country. They're just droppin' 'em into towns with a "See ya later", so people are waiting at airports and they have no place to go.'

Images of residents clinging to their rooftops and waving for help had stuck with me for weeks after Hurricane Katrina had submerged more than 80 per cent of the city. They weren't images befitting a so-called developed country, but one of gross negligence and government disregard, and it was miserable to hear Tiffany and Michelle's experiences confirm it.

Expecting (and hoping) to find breakfast options that would leave my insides crying, I was surprised (and disappointed) to find the menu listed modest items ranging from three-egg omelettes and 'steel-cut' oatmeal, to buttermilk pancakes and cheese quesadillas – with the calorific values listed alongside. We'd ordered quesadillas with a portion of apple and maple chicken sausages on the side that arrived just as Tiffany and Michelle got up to go back to their seats.

'You don't have to look hard to see what the hurricane did. But you both have a fun time, now,' Michelle said. 'And do not drink that coffee,' she added, her eyes widening at the pot on our table.

Considering the obsession with coffee in their TV shows and movies, and for all the thousands of Starbucks and artisanal brewers across the country, Americans have no idea how to make coffee. As I took a sip, I could smell the sourness, and the only two qualities that identified it as coffee were the colour and the temperature. It tasted like someone had poured boiling water through an ashtray. Edging the cup to one side, I noticed a pile of dollar bills on the table that Tiffany and Michelle had left as a tip, and broke out into immediate panic, unsure what the protocol was on a train trip. Given that we were likely to eat here again at lunch, did we tip at the end of the trip? Or at each meal? Amtrak meals weren't cheap, and there was something thoroughly irksome about leaving a tip for an attendant who hadn't so much as looked at us since she put down our plates. It wasn't particularly busy in the car and she had spent a significant portion of time flirting with another member of staff. But for fear of being singled-out as cheapskates, we left our share and wandered through to the lounge car as the train crossed in to Alabama.

The lounge car wasn't fitted with panoramic windows like the viewing cars on the Superliner services, so we were denied the full peripheral reach of Birmingham station's ugliness. Growing up in another Birmingham that was not known for its aesthetic appeal, I felt obliged to step out onto the platform with the smokers to pose for a photo in front of the station sign. Framed by dereliction, we looked like we'd been holidaying on a building site, with broken windows, steel bars, and hanging wires creating the backdrop to our increasingly odd holiday snaps. As we queued to get back on the train, a little man with glasses gestured towards me.

'Ladies first, always,' he said, standing aside to let me on. He then looked at Jem. 'You a dude,' he said, and boarded behind me as the smokers rasped and wheezed with laughter.

By a stroke of luck our bag of Trader Joe's groceries still smelt edible, so Jem and I stayed put in the lounge car for the rest of the day, filling up on limp sandwiches and Cheetos, chatting to passengers, and watching Alabama roll by at a pleasant pace. Since Birmingham, the scenery had transformed into unremarkable but inoffensive neighbourhoods laid with lawns and white wooden mailboxes spiked with tiny red flags. From Alabama the train dropped down through Mississippi where the ground reddened, and there was little to see but farmland and freight. Hundreds of cars of coal clattered by while we waited, waited, and waited some more. It transpired that there was a simple reason for the delays: of the 22,000 miles of track over which Amtrak operated, only 3 per cent was owned by Amtrak. The company essentially paid rent to private railroads to use the rest, and was supposed to be given precedence to proceed over freight, but in practice it didn't happen, and passenger trains were usually shunted to one side and delayed for hours – another reason for their unpopularity. Now, as the third freight drummed past the windows, I rummaged through my bag for company. We were in the right part of the world for my recent purchase, Harper Lee's *Go Set a Watchman*. Matching Mississippi's autumnal shades, the cover was uncreased and perfect. Opening up the book, I stretched the spine and read the first line with disbelief: 'Since Atlanta, she had looked out the dining-car window with a delight almost physical.'

Jean Louise Finch, better known as Scout, was, at that very moment, riding the *Crescent*. The previous time she had gone home she'd been scared after flying through a tornado, and had decided this time to take the train from New York to Maycomb Junction. From that point on, Jean Louise and I merged into one. I was, in equal measure, reassured that she had shared the same fears – 'lest the swaying train plunge down the riverbank and drown them all' – and appalled that she had drunk four cups of the train's coffee.

I couldn't remember the last time I had finished a book in one sitting. Our pseudo-busy, social media-driven lives had shortened our attention spans and tricked us into thinking we had no time for slowness and deliberation. Like babies, we were distracted by the slightest triggers, which were mostly trivial. For the first time in months, reading had become meditation again, almost medicinal in its healing. With a last look at the jacket, I left the book on the table for someone else to enjoy, and made my way back to my seat to pack up our belongings. In the final hour, what had been a less than visually arresting journey climaxed with a spectacular sweep across Lake Pontchartrain. After crossing the border into Louisiana, the train barrelled into a wilderness of water, chasing a sunset that teased and taunted from the edges. Bisecting the lake, nothing but a fine thread of track pulled us for more than twenty-four miles before we thumped onto dry ground past

Metairie Cemetery, rolling in the darkness, deep into the heart of the Big Easy.

It rained for five days. Not continuously, but enough for us to spend most of the day darting from one restaurant to the next, as miniature rapids gushed through the gutters and mud pools swelled in the roads. Cats watched from the windows as cars sloshed by, and Jem and I sat in the warmth of dark bars with my parents, drinking mint juleps and listening to old black men in suits play trombone. New Orleans was as I had imagined it – at least the French Quarter was – flashing with more neon than a Wham! video, the air layered with jazz and sweetened by weed. Coloured beads were tangled in the trees and crunched underfoot, as crowds stumbled from bar to bar, lured in by girls selling shots for a dollar. A morning stroll to 'Le Croissant d'Or' was like wading through the aftermath of the best house party, past hustlers and hardcores coming down on the kerbs, and kids wearing shades playing mouth organ. As Tiffany and Michelle had described it, the rest of the city was a patchwork of old white wealth, new white wealth, and black poverty – with pockets of Hispanics who had arrived as post-Katrina labourers and put down their roots. Areas like Esplanade Avenue housed regal nineteenth-century mansions with filigreed wrought-iron balconies, rocking chairs on the porch, and wind chimes shivering in the breeze. While across town, in the Lower Ninth, the carcasses of homes creaked with emptiness, covered by creepers, chipboard and graffiti. Stairs that had once led to porches and platforms stood alone, their houses swept away. It was easy to forget that this was America, so entrenched was the city in culture and history. With the exception of New York, it was also the first time I had wandered around an American city without worrying about my colour. When travelling in the US, race and segregation sat at the forefront of my mind in a way they never did at home. Here, in New Orleans, waiters called me 'baby' and my dad 'big daddy'. Each day we swapped numbers and made new friends with cab drivers, barmen, or other guests at our bed and breakfast, a grand old property on Esplanade owned by Patrick and Karma Ashton, whose spirit was as huge as their sugar-coated, butter-soaked breakfasts.

On the sixth morning, the rain stopped. As though the clouds had suddenly realised they had somewhere else to be, they dispersed, leaving an uplifting patch of blue. But it was a blue that we could only enjoy from the train window, as the *Sunset Limited* pulled out from New Orleans Union and began the journey along the country's southernmost route to Los Angeles.

'Fuck you.'

'Fuck you.'

'I'm serious man, turn around.'

'Turn yourself around.'

'Fuck you man, if I wanted my legs squashed I'd get your mama to sit on my lap.'

An altercation within the first three minutes of a two-day journey didn't bode well. Two passengers at the front of our carriage were arguing about legroom, and while I was dying to see how it panned out – stopping to search for nothing in my backpack – Jem nudged me down the aisle towards our seats. His sides were hurting and he wanted to sit down.

Formerly a Southern Pacific Railway service dating back to 1894, the *Sunset Limited* was taken over by Amtrak in 1971. Once a Pullman train comprising sleeper cars only, it was the oldest named train in service and one of the most coveted by American retirees and 'foamers', drawn to the vastness of its reach – spanning Louisiana, Texas, New Mexico, Arizona and California. 'Foamer' is a snide term coined by railroad staff for obsessive rail fans who get so excited about engines, gauge, hydraulics, mileage, dates and times, that they foam at the mouth. When it comes to measuring rail enthusiasm, I am nowhere near foamer levels, having absolutely no interest in anything mechanical or technical. I am positively a 'daisy picker' by comparison – the nickname for those more interested in the scenery, and usually to be found getting in the way of foamers photographing the brake rigging.

The argument at the front of our carriage had escalated into an exchange of insults about each other's family members, so we took our books and slipped off to the sightseer lounge, arriving just as the train began to thump across the frighteningly narrow Huey P. Long Bridge. Below, the Mississippi curled and enveloped the land in a hug, revealing why New Orleans was known as the Crescent City. A burly veteran was sitting in a window seat and strumming Simon & Garfunkel on his guitar, to the annoyance of an elderly lady who was knitting, peering over her pince-nez, oblivious to the view beyond her nose. Taking the opportunity, Jem and I settled into two window seats before the door burst open and four gum-smacking girls came giggling into the car and sat behind Knitting Nora, who rolled up her wool and left. Unable to disembark at the towns along the way, the next best way to tour the Louisiana bayous and swamps was from behind the glass. Granted a whistle-stop tour of sugarcane plantations and fields of corn, we passed streets named Railroad Avenue, and Bonnie, before rolling alongside trailer parks with ponies tethered to the fence. The glacial pace at which we were moving brought each inch into focus, if only for a second or two. The innards of these small towns and districts were hardly visited by tourists, certainly not open to dissection and examination in this way, and I felt privileged to be able to look upon the striped awning of the local bakery, a festive red bow left on a picket fence since Christmas, and an old gardener pruning a rose bush.

After Lafayette, the first diners swayed through to the lunch car and the smell of garlic drifted through the door. Reluctant to spend all our money on mediocre meals, I went downstairs to the cafe to see what was on offer. More a tuck shop than a cafe, it was staffed by one attendant who was sitting at a table playing cards with an off-duty colleague. He didn't look up. Standing at the counter, I glanced over at him every few seconds, then raised my eyebrows, wishing I had the balls to tell him to get up and do his job. Eventually he sighed, laid down his cards, and sauntered around the counter.

'What can I get you?'

Ordering an Angus cheeseburger, I waited for him to sniff, unwrap the burger with deliberate torpidity, then toss it into the microwave, all the while chatting over my head. An eternity passed as he sat back down and resumed his game. When the microwave pinged, he waited a few moments before heaving himself up and casting his friend a look of annoyance. As he dropped the burger into a cardboard carton, he nudged a tip box and shot me a challenging look. Suppressing every instinct to throw the burger at his head, I put $7.25 on the counter – the price of the burger – then after a pause, flicked another dollar bill into the box, disappointed by my own weakness. Fortunately, the burger was so good I'd eaten half of it by the time I'd sat down next to Jem, who, typically, had not wanted anything before and now wanted a bite.

'God, that's delicious,' he said. 'Can you get me one?'

'I've just been down there.'

'I know,' he stretched, then winced. 'My side still hurts, and anyway it's nice and sunny up here and I'm cosy.'

Counting up some cash, I went back downstairs to where the attendant was now on his phone watching a YouTube video of a man with a pellet gun being arrested in an Applebee's, then shot in the restaurant's toilet. He stuck his tongue into his cheek, then swaggered round the counter and gazed at me.

'And what can I get you now?'

'Another cheeseburger.'

My single dollar had pissed him off. Working as a waitress throughout my four years at university, I too had suffered the indignity of the minimum wage, and was in favour of tipping if the service was above and beyond the call of duty. I'd scrubbed stale beer at 3 a.m., been slapped on the backside, polished cutlery until my fingers stung, and endured all horror of customers – with no expectation of a tip. But a quick calculation suggested that I had just given this man a 13 per cent bonus for using a microwave, and he was expecting another. In the 1960s, Eric Newby had written about tipping, or more specifically, about who not to tip: 'Anyone in hotels or restaurants where a service charge is added to the bill, unless some member of the staff has rendered you an extraordinary service, such as carrying you upstairs and putting you to bed the right way up or cutting up your dinner for you if you have your arm in plaster.' The offending cheeseburger was plopped onto another piece of cardboard and shoved towards me, as was the tip box. There was no doubt that I had been rendered an extraordinary service, but for rather more different reasons from those Newby had described. Looking at the box, I paid for my burger, then fixing the attendant with a look of defiance, I picked up the burger and stomped upstairs, making a mental note to send Jem the next time either of us wanted food.

After a dreadful night's sleep, Jem and I were seated side by side in the dining car opposite Michael and Erin, who could have been father and daughter were it not for the way Michael kept glancing at Erin's dove tattoo as it winked from over her bra. Michael had the nondescript features of an All-American sitcom dad, and was travelling to his daughter's wedding in Irvine, California. I recognised Erin from our evening stop at Houston, where she had cornered me to ask where she could buy a ticket for 'LA or wherever'. The vagueness of her question suggested that not a lot of thought had gone into her travel plans, confirmed by the tiny knapsack now sitting on her lap. Jem was convinced she'd killed someone and was on the run. Erin was wearing a black Slipknot hoodie and had long black hair with purple streaks, and a tongue stud that she kept rubbing along her teeth.

'So, you're British?' she asked.

'Yes. How about you? Are you from Houston?'

'I'm from New York, but I moved to Houston two months ago to get away from everyone I know.'

'What's it like?' Jem asked, stepping on my foot as if to prove his theory.

'Oh, I hate it, I'm going to move back. Have you ever been on the Thames? And do Kate and whatshisname actually live in Buckingham Palace?'

'No, they live in Kensington Palace.'

'Is Henry VIII from where you're from?'

'I used to go to school in Hampton, which is where he lived,' Jem said, 'at Hampton Court Palace.'

'He had eight wives, right?' Erin asked, stirring three packets of sugar into her coffee, then reaching for mine.

'Six,' I said.

'And did he kill them all?'

'No, a good way to remember is *divorced, beheaded, died, divorced, beheaded, survived*. It's about the only thing I remember from A-level history.'

'I love that show, *The Tudors*. I'm obsessed. We don't have history in the States. I mean, we're like, 200 years old, we don't have anything, so we just pick off other people's.'

The Texas scrubland rolled by. Lonely cacti prickled the landscape, but the emptiness was terrifying. There were no roads, no homes, no signs of human life, and I wondered if anyone had ever walked this ground or if it existed for the sole benefit of train travellers to gaze at and muse over.

'It looks like *Breaking Bad* country,' I remarked to Erin.

'What's *Breaking Bad*?'

'It's an American show about a chemistry teacher with cancer who makes money cooking meth.'

'I like *Shameless*. It reminds me of my family. Can I get some more coffee?'

'What's *Shameless*?' Michael cut in.

'It's about this white trash, trailer park family,' Erin replied.

'Where are you from?' I asked.

'Staten Island. Go ahead, judge me.'

'I've never been.'

'It's not for tourists,' Erin brightened. 'Anyways, when I get to LA I think I'm going to drive to Joshua Tree. I don't know where my friend is, I think it's Joshua Tree. And then I'm going to go to the Dash store.'

'What's the Dash store?' Michael asked.

'The Kardashians have a store there. I like the Kardashians, I watch them on TV. *Keeping Up with the Kardashians* and *Shameless*.'

Having lost the best part of half an hour covering Erin's television preferences, we turned to Michael, curious about his story. For a journey of this length, it was unusual for someone middle-aged, middle class, single – and apparently of sound mind – to be travelling by train when flying was cheaper and two days faster.

'Oh, I hate flying, I won't do it. It's too stressful – the check-in, security, waiting for baggage. This is so much more relaxing. And, you know, I get to chat to pretty girls,' he shrugged, with an admirable lack of shame.

'I'm taking it 'cos it's cheap,' Erin replied. 'That's it.'

Michael laughed and stretched an arm across the back of their seats. 'I'm not too good at picking up pretty girls any more. When I was in my twenties I used to take the bus a lot, and when I got on I'd hover before getting my ticket and look around for the prettiest girl. I'd then go over to her and say: "You can take a chance on me, or you could wait and take a chance on a 300lb fat guy." And they'd look out the window and then say "Okay!" I mean, I didn't want to sit next to a 300lb fat guy either and it would work every time.'

The creepiness was remarkable, but I had to give Michael his dues for being open about his predatory agenda, which had done little to deter Erin, whose hand kept brushing his knee. Leaving them to their burgeoning romance, we finished breakfast and returned to our seats to find that someone else had suffered a worse night's sleep. Behind us, a man wearing an overcoat, trainers, and no socks, was kneeling up on the floor in front of his chair, sleeping face down in his pillow – or he'd collapsed and died in the night and no one had noticed. On reflection, jakeys and fuck-ups was not a bad call at all, and so far most people drawn to the Amtrak trains were unhinged to varying degrees, but there was still time, and three more trains to go, before making any firm judgements.

As the train rattled and banged along a nasty bit of track, Jem clutched his side, his face twisted in pain. Lifting up his T-shirt I found a series of speckles around his rib cage that looked no worse than a rash.

'Maybe you've got a bit of ringworm.'

'What?!'

'You might have picked it up from Patrick and Karma's kitten in New Orleans.'

'I didn't touch the kitten, you know I'm allergic to cats. Anyway, it doesn't itch, it hurts.'

Dropping the T-shirt, I assured Jem that his rash would go away, and went back to staring at the desert. Squatting on burnished hillsides was an abundance of prickly-pear cacti with flat pads like table-tennis bats, rimmed with red flowers. A single eagle soared overhead, and the occasional pick-up threw up dust in the distance. A copy of Cormac McCarthy's *Blood Meridian* lay in my lap, the bookmark where I had parked it the night before. Delays were for reading, but while we were on the move it was impossible to stay focused when there were so many conversations on which to eavesdrop. And it took just one sneeze or a glance into a bag of crisps to miss black-tailed jackrabbits springing into holes, and ground squirrels springing out of them.

Sleep crept up on us, and we woke to find the train had stopped at El Paso and passengers charging to the doors. Panicked, we leapt to the window and saw that a line had formed on the platform, leading to a lady wearing a checked shirt and a baseball cap. Next to her were two ice coolers packed with foil-wrapped burritos that she was touting for two bucks apiece. Burrito Lady was an icon of the *Sunset Limited*'s route. Joining the queue, we managed to scoop up two of the last hot beef and bean burritos, standing in line behind staff from the dining car who knew better than to eat their own wares. Boarding the train again, we noticed a number of security guards with dogs wandering the platform. Barbed wire looped along the station netting, and as the train set off along the Mexican border, a border patrol car raced alongside checking that no stowaways had slipped under the train or clung to the sides.

'I have stage four cancer.' Ernie tapped the oxygen cylinder by his side, which was wired into his nose. Staring at the Arizona

sunset, his bony hands in his lap, Ernie gave a little laugh. 'I can't
fly no more, not with the pressure on my lungs.' He paused for a
few minutes, pointing at the mountains wearing scarves of cloud.
'But why would I want to when I can sit here with a beer and
watch something this beautiful.' The sightseer car was crammed
with passengers who had gathered to witness the phenomenon
of an Arizona sunset. Two foamers had set up video-recording
equipment and were narrating the plums and purples that
streaked the skies, and Erin was now crying on Michael about her
ex-boyfriend. Sunsets had a strange way of gathering travellers in
a way they didn't at home. No one stopped cooking dinner or
switched off *EastEnders* to watch the sun set, and yet when abroad,
the entire day hinged on the six or seven minutes it took for an
everyday occurrence. Sunsets were an experience, a few moments
of movement and impermanence that by their very nature were
impossible to catch and contain – much like train journeys – yet
it didn't stop people from trying, their iPhones pressed up against
the glass.

Ernie was eighty-two years old and lived in Tucson, our next
stop, however the train was already two hours behind schedule
and he and his wife would only reach home around midnight.

'We've always wanted to take this train, but when you have
something on your doorstep, you never do until it's too late.
There is so much to see in this country, and most of us never
bother to look at it.'

'Have you travelled a lot outside the US?' I asked, untangling
Ernie's wires from my foot, wary of tripping over and killing
him off.

'Oh, I've fought in almost every war you can think of. Did a
lot of travelling that way. But I'm glad that I've had the chance
to ride this train, and with my wife. Not a lot of folks can say
that.' Ernie turned to us, his dentures holding up his smile. 'You
folks would be welcome to come and stay with us in Tucson. We
would love to have you and show you round our ranch.'

'Likewise. If you ever come to London, you should get in
touch,' Jem said.

'You're too kind.' Ernie raised his beer. 'But I won't live to see the end of this month.'

Jem had shingles. The rash had erupted into a belt of blisters around his chest, which explained the nerve pain whenever the train had passed over uneven ground. Through the magic of Facetime, my mother, a GP, had examined the vesicles and made the diagnosis, sending us a link to the course of antivirals he needed to take. Secondary to dying in a derailment, our next greatest fear had been falling ill in the US, and we were now sitting in the waiting room of a private clinic in downtown LA, about to experience the degradation of American healthcare. To Jem's annoyance, the walls were covered in posters for shingles vaccinations featuring wrinkled hands and Zimmer frames.

'Why have I got a geriatric affliction?' he whispered.

'It's not geriatric, anyone can get it.'

'Anyone over sixty-five.'

The door opened and we were called in to see the doctor. Grecian and bronzed with an abundance of wax in his curls, the doctor was wearing theatre scrubs beneath his open coat. The only surgery he was likely to perform was removing a splinter from a toddler in what was a glorified walk-in centre. Jem perched on the couch while I hovered in the corner. Lifting up Jem's T-shirt, the doctor took a casual glance at his rash.

'Does it itch?'

'No, it hurts. It tingles.'

'I can give you a cream.'

For what was set to cost at least $400 for three minutes of his time, I was determined to get our money's worth and spoke up from my corner.

'My mum was concerned that he might have shingles and suggested that we get a course of antivirals.'

'Oh yeah? And what does Mom do?'

'She's a GP.'

'Well, we specialise in this country. We don't do general medicine.'

'That's fine, but she suggested we keep a course of antivirals just in case it turns out to be shingles and we have no access to a doctor.'

'You can come back if it's shingles, which I don't think this is.'

'That's the problem: we're leaving tomorrow and will have to find another doctor.'

'So, you just want to take medicines without considering the side effects?'

'I won't take them unless it's actually shingles,' Jem said.

'Fine, have it your way. I can give you a three-day course of acyclovir.'

'Doesn't he need a seven-day course?'

Glaring at me, he wrote out a script for three days and booted us back into reception where it took more than two hours to process our insurance details and make the payment. Four days later, Jem's blisters broke down and wept, his chest seared with pain. Calling for another doctor, who diagnosed him with shingles – we both broke down and wept as he charged $400 to write out a script for a seven-day course of acyclovir.

'This is beyond a joke.'

After the shingles shenanigans, we'd upgraded to a roomette for the journey from LA to Chicago, our sixtieth train, in the hope that Jem would sleep better, and we were now being flung around in our berths as the train beat east through California. It was nearing midnight and I could hear our attendant fidgeting in the corridor as the train careered in the darkness, my head knocking against the wall. Without leaning forward, I could reach the door handle, so small was the space, which had come at the cost of around $50 per square inch. It was no bigger than a walk-in shower.

'I can't sleep up here,' said Jem.

'Why not?'

'It's so cramped, I'm getting claustrophobic.'

Kicking off my blankets, I ducked out of my berth, still banging my head, and offered to swap. There was no room for me to stand in the roomette as Jem climbed down, so I waited outside in my socks as he wriggled down and slid into my berth. Hauling myself up, I shuffled into a space no bigger than a luggage rack. For five minutes, I lay in the dark, reminded of the time I'd had an MRI for a stress fracture in my hip.

'Screw this. I'm coming down.'

'I told you, I could barely turn my head from side to side.'

Topping and tailing, we managed to contort like a pair of circus freaks in a box, and fell asleep as the train shuddered and groaned through the night.

As compensation, the journey on the *Southwest Chief* proved to be one of scenic enchantment. Unfurling ourselves in Gallup, New Mexico, we spent the day on safari, squashed in our roomette, drinking tea, and scouting for animals. Unable to hear the announcements on the crackling speakers, we had to guess where we were and make do with blunt responses from our attendant, who had shown no interest since we had boarded and failed to tip him for saying hello. Somewhere between New Mexico and Arizona – maybe Raton – nervous deer tensed and scarpered as the train came blaring through their homeland. Scores of stags lay in golden grass, their antlers tuned in like antennae, and punk cows with orange ear-tags watched moodily as the train inched up the Santa Fe Trail. Across Arizona, ponies wearing white socks drank from pools, creeks curved among orchards, and tiny white chapels remained coy behind curtains of willow. Unless embarking on an ill-advised hike, we would never normally be privy to this part of the country and its wildlife.

The curse of darkness eclipsed Kansas and Missouri, which slipped by overnight, and we spent the final morning in the dining car talking to Steven over breakfast. A six-foot-three Texan librarian with waist-length hair and acne, Steven was ferociously in favour of gun control, one of the reasons why he had left his hometown of Arlington, which, according to him, was full of 'open-carrying, homophobic, transphobic pricks'.

'I mean, what are you so frightened of? No one's going to kill you or your family except another white person with a gun,' he said, stirring sugar into his coffee.

A couple of heads turned to look in our direction. Being in favour of a complete ban on firearms, I was delighted to hear Steven voice an unpopular opinion with such force. I gently egged him on. 'Do you think that open-carry is unnecessary?'

'Guns are unnecessary. It's that simple. You just look at the stats. There are more gun-related deaths on American soil than the total number of American deaths in every war of our history – since the Revolutionary War.'

The car was silent but for the sound of the train rattling the tracks.

'Is that why you left?'

'Like I said, they're anti-LGBTQ, transphobic bigots, the kind of bastards who believe in conversion therapy. There's a whole young queer generation growing up terrified, and suicidal, and full of mental health problems because you can be refused service anywhere because of their "sincerely held religious beliefs".' Steven sat upright. 'And ... I myself actually identify as Ophelia.'

To my right, a woman literally stopped a glass from touching her lips. I was in heaven.

'Anyways, I'm getting off at Princeton.' Ophelia rose to her full height, tossing her hair over one shoulder and extended a hand. 'It was a real pleasure to meet you guys. I hope you enjoy Chicago, it's an awesome city.'

'Lovely to meet you too,' I replied. '*Really* lovely.'

Ophelia strode out of the car and we followed at her heels, basking in her wake.

With the subtlety of a right hook, I turned my back on the family behind me and eased out my notebook, ready to eavesdrop. Such cunning would usually have reaped great rewards were the family not speaking Pennsylvania Dutch dialect, leaving me and my pen with little to do but doodle. The twelve-strong Amish family had boarded at Columbus, Wisconsin, and were by far the most compelling aspect of the journey. Departing Chicago just after lunch, the *Empire Builder* had tunnelled through fog for two hours, before it lifted to allow for rain. The gloom had dulled the moods of most passengers, who were slumped around the viewing car, cajoling kids onto iPads and watching movies – with the exception of the Amish family, who appeared to be having a party. Known for their simple rural living, rejection of technology and desire to keep a distance from the outside world, Amish are Christians whose roots can be traced back to the early sixteenth-century Anabaptist movement in Europe. Fleeing religious persecution, Amish arrived in America looking for land to farm. As a result of family being the focus of their way of life – most families have an average of five children – their 300,000-strong population is one of the fastest-growing groups in North America, with the majority of settlements dotted around Pennsylvania, Ohio, Indiana and Wisconsin.

Dressed in bonnets and ankle-length skirts, the women were fussing over a toddler who was being passed around his bearded uncles, each one quick to smother him with cuddles. His hair was cut into the same pudding-bowl style as the men, and his romper suit featured a black ribbon tied under the chin. Two of his uncles sat him in the middle of a table and opened up a storybook called *Mei Bopp*, talking him through the pictures as his grandfather looked on with an all-consuming joy. The rest of the family were playing checkers and giggling. On the opposite side of the car sat another American family. Sipping his second can of Coors, the dad was scrolling through his phone. A couple of tables away his wife was trying to pacify two young girls whimpering for iPads. Side by side, the two families illustrated where we had gone wrong as a people. The toddler was thriving on the undivided attention of his family, while across the car there was disconnect.

Just before Tomah, the Amish family fastened their capes and adjusted their hats, buckling the toddler into a tiny coat. Smiling, the grandfather walked over to the two little girls, who were mesmerised by his teeth – half of which were missing, the other half decayed. Reaching behind their ears, he pulled out two dollar bills. Disappointed to see them go, I moved to the window and watched as they gathered on the platform like a portrait from the past, and waved as the train continued on its way.

'They're good, kind people,' said the passenger opposite me, reading my mind. 'Sure, they're a lil different than us, but who isn't? And their furniture is beautiful. Expensive, but top-of-the-range stuff.'

'Their furniture?'

'Carpenters, a lot of them. They craft with their hands. Clockmakers, cabinetmakers, and so on. Although some of them do use mechanical tools as long as it's not to benefit their own homes. If it's for a customer, then that's okay. Amish furniture is well known through these parts. You should check it out.'

'I thought Amish couldn't use anything but horses and carts?'

'For religious reasons, most use only horse-drawn vehicles known as buggies. It's a way of making sure that they restrict their movements to within their communities. Having a car is seen as a temptation to go further out. But Amish use buses and trains for long-distance travel, and they're a pretty common sight on Amtrak services in the northeast.'

'Do you take this route regularly?'

'I do. I didn't used to, but it costs me around $300 in fuel for a round-trip from Fargo to Chicago, and it's $440 for the four of us to travel on the train. For the extra $140, I don't have to drive through the city, I'm not tired, my boys can run up and down the train and play, and I can sit here and look out of the window and have a can – and be happy.'

'Don't the delays bother you?'

'You don't take the train to go nowhere fast. Nobody does. But it's a sacrifice you make for the upsides. And you know, sometimes it's nice to have a little time to just think. That's just me though getting old. I like to sit here and remember when I took the train with my dad. He was a railroader and he used to tell me how he saw moose and bears and stuff by the trackside. And you know why? Because they're smart. You're not allowed to hunt on railway property, so the animals still linger down there because they know they're safe.'

Playing musical chairs on an Amtrak was a guaranteed way to sponge up information, some trivial, but for the most part juicy little nuggets that I tucked away. The culture of these trains contrasted wildly with the way we conducted ourselves off the rails: cocooned within safe social circles, content to listen to the sounds of our own echo chambers, and clinging to the comforts of what was accepted and known. On board, there was only so long that you could sit in isolation before you became an outcast, as everyone else let down their guard and interacted. Perhaps it was the pace with which we lumbered along that catalysed the process of coming together in a shared experience of slowness and calm, where we were all compelled to listen, to speak, to question, to observe and to empathise with those who were different from ourselves. In just under a month I had met shopkeepers, chefs, NGO workers, pedicab drivers, predators, retirees, runaways, railroaders, the terminally ill, musicians, truck drivers and teachers, each one leaving a tiny but definite mark.

An announcement let us know that it was time for dinner and we left the families to unpack their Tupperware, and went through to the dining car. Wondering who would be joining us, we had just ordered roast chicken and rice, when the door opened and an elderly couple were directed towards our table. The lady was wearing a grey, button-down dress with a short cape around her shoulders, her hair tucked into a white bonnet. Her husband was dressed in a green shirt with a waistcoat and thick braces. His beard was shaved into a thin strip so that he looked like he was wearing a bicycle helmet strap under his chin. Arlene and Russell were from Ohio, and nodded when they sat down. Jem arranged the condiments in a line as a long silence filled the space between us, the cutlery clinking as the train dipped to one side.

'So, you're clearly Amish,' Jem said finally.

'No ... we're not,' said Russell.

I cringed and stared at the tablecloth.

'We may look like it, but we're actually German Baptist Brethren.'

'Are there any similarities?' I asked.

'Some,' said Arlene, looking at Russell. 'But we drive. I couldn't harness a pony trap to do my errands. And we have electricity, too. I can't imagine living with no electricity.'

'Me neither,' I said, pleased to find common ground.

'Amish have a telephone at the bottom of the drive of their family home, as they say it disturbs family time, but we use normal cell phones. A lot of our beliefs are the same, I guess.'

Russell and Arlene had wonderful enunciation whereby a bus could fit through each one of their pauses, but it made listening to them so much more enjoyable.

'What do you do?' Russell asked Jem.

'I work in tech … technology?'

'Well, good for you. If you've found something that you enjoy.'

Our meals arrived at once and Jem ripped open a sachet of balsamic vinegar and began pouring it over his chicken. Russell cleared his throat.

'I hope you don't mind … but we're going to take a moment before we eat our meal.'

'Of course not.'

Jem quickly squeezed out the remaining drops as Russell and Arlene waited with their hands clasped, watching him roll up the wrapper like a tube of toothpaste. Touched by the sight of their bowed heads, I decided to join them and said grace before my meal, something I hadn't done since primary school. The gesture warmed the relationship between us and we began to eat together. Arlene and Russell were on their way to visit their daughter and grandchildren in Idaho for two weeks and were keen to hire a car and drive across the border to Jasper to see the wildlife while they were there.

'Do you hunt?' I asked Russell.

'Oh, I used to, but not any more. Used to like pheasant … quail.'

'He can't shoot deer,' said Arlene, 'not with those big brown eyes. There was a squirrel the other day eating up my yard and we shot that … and we deep-fried it and ate it. We liked that.'

'Sounds good.'

'Oh, it really was.'

'Do you take the train often?' I asked.

'We like the train,' said Russell, dabbing his beard with his napkin. 'We have our pillows and blankets. And we appreciate that we have the chance to make acquaintance with different folks such as yourselves. We like that.'

'But these trains are delayed plenty often as they have to wait for freight,' said Arlene. 'We arrive in Idaho around 1 a.m. and then we have to drive two hours to our daughter's home. Without the train, we wouldn't be able to see her. It just makes you so grateful for what you have.'

That night, the *Empire Builder* swept across America, shadows of cliffs and hills rising and falling like ghosts creeping up on the train. For all its failings, Amtrak was powered by human spirit and an intimacy of interaction that I'd once given up on. There were jakeys and fuck-ups aplenty, but for people like Ernie, the train was a dream fulfilled, for lost souls like Erin it was therapy – the anonymity emboldening. The train was a sanctuary for loners to find company, children to find play, and daydreamers to reminisce. Americans who have never ridden on their own railways have no idea what they are missing. Over two days we ploughed through rain and fog, forests and falls, rolling by rivers and shuddering through towns so small they were no more than a gas station, a church and a school. Sighing into Seattle, the train came to rest, abandoned by its passengers who waved at friends, kissed lovers, hailed taxis or simply picked up their bags and walked away, slipping back into the rhythm of their lives.

8

Keeping Up with the Kims

Shortly after arriving in Seattle, our Amtrak passes expired and we completed our American circuit with a flourish, threading in and out of bays and islets up the coast on the *Amtrak Cascades* back to Vancouver. There, we discovered that Sarah and Scott were now Sarah, Scott and Stella – who had arrived a week after we boarded *The Canadian*. Eric the cat was ambivalent towards his new flatmate, picking his way round the room, as we sat on his sofa having cold feet about the next country on our route.

'What do you think? Are we mad?' I asked.

'I think you'd be mad not to go,' said Sarah.

'Really?'

'Definitely. When are you going to do something like this again?'

I watched Sarah rocking the little bundle, and realised that I had a finite window of opportunity for taking such risks.

'But what if something goes wrong and I get detained?'

'You're not going to be detained,' said Jem. 'And if you are, I won't let anything happen to you.'

'I'm not sure you'd have much say in the matter.'

'Unless you do something really stupid like steal stuff or sneak off to the fifth floor of the Yanggakdo, there's no reason why anything should happen. Thousands of people visit every year and they're fine,' said Jem.

On this point, Jem was right. Until recently, I was unaware that tourists have been allowed to visit North Korea since 1953, when an armistice ended the Korean War. However, until

1988, tourism was restricted to visitors from fellow communist countries, or 'friendly' countries of the Non-Aligned Movement, which included India, Egypt, Indonesia, Yugoslavia and Ghana, among a handful of developing nations that refused to identify with the collective ideologies of the Western and Eastern blocs. Getting there isn't as simple as booking a flight and turning up with a Samsonite in one hand and a Lonely Planet in the other; independent travel is impossible. But more than 5,000 Western tourists – and almost 100,000 Chinese tourists – visit North Korea each year through privately run tour companies that offer everything from cycling tours into the countryside, and hiking trips up Mount Kumgang, to running the Pyongyang marathon, or travelling around the country for ten days by train. It was this final itinerary that had piqued my interest. Beginning in the capital city of Pyongyang, the chartered train travelled up to Hyangsan before turning east to the cities of Wonsan, Hamhung and the port city of Chongjin – the last of which had only recently opened to foreigners. Pyongyang is depicted in the media as North Korea's showcase city, where a carefully choreographed performance is put on for tourists. Whether or not this was true, it was certainly less easy to frame and control what tourists could observe outside the capital, particularly along the train routes. The trip also included a visit to the mausoleum to view the embalmed bodies of both President Kim Il Sung, and his son General Kim Jong Il, and the final day of the itinerary coincided with the seventieth anniversary celebrations of the Workers' Party.

The decision to go was not taken lightly: conscious of UN reports of human rights violations, famine and gulags, I'd given careful consideration to how wrong it would feel to top up the coffers of a dictator by visiting. But ultimately it boiled down to human curiosity. I had no interest in gathering stories to thwart dinner-party bores, or to brag on social media; nor did I harbour any secret desire to unfurl an anti-Kim banner from a hotel window or get myself arrested in order to sell my story. What I did yearn for, though, was the opportunity to visit and observe a relatively unknown country with some semblance of objectivity. Unapproved journalists are not allowed to enter and newspapers regularly preyed upon foolish couples and American students willing to ham up tales of their visit for a tidy fee, while most documentaries featured faces filled with terror to the soundtrack of Prokofiev's 'Dance of the Knights'.

In our digital age, a tap of the fingertips can produce satellite images of almost anywhere on earth – and outside it. From a sofa in Suffolk you can look down on Moscow's Kremlin, or dive off the Great Barrier Reef while wearing an Oculus Rift headset in Glasgow, but North Korea is one of the only countries in the world to remain watertight when it comes to allowing information in and out, so that testimonies from defectors are one of the only ways to gather reliable information about the so-called 'hermit kingdom'. But even defectors are known to embellish their stories, which makes it impossible to definitively sift out fact from fiction.

While North Korea spins stories, the Western media is just as guilty of indulging its own agenda, painting North Koreans as one-dimensional robots serving their great leader. I was under no illusion that ten days in North Korea would uncover anything more than a stage-managed performance, but I wanted a front-row seat at the show. The country had just lifted a four-month travel ban, imposed over fears of the Ebola virus, so now was as good a time to visit as any. And more than that, I was looking forward to seeing who else would be travelling there; what kind of person chose North Korea as a holiday destination?

It did not take long to find out. From Vancouver we flew into Beijing and arrived at the tour company's offices for a briefing, and to meet the other thirteen travellers signed up for the tour. This included Alice, an Australian mother who hadn't told her family where she was going; Pyotr, a red-faced Russian who would repeatedly get us all into trouble; Alan, a tech consultant from Cheltenham; Victor, a Canadian retiree on his fourth visit; Satoshi, a Japanese businessman; Nick from Notting Hill; and Tommy and Anna, newly-weds on honeymoon. Leading our group into North Korea was Sarah, a lovely Londoner in her mid-twenties with shiny bobbed hair, high-top trainers and a bright smile that masked all manner of annoyances when it came to handling our group.

Hand-painted propaganda posters brightened the walls of the office, which was stacked with North Korean memorabilia, ranging from books, DVDs and T-shirts, to paintings, badges and postcards showing stills from the popular film *Comrade Kim Goes Flying* – the story of a female coal miner who wants to become a trapeze artist. It had played at the Pyongyang International Film Festival and become a hit with North Koreans, so we were given a handful of the cards to offer as gifts to the guides when we arrived. Seated at a semicircle of school desks, I skimmed over Sarah's handout. From what I'd read, phones, computers and Kindles had to be surrendered on arrival and photography was banned; wearing jeans was illegal and men with long hair would not be granted entry. But as Sarah talked us through the rules it transpired that this was all nonsense.

'While a lot of what you've probably heard isn't true, there are a few things that you need to be aware of,' she said. 'If you have a copy of a newspaper with Marshal Kim Jong Un on the front, please do not fold it down the middle of his face. Don't deface it or scribble anything on him. Similarly, please don't place cups or glasses on top of his face as it's seen as really disrespectful.'

Alice put up her hand. 'Are we allowed to take photographs using proper cameras or just with smartphones?'

'Cameras are fine, but please ask the guides first if you're not sure. You'll see quite quickly that local people don't like having their photo taken, as they don't know who you are and they don't know what the picture is being used for, so it's always better to check first. And remember, if you take any photos of statues of the Kims to make sure you include their whole body from head to toe. Don't crop them at the shoulders or waist as it's seen as decapitating the leaders, and the photos will be deleted by the guards who check phones and cameras when we leave.'

Sarah went on to detail a number of items that were banned: books about North Korea and the current political situation, including guide books; American or South Korean flags or any clothing displaying them; literature from South Korea; and clothes with political slogans that officials would demand to have translated. Lastly, taking a Bible was vehemently discouraged. Proselytising in North Korea is a serious offence and showing a Bible to North Koreans or leaving one behind would probably result in detainment.

In 2014, Jeffrey Fowle, a father of three from Ohio, was arrested for deliberately leaving a bilingual English-Korean Bible under a bin at the seamen's club in Chongjin, and was imprisoned for six months. He claimed at the time that it had merely fallen out of his pocket, but later confessed that he had known exactly what he was doing. 'I thought I could do a little evangelical work on the sly and left the Bible in the restroom,' Fowle said in a Reuters interview. 'Having seen the plight of the people, I knew about the severe Christian persecution. I wanted to help them.' Fowle was one of a handful of Christian missionaries who had been detained in the recent past for trying to bring in religious texts in order to 'save' North Koreans who grow up believing in the supremacy of their founding father, Kim Il Sung. The previous year, another American tourist, Matthew Miller, had ripped up his visa at the airport in Pyongyang and sought asylum, admitting later that his main fear was that 'they would not arrest me' – so desperate was his desire to be detained so he could see North Korea 'beyond the tourist trail'. Not long after our trip, an American student named Otto Warmbier travelled out with another company and was detained and sentenced to fifteen years' hard labour after allegedly being caught on video attempting to steal a poster from behind the reception area of the Yanggakdo Hotel, a staff area that was strictly off-limits to guests. In a horrifying turn of events, Warmbier was released after seventeen months and returned to the US in a coma with a serious brain injury, and died within days. North Korea claimed he had contracted botulism after being given a sleeping pill, but American doctors denied that he had any signs of the toxin in his system. Soon after, the US State Department issued a ban on Americans travelling to the country.

I glanced around the room hoping there were no Bible-bashers, sociopaths or Americans in our midst. I couldn't help but marvel at the arrogance of those who had been detained, and with the exception of Warmbier, was unsympathetic towards their fate. Observing the regulations of any country is simply good manners: if you don't feel you can comply or you disagree with the rules, then you need not go. But it's reckless to visit, flout the laws, then plead forgiveness having jeopardised the safety of fellow travellers and also put the North Korean guides at risk, who are likely to be punished for not properly managing their group. Fortunately, the rest of our group looked like a fun bunch, indifferent towards wilful incarceration, and I was looking forward to undertaking what was geared up to be a trip of a lifetime.

Having decided it was safest to leave behind my laptop, notebooks and Dictaphone, I had a last-minute panic with my Kindle. On it was a book on North Korea by a *Los Angeles Times* journalist, Barbara Demick, called *Nothing to Envy*. Compiled over seven years using the stories of six defectors, it was a fascinating piece of work, and the only real reading I had done in the hope of projecting as few preconceptions as possible. However, it was one of the main texts that customs officials would search for on arrival, and it refused to vanish from the Cloud despite having been deleted. Giving up, I chucked the Kindle to one side and decided that time would be better spent keeping my eyes open rather than fixed on a book.

Instead of taking the train into Pyongyang, we were booked – for the sake of ease – onto a ninety-minute flight from Beijing, much to Jem's horror. Part of the reason that he had been so keen to join me on my travels was that he had a fear of flying and was relieved to be able to globetrot without the threat of going down in flames. As the engines roared and the plane tilted up, a cold wet palm would usually find my knee and squeeze for reassurance while he blinked his way through the trauma and ordered several Bloody Marys. Normally amused by this routine, I understood his concern. Two airlines operated between Beijing and Pyongyang: Air China and Air Koryo, the latter being ranked by Skytrax – the air-transport research company – as the worst in the world, although this was largely a publicity stunt for the company, based on little more than hearsay. Sanctions imposed by the US and EU prevented Air Koryo from buying airliners from either Boeing or Airbus, leaving them little choice but to use old Russian aircraft. In 2007, in an attempt to rebrand, Air Koryo had bought two relatively modern Tupolev Tu-204 aircraft but was still left holding a one-star rating for service.

Jem was seated in the middle of the row with Pyotr, his stomach spilling over the armrest into his lap, while I had the luxury of the window seat from where I could gaze at the bends and twists of the Great Wall that embroidered the crags below. It did not take long for me to tire of this, when the flight attendants, in natty blue outfits and white gloves, handed out their glossy brochures to commemorate the 'Seventieth Anniversary of the Founding of the Workers' Party of Korea'. It was the most delicious propaganda, showing the three generations of Kims 'acknowledging the enthusiastically cheering crowds', 'giving field guidance' at the Chongjin lubricant-oil factory and meeting the women's national football team, who were all in tears. Beneath each photo was the date: Juche 71 (1982), or Juche 58 (1969). The year of Kim Il Sung's birth, 1912, was deemed Juche 1 and the North Korean calendar still counts the date this way.

While I marvelled at the sheer size of Kim Jong Un, an old-fashioned folk tune started playing through the speakers and the screens overhead displayed footage from parades and concerts, including one given by the Moranbong Band – North Korea's popular, short-skirted troupe of around twenty young women; they sang, played violins, cellos, keyboards and drums, and were supposed to have been handpicked by Kim, not only for their musical prowess, but for their modern look, which would appeal to North Korea's youth. Halfway through the flight, there was a buzz of excitement at the arrival of the infamous Koryo burger. Phones were whipped out amid a lot of rubber-necking to see who was going to dare sample the food item that was rumoured to contain rat, dog, and anything in between. Wrapped in cling film and plopped straight onto the table, the cold burger was a sludge grey and garnished with what looked like a wet autumn leaf. I nudged mine away while Jem munched through his, which he remarked tasted much like his great-grandmother's fishcakes.

As the plane began to descend, I scoured the mountains below with a mix of nausea and excitement that we were about to enter the forbidden kingdom. Approaching the runway, the plane began to lurch so hard that Jem grappled for my hand and closed his eyes as we accelerated in to land with a slam. We shot down the runway and I glanced out of the window, catching sight of five men in uniform crouched in the long grass.

'Did you see them?' I whispered.

'I did. What do you think they're looking for?'

'Maybe making sure no stowaways are going to drop out of the plane? Bit like the border at El Paso.'

'Surely stowaways would want to escape North Korea, not sneak in,' Jem whispered back.

'True. Maybe they're looking for foreign journalists or something?'

'Don't be ridiculous.'

We had barely touched the ground and paranoia had already kicked in. Having a quiet word with myself to treat the next ten days with an open mind, I pulled on my satchel and followed the group through to arrivals.

Immigration was a pain-free, pleasant experience. Officials scanned each bag, writing down the names of our books, before sending us on our way. We were out so soon that I was able to slink off to nose around the arrivals area, while the rest of the group were held up with laptops, digital SLRs and iPads. Shiny and new, Sunan International Airport seemed outsized for one that linked to only four cities: Beijing, Shanghai, Shenyang and Vladivostok. After one lap around the building, I came across a photo gallery featuring missiles, military parades and Kim Jong Un, when a tiny caption caught my eye: 'School Children in Pyongyang with Nothing to Envy'. Nothing to envy. Demick's book came back to me and I realised how she had come about the title. Waving me over, Jem gestured that we were ready to leave now that our four North Korean guides had arrived to escort us.

The guides worked for one of the state-owned tourism companies and were occasionally the children of diplomats, who spoke excellent English, and had often lived abroad for significant chunks of their youth. It was assumed that they were there to control – rather than host – tour groups, and while I didn't doubt that the former was probably true, they certainly livened up the trip. Whether they were guides or minders, Mr Lee and Mr Pak were old hands who often worked with Sarah and greeted her like two big brothers. They were mentoring two new guides, Mr Song, a pale, nervous-looking man, and Miss Kim, a princess with a perm, wearing a white fur-trimmed jacket. She looked distinctly unimpressed by our group and was more interested in taking selfies, which she then whitened with a special app. Pyotr had managed to get lost between the exit and the coach, so once the rest of us were on board, Lee took the mic to kill time while Pak was dispatched to look for Pyotr:

'"*Annyong hashimnikka!*" This is a respectful way to say: "Hello, how are you?" in Korean.' He paused and beamed at all of us. 'We know that you are used to saying "North Korea", but we do not believe in north and south,' he said. 'We are the Democratic People's Republic of Korea, or the DPRK, so please remember that while you are here. And this ...' he added, having spotted Pyotr being herded up the steps, 'will be useful for the next ten days, "*Bballi kapsida!*" means "Let's go quickly!"'

Lee had the japes and jollity of a Butlin's Redcoat and knew how to engage an audience, but as we set off into the city his voice faded to white noise as I became magnetised by the view from the window. We were really here, in North Korea.

Pyongyang's roads were tank-wide and newly surfaced, with few other cars in sight. One tractor bobbed along the edge of the road and a couple of cyclists rode on the pavement wearing khaki clothes, but there were no pedestrians. A tram packed with grey-clothed passengers went past in the opposite direction and I craned my neck to get a proper look, while the rest of the group had cameras up against the glass and were photographing every tree, every car, every sign. No wonder the local people became suspicious and annoyed. A white, listless sky deepened the absence of colour and energy, two things I most associated with Asian cities, but as we neared the centre, reds, yellow and blues flashed from revolutionary billboards bellowing messages of pride and glory. Strong-faced young men in dungarees held aloft scythes in one fist and the national flag in the other, as a missile rose in the background. Another depicted Kim Il Sung and Kim Jong Il among a field of flowers and children. Apartment blocks were no more than four-storeys high and painted an anaemic peach with pots of red flowers perched on the edge of each balcony. A Mercedes 190E pulled up at the traffic lights alongside us, a model that my parents had driven in 1991, capping off the feeling of having travelled back in time. We soon slowed and Lee gestured outside: 'We have now arrived at the Mansudae Grand Monument, so you may bring your cameras.'

Even from the bottom of the hill, the tops of the two Kim statues were visible through the trees. Standing at around twenty-two metres high, the bronze monuments that overlooked the city marked one of Pyongyang's most sacred spots, drawing both tourists and North Koreans who gathered to pay their respects. Surrounding the statues was a well-tended lawn, upon which crouched more than fifty middle-aged women wearing long shirts and identical rubber-soled shoes, and who appeared to be hand-picking weeds, even though the grass looked immaculate. They turned away from the cameras, putting up their hands to shield their faces. Lee ordered us to form one long line, tuck in shirts and zip up jackets. Sarah was holding a large bunch of flowers, which she then handed to Victor, who was selected to walk alone to the foot of the statues, bow, lay down the flowers and then turn and walk back to the line. Meanwhile, the women had vanished. Tommy sidled up to me in his cagoule.

'Do you think they were actually gardening or just put here to spy on us?' he whispered.

'Who knows? They probably just didn't want to be in any of the photos.'

'Maybe, but don't you think it's a bit weird that they've completely gone in less than two minutes of us arriving?'

'No talking please,' said Lee, standing a little in front of us before taking a deep bow. We followed in sync. As I looked down at my shoes I felt unease. I certainly did not respect the leaders and was disappointed in myself. Later I was told that North Korean officials use photos of tourists bowing before the statues to tell their people that foreigners come on special pilgrimage from all over the world just to offer their respects, so greatly revered are their leaders. If this was indeed true, then I felt even worse for being complicit in the deception. Then again, I had made the decision to come and could have stayed on the bus if I did not want to abide by their rules. And placing flowers at their feet was no different from the servitude expected at most places of worship.

On the walk back to the coach I noticed how pristine the surrounding park was. There was not one fallen leaf on the grass, and rows of red flowers bloomed in perfect alignment. Miss Kim came over and linked her arm through mine.

'What were the ladies doing here earlier?' I asked.

'All the ladies are working voluntarily out of respect.'

I looked down at the circular red pin on Miss Kim's lapel, which featured the avuncular face of Kim Il Sung. Lee wore a pin that featured both Kims, as did Pak and Song. I was curious as to why none of the pins showed the current ruler, Kim Jong Un, but decided it was too soon to interrogate the guides. Unsure whether she was being friendly or stopping me from dawdling, I felt Miss Kim steering us back to the coach and took the chance to ask if I could get a badge for myself. She looked momentarily offended, then resumed her default setting of being unimpressed.

'This is not for foreigners. When we join the Youth League we are gifted the badge.'

'Do you ever take it off?'

'No. It is our dear father, I am so proud to wear it. He is a great, great man who has done so much for us.'

I found it odd how Miss Kim kept referring to him in the present tense, but didn't give it much more thought and flopped down in my seat, ready for dinner and a hot shower before bed. Miss Kim sat in front of us and shoved in her earphones for the journey; they were playing the theme song from the film *Titanic*.

The Yanggakdo Hotel was a tower block of gloom located on its own island, offering a panoramic view of Pyongyang from the windows, which, rather worryingly, could be fully opened, even on the fortieth floor. Neon-lit and charmless – and packed with foreign tour groups – the Yanggakdo housed a pool hall, a bowling alley and karaoke facilities in the basement. But after a dinner of egg fried rice, pork and pickled cucumber, we were too tired to even consider a verse of 'My Heart Will Go On' and took ourselves off, leaving the rest of the group in the bar. In the lift, Jem pointed at the panel where the numbers jumped from '4' to '6'. The fifth floor was indeed missing. The Yanggakdo's mysterious fifth floor was akin to the twilight zone. It definitely existed, but it was strictly out of bounds. Unsurprisingly, an American blogger had once gained access through a staff staircase and posted up photos of an empty floor covered in the standard propaganda posters, and an office with what he claimed was Soviet recording equipment, which I later discovered recorded little more than footage from four video cameras in the lobby and one in the car park. We had read all about this and now that we were here and unsupervised in the lift, we were just as uninterested. Even if our room was tapped no one would hear anything more incriminating than Jem snoring and my moaning about being cold and tired, and I had no intention of sniffing around where I was not wanted.

Our room smelt like my grandmother's cupboards. Layered with dust, but warm and carpeted, it contained two single beds separated by a heavy radio unit, so there was no way for us to push them together and whisper across our pillows. There was a TV airing Al Jazeera and the BBC politics programme *Dateline*, in addition to the state news channel, which featured a terrifying middle-aged woman wearing a *chima jogori* – a traditional skirt and top. She never moved from behind her desk and boomed out details of Kim Jong Un's movements like an opera singer. There was no sound accompanying the footage of him at department stores or being chased in his bus by weeping subjects. It was fascinating stuff, yet I couldn't quite imagine twenty-four-hour footage devoted to the Queen riding horses, cutting ribbons or wandering around Chelsea Flower Show.

Having ferreted away the toothbrushes, combs and soaps from our bathroom as souvenirs – or to sell on eBay – Jem ran the hot tap and examined the earpiece of the phone for electronic bugs. He unhooked the hairdryer, which let out little more than a wheeze. Contrary to all the doom-mongering, everything else was in working order. Before drawing the curtains, we slid open the windows and huddled together as a slap of icy air took us by surprise. From the twentieth floor, we looked out across the blackness of the Taedong river. It didn't look right. Two bridges were lit up in green and blue neon, the curves reflecting in the water, and the red flame of the Juche Tower was aglow, but the rest of the city lurked under shadows. Freckles of light revealed the odd high rise, but in the absence of street lights, traffic and advertising, it appeared that the city had been turned off. Shivering, we drew the curtains and called it a night.

As the clock struck six o'clock, a tuneless wail crackled from the speakers of Pyongyang railway station. Played every hour on the hour, the eeriness continued for more than five minutes as I gazed up at the two Kims beaming beneath the clock. From behind the station, there came the hint of the first sunny day as dawn broke across the sky and my heart leapt. I was dying to get back on the trains and sunshine was just what was required for hanging out of train windows en route to Hyangsan. Around four hours' northeast of Pyongyang, this was the closest station to reach Mount Myohyang, and few tourists had ever taken this route by train. Counting heads, Sarah noted that Pyotr had gone missing again and he was soon spotted shuffling across the street with his camera. Pak was dispatched to collect him while the rest of us gathered our things and went in to find our train.

The station was as empty as a disused airport hangar. It echoed with the squeak of our shoes, for there was not a single other person present. Expecting the slamming of doors and thud of engines, the frenzy of hawkers and whistling announcements, I felt cheated. There were no more than three or maybe four tracks, yet the first platform covered an expanse the size of a football pitch and just one train stood at the furthest end. Its diesel engine was Korean, but the carriages were taken from a 1970s vintage Swiss train chartered just for us. We were not allowed to travel on local trains with citizens, so this was our home for the next nine days. I took great pleasure in watching the rest of the group run around bagsying seats, inspecting the loos and fondling the blankets in the sleeper car. It felt like Christmas morning and it only convinced me further that trains would always have a charm that could soften even the grumpiest traveller: a spot of sun warming your cheek while you read; the clackety-clack of wheels as you slept; or the thrill of a smile and a wave from passers-by. The guides had commandeered the first compartment and had already taken to teasing and taunting Miss Kim, who had changed into a pair of bedroom slippers and a fur gilet. I slipped into their compartment and sat down opposite her, armed with a notebook and a weak smile, in the hope that a little female solidarity would help her to open up a bit. After chain-smoking a number of Marlboro Golds, Lee and Pak changed into towelling slippers and settled down to rifle through Sarah's handbag. Mr Song, the antithesis of what his name suggested, remained mute in the corner.

The Swiss carriages began to glide with such stealth that I didn't notice we were on the move until sunshine flared at the window, and I moved into the corridor for a better view of the city. Free from the fumes of factories and traffic pollution, the sky burned an unusual blue that set the city alight. Gone was the greyness and desolation. Pyongyang's tower blocks were now the embodiment of twee perfection, like Disneyland towers in bubblegum pink and peppermint green. Florets of green bundled around the treetops and a lace of purple flowers lay by the track. Victor joined me at the window just as an ominous but familiar sight loomed into view. Driving up from the ground, the rocket-shaped Ryugyong Hotel was almost four times the height of any other structure in the city and five times as wide. Dubbed the 'Hotel of Doom', construction of the 105-storey building had begun in 1987 but had come to a halt during the collapse of the Soviet Union, which had devastated North Korea's economy. The glass exterior had since been completed but it was anybody's guess as to whether or not it would ever be opened for service. It looked like it might take off at any moment.

'Monstrosity,' Victor said, as we rolled past the Ryugyong and began to pick up pace. 'But I tell you, it's fascinating how fast this country is changing.'

'This isn't your first time?'

'Fourth,' Victor replied, staring straight ahead as the wind began to tease the slicked-back strands of his hair. Victor was from Vancouver, in his late sixties and looked like a dark-haired version of Robert Redford. Not overburdened by modesty, he had let it be known that he had made a fortune in business and was now indulging his love of travel.

'Fourth? What's the attraction?'

He looked me dead in the eye. 'The same reasons you're here. Curiosity. Intrigue. Wanting to witness history as it unfolds. And of course, this ...' Victor waved an arm through the window. 'You can't beat train travel. You know there's a real beauty to it. You can fly, you can drive, but nothing can show you the bowels of a city like standing at a train window. Do you like train travel?'

'I do. That's why I chose this particular trip.'

'That's unusual, you know.'

'What is?'

'A girl, enjoying this kind of travel. I think it's highly commendable that you're doing this.'

My nostrils flared, but I stayed quiet. In fairness to Victor, the group more or less comprised single white men on an adventure.

'I was here a couple of years ago and when I read about this trip I couldn't resist the chance to get out of Pyongyang and see the rest of the country,' Victor said. He glanced into the guides' compartment. 'They hide a lot, as you've probably realised.'

The truth was that I hadn't realised – or rather, that I couldn't. I knew that the surface belied an ugly reality, but there was no way of confirming the degree to which it was true. People were polite – albeit reserved – and the infrastructure appeared in better shape than a lot of cities we'd travelled through. Moreover, I had been reluctant to quiz the guides for the first few days for fear of putting them on their guard or making them feel awkward. Both Pak and Lee had spent their adolescent years living abroad and it beggared belief that they would come back to live in North Korea and continue to peddle a myth when they must have been fully aware of the truth behind their leaders and their country's standing in the world. I also wondered why their families had bothered coming back, but it transpired that when diplomatic families are posted to other countries, one child is often left with extended family to guarantee their return.

Victor rummaged around in his bag, pulled out a twelve-pack of Crispy Crunch bars and broke one in half to share. 'I packed all my food for the ten days. Last time I was here the food was awful, barely edible, so I brought my own stuff – tins of tuna … lots of nuts. But I can't tell you how different it all is. I mean the food is great now. You wouldn't have touched the stuff back then and everybody got sick. This is why I keep coming back. I like to see the progress. It's going to be so different in ten, maybe fifteen, years. I think we won't recognise it. I'm so hopeful for the people.'

'You don't feel guilty about coming?'

'No, why should I? The US has nuclear weapons, so do you guys. America has committed some of the worst human rights abuses on this earth and continues to do so every day. The Saudis flog their citizens and treat their women like dirt, but no one issues sanctions against them. What do they do? – the UK and the US give them aircraft and munitions to murder civilians in Yemen.'

Sarah came padding through in her slippers. 'Everyone okay?'

'Fine thanks. Loving the views,' I said.

'I know, it's amazing, isn't it? So nice being out of the city.'

I nodded towards the compartment where Pak and Lee were fidgeting with Sarah's iPad amid gales of laughter as Miss Kim glared out of the window.

'They were going through your bag earlier,' I said.

Sarah started laughing. 'They don't really get the concept of "mine" and "yours" or the idea of personal possessions.'

'Socialists,' Victor muttered.

'The guides regularly go through my bag looking for snacks or my iPad, which I don't mind. In fact, I find it quite funny. I remember on one trip coming back to the compartment to find Lee and Pak had got my make-up bag out and Pak was holding the compact mirror and applying BB cream.'

She looked over at them with an expression of genuine fondness. 'Although the one thing that does annoy me is when they call people fat, especially when they do now understand that Westerners find it rude. I once had a massive fallout with Lee when he told me how fat I'd got since our last trip, but the best way to get back at them is to tell them they have a lovely dark tan and then they get super offended.'

As was the case in all Asian countries, darker skin implied a low-class life of labouring in the sun, whereas a complexion the colour of milk was more indicative of higher social standing – which explained Miss Kim's penchant for whitening up her selfies, even though she was evidently from an 'elite' family.

Victor went back to his compartment while Sarah checked up on the rest of the group, granting me a few moments of peace. The train had left the city and entered the countryside where we were now surrounded by fields of maize, gathered and bound like scrolls of burnt gold. A spritz of cloud hovered in the blue and my bare arms began to warm as I absorbed the stillness. It had been a frenetic few days and my mind was brimming. The North Korea of tanks, missiles and the Kims was already a world away: oxen ploughed the fields; clusters of cottages had roofs of red chillies drying in the sun; and beautiful children squatted in the yard sifting piles of corn. Their parents paused their work and watched stony-faced as we swept by. Buffalos huffed and bowed, drawing wooden carts piled with people, and cyclists stopped to inspect the train as we slowed into a tiny station. Pak appeared at once at the door. 'Do not take any photographs at the stations. It is forbidden,' he warned, going to each compartment in turn.

Disappointed I pocketed my phone and leant out of the window as a wiry man with a stick attempted to guide a frenzy of ducks flapping and honking their way across the tracks.

'NO PICTURES!' came a shout from on the platform. While we weren't allowed to disembark, Pak had hopped off to have a cigarette and was yelling at Pyotr who was leaning out of the window and photographing a group of soldiers waiting with their bags. Despite the widespread belief that North Korea's military comprises mindless warriors waiting for orders to launch the next warhead, soldiers are often no more than free labourers engaged in any number of construction projects, and are commonly referred to as 'soldier-builders' by the state media. Lee had also gone out for a cigarette and was chatting to Pak when I saw then how much taller and broader they were compared with not just the soldiers, but every other person we had seen. Pak was well over six-foot and Lee wasn't far off, while everyone else averaged around 5 foot 5. Having lived abroad in their teens, they had obviously escaped the effects of the 1990s famine, which were now only clear when witnessing them all side by side.

Tommy banged on the door and waved, yanking it open before I could protest. 'Bloody Russians,' he grinned, taking off his cagoule. Nick, Geoff and Tommy's wife Anna wandered in and I gave up on peace and quiet for the present. As we began to move, Geoff joined me at the window. A former journalist doing a PhD on North Korean studies in Seoul, Geoff occasionally came over to the North to keep up to date with affairs. He had a huge bottle of *soju* – rice liquor – in one hand that he readily shared around as he wasn't allowed to take it back to the South. Putting on a pair of plastic sunglasses, he smiled up at the sun, which beamed in return. The train began to roll past a village and I watched the women carrying bundles of crops and children on their backs. They exuded health and strength, as did their offspring. Their clothes, while drab, were clean and in good condition. There was little to suggest poverty and I remarked as such to Geoff. He pushed his sunglasses onto his head before glancing back at the others and saying in a low voice: 'That's probably true, but like with everything in this country, there's always more to the story. North Korean towns and villages operate on a tiered system. If you're from a politically favoured family,' he continued, 'you would get the privilege of living in Pyongyang or somewhere pretty good, whereas lower-tiered people have to live elsewhere. Privileged people get access to better railways, infrastructure, education and whatever else. This is how the Workers' Party dispenses patronage. Elite compounds, for example, have their own private railroads for high-ranking cadres.' His voice sank to a whisper. 'We also know from defectors that smaller railway lines have fallen into disrepair. We aren't seeing any of this on our route, so we can reasonably assume that we've been granted access to approved areas that have probably had the economic advantages of being on the railway artery.'

At that moment, Sarah poked her head into the compartment and announced that we were about to arrive in Hyangsan.

A short drive from Hyangsan brought us to Mount Myohyang, a national park of sorts that stretched around the river Chongchon. Waterfalls slid like silk down the granite cliffs, before being bundled along by the river as it rushed over fallen trees and boulders. A blanket of conifers covered the hillsides and the slopes of green looked so Alpine that I half expected a tearaway nun to come twirling around in song. Having wound down into a valley, we eventually pulled up outside a pair of grey buildings. This was the International Friendship Exhibition, which housed all the gifts that foreign dignitaries had ever presented to the Kims. It looked like a Bond lair. The entrance was concealed by a four-ton copper door, which had a protruding sphere at the centre. On closer inspection, it appeared to be a model of the earth. A high-pitched creak suggested wheels were in motion and the earth split into two as the doors slid back to reveal a woman wearing a black velvet *chima jogori* embroidered with silver stars.

After handing in our coats, cameras and phones, we followed the guide as she glided through the windowless building, her hemline sweeping the floor. In the main hall was a treasure trove of rhino horns, swords, vases, shields and spears gifted to the Kims, which included a gold sword from Colonel Gaddafi, a rugby ball from Wigan Warriors and an NBA basketball signed by Michael Jordan that Madeleine Albright had presented Kim Jong Il when she visited in 2000. I was relieved that the cabinet of UK gifts looked like the world's worst charity shop and featured two chipped glass plates and one faded vase. Miss Kim walked alongside us, pointing out the plethora of international newspaper front pages that featured the Kims, the best of which was from the *New York Times:* 'Kim Jong Il Emerges as the Lodestar for Sailing the 21st Century'. 'All over the world the dear leader was known for his greatness,' she said as I winced with embarrassment. From the 1960s until as late as the 1990s North Korea regularly placed adverts in leading Western newspapers that the state media then reported as editorials or news. Miss Kim's parents had grown up abroad, so it seemed unlikely that she had no awareness of the Kims' regime. Did she believe this illusion? Or was she simply playing the role that was expected of her? Elite families were the first to benefit from the regime's patronage – the same the world over – so perhaps it was in her best interest to toe the line and reap the rewards. Overcome by a rush of frustration I was relieved when the tour ended and we were free to have a cup of tea, buy some souvenir stamps and breathe in the greenery of the surroundings, which held far more allure than anything we had been shown.

Jem was snoozing on the train to Hamhung, so I stationed myself by the windows. Overwhelmed and drained from keeping up with the Kims, I felt most at home on the train, where I could stand at the window alone and take in the sounds and sights without being told what to see and how to feel. This was one of the most remote regions on the east coast and one of the most scenic. Sand-coloured mountains dipped softly in the distance, curtained off by a haze of light. Villages of white stone houses were scattered around the foreground. Their roofs were tiled with curved red slabs fitted together like fish scales, or lined with dried wooden logs. Behind each house was an allotment of cabbages and potatoes, which completed the scene of bucolic prosperity. I thought back to my earlier conversation with Geoff and wondered what the rest of the country looked like. A series of hoots and yells came from the guides' compartment and Miss Kim appeared, slamming the door behind her, her cheeks the colour of pomegranate. She linked arms with me again. After a few moments, she asked where Jem was and I told her he was having a pre-lunch nap.

'I like your boyfriend's face,' she said.

'Oh. Okay, that's nice, thank you.'

'He reminds me of my own boyfriend. He has the same shaped face. He has big eyes and a soft mouth, just like a girl.'

Unsure where this conversation was going, I picked up the thread nonetheless.

'How often do you get to see him with your work?'

'We don't see each other any more. He had to move after university to live in Paris with his family.'

'I'm sorry to hear that, when will he be back?'

'I don't know, but we never broke up, so I hope one day I will see him again.'

'Can you call or write?'

Miss Kim appeared not to have heard me and I realised that she might not be allowed to do either without having her correspondence intercepted.

'Did you meet him at university?'

'Yes, we were both studying English. I wanted to study music, but my father told me I would study English at Kim Il Sung University.'

'What was it like?'

'Studying English?'

'No, Kim Il Sung University.'

'I felt very proud. I studied very hard every day for five years.'

'What sort of things did you learn?'

'We learnt good things about all countries except the US and Japan. I want to travel to as many countries as possible, but especially to countries that have world miracles.'

'Like?'

'London, to see the London Eye, Paris for the Eiffel Tower, and the Spinx.'

'*Spinx?*'

'In Egypt. Also, the Nicaragua Falls. I also enjoyed learning about the Second World War.'

Given the distorted version of the Korean War – known as the Victorious Fatherland Liberation War – taught by the DPRK, I was curious to hear what Miss Kim had learnt. 'What aspect did you enjoy the most?' She fixed me with a long stare. 'I learnt that fascism is a very bad thing. Each country should be left alone to live as they want to. And big countries always want to make small countries adopt their culture. It is bad.'

Before I could probe further, she wedged her earphones into her ears and turned towards the window, signalling that the conversation was over. Pak and Lee hollered that lunch was ready and I caught up with Sarah on my way to the dining car. Feeling a bit sad, I relayed my conversation to her about Miss Kim's boyfriend moving to Paris.

'That's odd.'

'Why?'

'There are no diplomatic relations between North Korea and France. France and Lithuania are the only two EU nations not to recognise North Korea.'

'So ...'

'So, either his family were moved somewhere else or he just didn't want to dump her and is probably seeing someone else. Poor girl.'

In the very last car of the train, three women were crowded into a kitchen with one gas stove and a cupboard of cups, saucers, Nescafé and Coffee-mate. They brought out tomato and onion omelettes swimming in butter, and placed them on two wooden tables covered in laminate, which only just allowed for the fifteen of us to squeeze up. Pouring out beakers of good Korean beer, they piled on plate after plate of fried wings, kimchi, slabs of luncheon meat, rice and soup and a large platter of blood sausage – a speciality that looked like big scabs and which no one touched. Meal times on the train were the only occasions when we were all obliged to sit together, and the spectrum of personalities on board reminded me why I never travelled with groups. However, over the previous two days I'd spent time in the company of Tommy's wife, Anna, who had an abundance of Twixes in her handbag, and I was starting to warm to Boston Bobby, a gentle Cold War veteran in a Red Sox hoodie and trainers. He'd spent much of his time sitting with us, when he wasn't wearing a fake red nose to amuse passing schoolkids, or clowning around and running down the corridor waving rolls of toilet paper. Retired, Bob now worked as part of the welcoming team for Red Sox games, in between taking off on solo trips to Iran, India and Mongolia in search of adventure. His wife Brenda was more than happy to stay at home during these trips and he had so far managed to steel himself against the anti-American rhetoric and the propaganda posters of 'American Imperialist' soldiers having their eyes pecked out by crows – but I sympathised and admired his willingness to visit the country by himself.

'How are you finding it all?' I asked. 'It must be quite tough.'

He shrugged. 'I feels bad for 'em. You can't live just for revenge. Look what it does, it destroys you. You gotta keep moving.' Bob poured another beaker of beer and speared his chicken, or what we assumed was chicken. 'Being unable to forgive or forget does nothing but stunt your own growth. Obsessing over us and Japan seems so petty and short-sighted. Imagine if every country in the world had grudges against every other country that had ever invaded or colonised. We'd all be lost.'

Just then a freight train began to draw parallel with our carriage. It was the closest we had ever been to local people: I could see right into the driver's cabin where three men were sitting together in grey overalls; five others were perched on top of the load and as we attempted to wave they all waved back and started laughing. It was the first positive response. The engine eventually ran alongside us and the three staff gave us a thumbs-up as the sunlight streamed through the window, warming the men's faces. They were no more than an arm's reach away and we all jumped up and stood at the glass like children, that piece of glass representing so much that I wished we could break. Eventually they drifted further and further back until we had lost them and we retook our seats in silence. Alan, who had rarely spoken since the first day, looked up:

'If we could just sit down and have a cup of tea with them it would be lovely.'

It was the saddest I'd felt so far.

The Majon guesthouse in Hamhung made the Yanggakdo look like the Ritz. Having spent the day touring a fertiliser factory, the brutalist Grand Theatre and more statues of the Kims, we retired for the night to this spot that was fast becoming popular with North Korean tourists – at least those with the papers to travel. Stumbling across the gravel by torchlight, I could hear the rush of waves against the beach below as we found our cottage and offloaded our bags. Someone had left the plug in

the bathtub, which I immediately drained, and then opened the
sink tap to wash my hands. There was no running water. A red
plastic barrel by the sink contained boiling water and a mug and
it transpired that the tub had been filled earlier in the day so
we could wash. The barrel was expected to stay warm until the
following morning in spite of the room being colder than the
fridge, which smelt of old milk. I was used to squatting to bathe
in India and had taught Jem to do the same, but it presented
quite a puzzle to the rest of the group. At breakfast Tommy said
he had simply climbed inside the barrel and used it as an upright
bath, while Alan was so repulsed he had taken a bar of soap and
gone down to bathe in the ocean at dawn. It didn't bode well for
the citizens of Hamhung if this was the best the city had to offer.

After breakfast, we were back on the train for the twelve-
hour journey up the northeast coast to the remote port city
of Chongjin. So far, few passenger trains had passed by, but
abandoned trains were in abundance. Green with a yellow stripe
down the middle, their blistered carriages wore petticoats of
rust, but the windows remained intact, unlike abandoned trains
in England, which were a magnet for graffiti artists and vandals.
I cornered Pak and asked him why they hadn't been taken away
for scrap and he shrugged and went into the vestibule for a
smoke. Less than half an hour later we passed one such carriage
with pretty curtains in the windows. They were clean and tied
back to reveal a line of washing drying inside. A moment later
a girl with wet hair poked her head out of one of the windows
and watched our train roll by: they had been adopted as homes.
This was a wonderful example of the *juche* ideology of self-
reliance established by Kim Il Sung. It made perfect sense. Inside
was warm, protected from the elements, and there were sleeper
berths for all the family.

The train to Chongjin clung to the coastline, disappearing
into hillside tunnels and emerging by stony beaches where kids
in brightly coloured anoraks chased one another along the shore.
As we passed through local stations, the sweet smell of rubbish
that often rotted between the tracks was noticeably absent. For

all the criticism of the regime it had some reasons to be proud. The cities looked as though they were scrubbed and washed every night. Elderly women carried dustpans and brushes and even a handful of leaves would be swept up in an instant.

Pyotr was still taking photos at stations, so much so that a few hours into the journey we were summoned by Sarah and Pak. Someone along the route had reported us and we were now being monitored. Furious with Pyotr and also Satoshi, who, since the first day, had been wandering around filming and trying to chat to passing children, the group was beginning to show signs of strain. No one wanted to jeopardise the trip or get Sarah and Pak into trouble, who would inevitably be the ones to bear the brunt of punishment.

The city of Chongjin was a concrete dump. Once a small fishing village, it was now a centre for trade owing to its proximity to Japan and China. While the outfits were in stark contrast to the drab dressing in Pyongyang, I felt like we had taken the train into 1988. Women in black flared trousers and quilted bomber jackets cycled by wearing black platform shoes with big buckles, their hair styled in shoulder-length perms clipped at the back with a giant sprayed quiff, much like Janet Jackson in her heyday. Younger girls wore state-of-the-art trainers covered in sparkles and spangled laces – including a pair of tangerine-coloured boots splashed with rainbow stripes – and carried trendy handbags. With the exception of one Lexus and a battered old Volvo there were no cars on the road, just trams and people riding past on bikes, chatting on mobile phones and wearing sunglasses.

On a short walk around the city centre I was able to peer into windows and shop doors with ease and found that the quintessential red flower that sat on every balcony was no more than tired silk. Net curtains parted to reveal two framed photos of the Kims on every wall, and shops stocked Hennessy cognac and Courvoisier. Given the anti-Japanese propaganda it was odd that women were carrying Mizuno shoulder bags and riding

Honda bikes. Lee was walking alongside, winding up Miss Kim, so I asked him about the Japanese brands.

'There is so much Western propaganda against us and I don't know why,' he replied. 'We use Mitsubishi, Sony, Japanese brands, American brands. They're just items created by other human beings.'

'But aren't they considered your enemies?'

'Enemy is a strong word, hostile is better, but really it's okay. We read Western media. Our tourism company gives us the *New York Times*, we watch BBC news, ABC news from the States, once it's been approved through the government we have access to it. That's why we want people to come here and see it for yourself. Because seeing is believing. What you see is how it is.'

And yet that afternoon we were treated to a spectacular show of propaganda at a 'local' school. The Steelworks Kindergarten, which had a delightful little playground for the kids featuring all the usual items one would expect for four-year-olds – a tank, a submarine with a torpedo on the side and a merry-go-round of fighter jets – put on a one-hour show that involved some of the most complicated dance routines I have ever witnessed. The children, who were no higher than my waist, were dressed in the sort of outfits worn by Olympic ice dancers, and grimaced with red lips as they flew around the room, pirouetting, punching the air and cartwheeling in perfect harmony.

'Dwarves, I tells ya, definitely dwarves,' Boston Bobby whispered to me during the performance. Even for my sixth-form production of *Guys 'n' Dolls* we had been unable to generate the coordination and precision of these toddlers.

'You can just imagine all the Notting Hill parents wanting to send their kids here,' Nick said, when the show had ended and the children bowed and forced smiles through clenched teeth.

On the way back to the train we made an obligatory stop at the city's Kim statues and were hovering about when some sort of commotion began to brew among the guides. Lee and Pak were engaged in a heated discussion with Mr Song, who was hanging his head. While taking a photograph for Pyotr, standing in front of the statues, he had accidentally cropped out one of the Kims' heads. In his panic, he had tried to delete the photograph to avoid any trouble and had managed to delete Pyotr's photographs from the entire trip. A shadow of schadenfreude passed over me – the constant photographing of local people reduced them to little more than zoo animals – but I felt terrible for Mr Song, who became known for the rest of the trip as The Deleter.

Fumbling for my watch, I rolled over and squinted at the window wondering why we had stopped. I propped myself up on my elbow and listened. The air was sour with the smell of the guards' old Marlboro Reds so I buried my nose in my scarf, waiting for the jolts and wobbles from engine changes or the reassuring clump of boots from guards pottering around.

Nothing.

For a few minutes I lay staring at the mound that was Jem, willing him to be awake, but his breath whistled into the blankets, suggesting otherwise, and there was no sound of movement from our companions in the adjacent compartments. Roald Dahl had called this 'the witching hour' – a special moment in the middle of the night when every child and every grown-up is in a deep, deep sleep and all the dark things come out from hiding and have the world to themselves. Gathering the bulk of faux-fur blankets around my shoulders I shuffled up to the end of the berth and peered around the edge of the curtain, which was damp with cold. Blackness greeted me. We had stopped in the middle of an empty expanse. There were no lamp posts, houses or other trains in sight; no torches bobbing along to suggest human activity. We hadn't even stopped at a platform.

So far, I had taken the trip in my stride, but I was aware now of a quiet hysteria building in my gut. Had we been reported again? Had Pyotr been hanging from the windows taking more photos? Or maybe it was me? I usually slipped away to make notes on the sly, but for all I knew I had been watched and was now going to be arrested by the authorities. They would force me to write an apology and read it at a press conference, or make me serve fifteen years of hard labour. It had finally happened. The paranoia had sunk in its claws and I was convinced I would never be able to leave the country. Shivering, I crawled back up the berth and lay down, turning foetal with anxiety when the train started to glide away from its spot and a blade of white light cut through the curtain. I saw that we were rolling into a station. And there, side by side, high up on the station wall, were the two illuminated faces of Kim Il Sung and Kim Jong Il, beaming down. They were the picture of jollity: paternal and kind, watching over the fatherland. Without stopping, the train began to pick up pace and their light was soon shrinking into the distance. It was just a temporary stop outside a station. Pacified, I lay down, took out my phone and began to watch videos of the kindergarten children as the train swept down the coast to the port city of Wonsan.

Loudspeakers played a crackling piece of dated music. It was early evening, and we had gathered at the edges of the main square in Wonsan to watch more than a thousand Korean students take part in a mass dance in preparation for the upcoming seventieth anniversary celebrations. The women were dressed in colourful *chima jogori*, and the men were wearing white shirts and red ties. It looked much like a barn dance; linking arms and dancing do-si-do in circles, they appeared to be enjoying themselves and the guides clapped and cheered in support. Mr Song grabbed us one by one and told us we could join in. Uncomfortable at the thought of interrupting them, we hovered at the edge waiting for someone else to go first. It was like being back at school again. Geoff ventured forward and Mr Song appeared from nowhere, grabbed my hand and thrust it into the palm of a tall man who let go of his partner and led me as though it were the most normal thing in the world. Too embarrassed to make eye contact, I noticed that Jem was dancing with the girl who had been thrust aside to make way for me and she was struggling to keep him within the formation, but laughing and patiently guiding him. This was what I had longed for all week. As we held hands and twirled, we became an unbroken chain of young people having fun. Little stood between me and the tall North Korean with warm hands but music and energy. A surge of heat flushed under my skin and I could feel tears at the corners of my eyes. They weren't out of sadness, sympathy or pity, but a sense of nostalgia, for when we were small kids unburdened by prejudice – when we played with everyone without caring who they were or where they came from.

The music stopped and the group broke apart into applause and we bowed, thanked our partners and darted back to the side, exhilarated. As the others joined the next dance, I wandered over to Nick, who was enthralled by the scene. Leaning in, he said: 'Do you know, there's nothing here – apart from violent oppression – that isn't reminiscent of European society a hundred years ago, where everyone respected the heads of state, and for an event they would all come out onto the town square for a dance. If it's all been propaganda, then it's been a triumph. I've bought it.'

'Really?' I asked.

'Oh, absolutely. I'd recommend most people come and see it for themselves and make up their own minds. I've seen worse in Glasgow and the north of England than here. Even their poor neighbourhoods are clean and painted and they have very neat-looking houses. The people don't have an obesity crisis, they look healthy, it's not all soviet grey. There's a lot that's really good about it and I think that people ought to get out here and see it.'

For the first time since we had arrived, we were allowed to walk back to our hotel unchaperoned and it felt like we had just been given permission to strip naked and do somersaults. The buzz of crowds coming down from a high reminded me of walking home from Hyde Park after a summer festival and yet there were no empty cans of Strongbow in the street, no pissed-up idiots collapsed under trees, no remnants of goat curry and wooden forks in the gutter. Everyone ambled along, elderly women swept up leaves in the road by torchlight and, although

em and Monisha suffering the effects of altitude sickness

Monisha enjoying the view on the approach to Lhasa, Tibet

The Chinese flag flaps in the wind as the train draws into Lhasa

Armed military trucks patrol the streets of Lhasa

A Tibetan nomad looks into a Chinese shop selling skin-whitening products

Nomadic pilgrims enjoy bananas outside the Potala Palace, Lhasa

Marc, Monisha and Jem inside the entrance to the Potala Palace

The Tibetan nun shows Jem and Monisha videos on her iPhone

A night-train passenger sips from a bowl of noodles

Discs of soft cumin bread are baked on the streets of Turfan

Trains pull into Turfan, Xinjiang Province, China

Surveillance trucks with armed police parked in central Urumqi, Xinjiang Province, China

Marzhan and Azamat wave off our train at Almaty station, Kazakhstan

A storm gathers on the mountains as the train crosses from China into Kazakhstan

The *Venice Simplon-Orient-Express* stops at Innsbruck, Austria

Dressed up for dinner in the Côte d'Azur dining car

it was dark, tiny children walked home alone, so safe was it for them to do so unaccompanied. There was much to Nick's observations that appeared true.

The following morning, I was sitting on the coach and waiting for the others to emerge from the hotel. A couple of men were milling around, smoking and chatting to our driver, when a man on a bicycle sailed past them, slowing briefly to reach into his jacket and pull out a digital camera. In a flash, he passed it to one of the men, who pocketed it without saying a word and carried on smoking like nothing had happened. It all took place with such speed that I wondered if I had imagined it. Either I had just watched something underhand take place, or my paranoia had got the better of me. I resolved to bring it up with Geoff when I saw him.

As we boarded the train for the last time I was overcome with sadness that the trip was coming to an end. The journey from Wonsan to Pyongyang would take just over eight hours and we had only one more day in Pyongyang before taking the train back to Beijing. Yet I was relieved. It had been a long nine days and the strain of being polite and vigilant was taking its toll. Even Bob was subdued and had on his lap a brown envelope of family photographs to keep him going. He had spent the last couple of days trying to ring his wife, with no success. He passed the photographs to me and Jem, and pointed out his grandchildren and Brenda, a smiling lady with blonde curly hair.

'Oh, I loves 'em,' said Bob. 'She's such a good woman. It was our fifty-fifth wedding anniversary a few days ago, but we're going to celebrate together when I'm home.'

I was touched by how much Bob yearned for his family and hoped that I would be the same in fifty-five years, struggling to be without them for ten days.

In the autumnal light, Kangwon province throbbed with life and colour. Curving through the bottom of a canyon, the train raced against a river throwing itself around the bends and banks of green. The canyon appeared aflame with maple trees, draping a shawl of gold and red over the valleys, and once again the sky burned that beautiful blue. Lee was sitting in his compartment going through notes about the next day's activities, so I stepped in to ask what we would see at the mausoleum. In addition to the embalmed bodies of the Kims, the mausoleum housed the private train carriages in which each leader had travelled and – in the case of Kim Jong Il – died. The official story was that he had been out in the countryside inspecting a dam and had succumbed to a heart attack having worked himself to death. His body was found in his train carriage. However, the story was quickly challenged by Won Sei-hoon, the then director of the National Intelligence Service in Seoul, who declared that Kim's train had remained stationary in Pyongyang at the time of his death and cited US satellite surveillance photos as proof. Like most stories, it was impossible to corroborate. Lee described how important the railways were to North Korean pride and identity before disappearing for another smoke. Geoff, who had been listening in the corridor, sat down with his bottle of *soju*, which was almost finished, and checked that everyone else was out of earshot before drawing the door closed.

'What Lee said isn't untrue, but the railways are basically the product of Japanese militarism during World War II. They weren't necessarily a communist or Stalinist creation. When Korea was a unified colony under Japanese rule, Japan built many of the current lines as part of its expansion across Asia.'

'They loved their railways,' I said, thinking of Sir Harold Atcherley.

'The Japanese loved infrastructure and railways. They even had their Korean military headquarters at the same place as the main US military base in South Korea now, in large part because of the major railway nearby. They could quickly sling their soldiers across the whole of Korea – as in what is now the North and the South. Long before the Korean division, a lot of battles between Russia, China and Japan were fought over the railway arteries.'

'I have a question: why do they not wear Kim Jong Un on their badges? And why does Miss Kim refer to Kim Il Sung in the present tense? Given that the current leader is so dictatorial

I'm a bit surprised that he doesn't enforce the wearing of his own badge.'

'Kim Il Sung rules from the grave. North Korea is a necrocracy, if you will.'

I had never heard the word before.

'And as for Kim Jong Un, let's just say he hasn't yet earned his colours.'

The more I learnt about the Kim dynasty and its relationship with the people, the more it made sense. North Koreans were sold a story from birth and grew up believing it to be true because they received little information to the contrary. It was no more ridiculous than any other world religion, in fact their belief system invited minimum mockery as they at least acknowledged the supremacy of a living, breathing human being, rather than an invisible entity. The Kims had taken pains to be viewed as an enigma by rarely speaking in public, having no known official residence and appearing around the country unannounced. Kim Jong Un first spoke in public on 15 April 2012 at his grandfather's hundredth birthday, ending a twenty-year period of silence from the family. North Koreans hadn't heard any leader speak since Kim Jong Il had shouted 'Glory to the heroic Korean People's Army' in Kim Il Sung Square in 1992. Kim Jong Un was in his late twenties before anyone in the country had even heard of him, and it was only after the American basketball player Dennis Rodman had gone to Pyongyang to film a documentary that it was revealed to the world that the leader had a baby daughter of whom his own people were still unaware.

Things were changing, though. Defectors to South Korea had begun to describe how fewer and fewer people bought into the state media propaganda machine and North Koreans were growing more aware and more trusting of foreign media that had started to find its way into the country on USB sticks and DVDs. I realised then that I hadn't imagined seeing a camera being passed from the cyclist to the man standing next to our bus. Memory cards and USB sticks were easy to hide in a search. Cities on the borders of China and South Korea were often able to pick up foreign radio and TV signals, allowing North Koreans to tune into a new reality. South Korean soap operas and movies showed a different world, and it gave them a taste for more. That was not to say that everyone wanted to defect across the border; they just wanted to enjoy a few luxuries and some light entertainment, and those caught indulging were now far more likely to be fined than imprisoned. The chance of an uprising was still remote, as the money and power lay with the upper echelons of society, who were quite happy to maintain the status quo so long as it worked in their favour.

Jem had joined us by the window to fill up on the last we were going to see of the countryside, and Victor came in with a tin of pistachio nuts and sat down opposite us, staring at the hillsides and arranging the shells on his knee.

'Do you think you're going to come back again?' I asked him.

'Not for another few years, but surely. And yourselves?'

I glanced at Jem. 'I'd love to come back in about ten years and see what the changes are, but I don't think I'd rush back. Having said that, I've not been entirely appalled by what I've seen.'

Victor sat up and waved his palm at me.

'This is all an illusion. Don't drink the Kool-Aid. The most hostile classes in Chongjin will never get to leave and come to Pyongyang. The gap between them and Pyongyang is gigantic. Did you know there is a thriving black market here that enables the local people to survive?' he said. 'They have their state job, but almost everyone has another job or jobs on the side.'

'I thought private trade was illegal?'

'Of course it is. On the surface.' Victor glanced up at the heater in the wall that often carried sound from the guides' compartment and vice versa, then leant forward. 'But after the famine, people realised they really had to look after themselves because the state wouldn't. And couldn't. Not quite the *juche* that Kim Il Sung had imposed, but a real self-reliance. All those cigarettes and beauty products we bring as gifts for the guides? And the tips in euros? They can sell all of that and live wonderfully for a couple of months.' He pointed a pistachio at me. 'Don't be naive. Everyone is involved, from the top to the bottom. Like you and me, people just want to live well. Most of them know now that South Korea is not the impoverished state that they've been led to believe – although that was once true in the sixties – and they want a piece of the pie. You know that right now the official exchange rate is around 130 won to the US dollar, but on the black market it's around 8,200 won.'

That evening, as we drew into Pyongyang, I cupped my hands to the window, unable to discern anything through the glass. Switching off the light in the compartment, I peered into the blackness, where there was little more than a spattering of light on the ground floors of the odd building. Contrary to the Western ideal of penthouses being the preserve of the wealthy, the elite lived on the ground floor in North Korea. With electricity being in short supply, having no lift to reach the top floor soon became a problem. In the absence of car headlights, streetlights and advertising hoardings, the city was all but invisible. The glare that usually heralded the arrival into a major hub was nowhere to be found. But as we gathered our things and disembarked, I sensed that the station was heaving with bodies. Two other trains had arrived and people were pouring out of the carriages, which were dimly lit and poorly maintained. In the dark, I was just able to make out their loads of cardboard boxes, paper bags, and children tied to their backs, as the guides steered us through the crowds thronging towards the exit. Grappling for Jem's hand, I felt my way out and we were soon on the coach back to the loving arms of the Yanggakdo.

'Men, please all wear your ties and make sure that your shirts are tucked in,' said Lee, who was wearing a smart black suit and polished shoes. We were on the way to the mausoleum, and having forgotten to bring a tie, Jem was examining the spares that Victor had thoughtfully brought with him. Anna was wearing a prim dress and heels, but, refusing to pack either into my Osprey backpack, I had zipped up my fleece and tied my laces into a pair of fetching bows, which was as far as I was willing to go for the Kims.

It was as though everyone had gathered in their Sunday best at the mausoleum, smoothing down skirts and checking side partings. Lined up in rows of four, we were instructed not to talk and to bow at the feet of each leader before walking to the left and bowing again and then bowing at the opposite side before leaving the room. Bowing at the head was forbidden. After what felt like miles of moving walkways, gold hallways and trophy rooms, we passed through a tunnel that blasted air onto us, apparently to banish dirt from our clothes before we entered the first hall. Lit by a blood-red glow and hung with velvet drapes, the windowless ballroom looked like the set of a Kubrick film. And there, spotlit in the centre, was a glass case containing the Great Leader. Roped off on all sides and watched by armed guards wearing white gloves, lay the body of Kim Il Sung dressed in a black suit and tucked in under a red blanket. He looked like a waxwork. A number of North Korean visitors were crying in the row behind us and I couldn't work out whether it was genuine or for show. Bowing at the feet made my stomach turn and I noticed Bob barely nodding. On the way out he was shaking his head and mumbling.

'It's all about them, it's not about the people. I'm a guest in this country, but I don't kowtow. It's way over the top and ostentatious.'

Kim Jong Il was lying on a different floor – which gave me an awful sense of déjà vu as it was designed to mirror the first room – yet the figure in the middle was dressed in his signature khaki outfit and looked puffy and grey, a far cry from the familiar images of the robust man with the shock of black hair. Next door housed Kim Jong Il's private train carriage, which comprised an office suite with two cream leather sofas, next to which sat a pair of his little black shoes with heels, like Cuban dance shoes. On his desk was an open, very American, MacBook, and beneath his desk was a foot massager. I was soon stopped by a guard and made to unfold my arms and put them by my sides, at which point I decided I had had enough and made for the exit.

Our special day was far from over. Today was the seventieth anniversary of the Workers' Party and a good number of the world's press had descended on the Yanggakdo to cover the celebrations, which were taking place in the stadium in the city centre. Foreigners were not allowed anywhere that Kim Jong Un might be present, so a large portion of the afternoon was spent wandering through the crowds, watching jets and bombers scream across the skies to the stadium. The equivalent of the Red Arrows, they left trails of blue and red in their wake, the number '70' written in the sky in clouds of smoke. The Youth League were dressed in white shirts with red baseball caps, and were carrying pairs of what looked like drumsticks for the ceremony. Women wearing *chima jogori* carried cheerleading pom-poms like giant balls of candyfloss and gathered on the pavements, waiting for the parade to leave the stadium. Huddled together to fight off the winds, we waited until dusk when the first growl of tanks appeared on the horizon. With soldiers perched on top, they rumbled past, headlights blazing, lighting the crowds who cheered at the roadside. Red flags waved from the sides and the flame of the Juche Tower glowed over the scene. As night drew in, the clouds darkened to purplish bruises that striped the skies, creating a setting fit for *Apocalypse Now*.

Next, jeeps packed with soldiers waving and cheering bounced past followed by trucks carrying missiles and rockets the size of houses. When it came to artillery, the North Koreans didn't fool around. A rocket rolled past on the back of a juggernaut, and Jem and I looked at each other in disbelief. There was nothing comparable. We knew that history was unfolding around us, and that one day we would tell our grandchildren how it felt to stand at the edge of a North Korean military parade. As the smoke began to build, and the rain pelted down, my socks became soaked through and I lost all feeling in my hands and feet. Winding through the crowds, we sought out the coach, passing hundreds of children crouched in the middle of the road waiting to join the parade. Their white shirts were now stuck to their bodies and rain ran off their hair, rolling in lines down their faces. Shivering, they stayed in perfect formation. Horrified by what the children were being forced to endure, I looked away. They had been in the streets for more than ten hours and who knew how much longer they were going to have to stay there. It was a relief to know that we would soon be back at the Yanggakdo for a hot dinner, shower and bed.

At around two o'clock in the morning Jem and I were asleep when the building was rocked by an explosion that shook us both awake. Over the previous few days, rumours had been flying around that Kim Jong Un was planning to test a ballistic missile on the night of the celebrations, while the world was watching, and we were convinced it had happened. Leaping to the window we pulled back the curtains and found smoke drifting above the river and the sky emblazoned with fireworks. Fountains of red, green and gold burst over the city, then scattered like showers of electric rain.

9

Night Train to Beijing

Through no fault of our own, we had entered North Korea without return visas to China – the only two in the group to do so. Having used our single-entry visas to come into China from Mongolia in July, we'd used a transit visa to fly back in from Vancouver, and had had no other option but to apply for a re-entry visa from Pyongyang the day we arrived, and hope that it was granted by the time we took the train back to Beijing. Now, as we stood on the platform watching the others board the train, the extent of our recklessness sank in. On Lee's advice, we had filled in the forms with terrible handwriting so the officials would tire of deciphering our scrawls and wave through the applications. It had seemed cunning at the time, but now I worried it might have had the opposite effect. Surely the North Koreans wouldn't want us hanging around in their country and would be keen to boot us back over the border, but it was up to the Chinese embassy to grant the visas and I hoped the numerous stamps in our passports wouldn't raise suspicion. Everyone had had to surrender their passports for the ten days, which hadn't bothered me, considering the furthest we could reach without a chaperone was the Yanggakdo's car park, but now I was nervous that we would be left to mooch around for a few more days, and I was more than ready to leave the DPRK.

Seeing Nick wave from the windows, I was beginning to lose faith just as Lee appeared with Sarah and thrust both passports into my hands. Before I'd even pulled on my rucksack, Jem had got one foot on the steps and was squeezing his way into the carriage. Turning to Miss Kim to say goodbye, I gave her a hug as she tried to negotiate her arms around my bag. Her crisp perm smelt freshly sprayed, and I was stabbed by sadness, knowing we would never see her or any of the guides again. She gripped my hand, and I made her promise to get in touch if she was ever able to find her way to London, knowing full well this would never happen. Exhaling with relief as I stepped into the train, I found Sarah had set up shop in the first compartment, taking one of the top berths of the soft sleeper, with Nick below, leaving the other side for me and Jem.

Tommy, Anna and Alice had also chosen to take the overnight train back to Beijing, but as American tourists weren't allowed to take the trains in and out of North Korea, we'd had to part ways with Geoff and Bob, who now had another Koryo burger to look forward to. The rule was an odd one, as American teachers at the Pyongyang University of Science and Technology often used the trains, and there was no official ban in place for tourists: they simply weren't allowed to travel on them. Tommy and Anna were next door, and Alice was two carriages away in a hard sleeper, bunking with rowdy North Koreans for a few hours as she was hopping off early in Dandong. Travelling on the Pyongyang–Beijing service provided one of the only opportunities granted to tourists to interact freely with North Koreans, but the language barrier hindered probing of any real value.

Having spent the previous few months sharing compartments with strangers, it was a treat to be travelling with friends. Even though our companions had usually been a good-natured mix, there were always personal boundaries to respect, which required a certain level of train etiquette lest we disturbed meals, interrupted conversations or kicked anyone in the head while climbing down for late-night trips to the loo. This, however, felt like the sleepovers of my childhood, as we shook out blankets, pooled bags of sweets, and sat cross-legged waiting for the train to leave, lifted by the aura of relief that the trip was over and everyone could relax. Nick appeared at the door.

'Is it all right to leave my things here, do you think? I'm going to find my seat once we're on the move.'

'Your seat?' I asked.

'My seat … in the seating carriage.'

'This is your seat, Nick.' I pointed to where his bag was placed. 'During the day, that's your seat, the one next to it is Sarah's, and at night she goes up to the top berth and this becomes your bed.'

Nick looked confused. 'You mean this is it? There's no other seating carriage?'

'Nope. That was a fancy chartered train so we all had nice seats and a separate compartment for sleeping, but not here I'm afraid. But there is a dining car,' I added, hoping to soften the blow.

'Pffffff.' Nick sat down and plopped his hands in his lap. 'I shall have to get a drink once we're moving,' he huffed.

It was barely ten o'clock in the morning.

As we began to pull away from the platform the guides crouched down and waved through the windows. With the exception of days off to celebrate the Kims' birthdays, and the odd anniversary thrown in here and there, they received no holidays and would be back to work the following morning as soon as the next tour group arrived. As the Ryugyong Hotel sailed by, it was with mixed emotions that I watched the city of Pyongyang slip from view. Victor was right: it was a selfish need that had brought me here, the need to paint myself into a moment of time before it was confined to the history books. But what we had witnessed wasn't the same as watching the Berlin Wall come down or protesting in Tahrir Square. Those events had a finality that birthed a beginning, but none of us could predict what the future held for North Koreans.

The previous evening, we had gone to a barbecue duck restaurant for our farewell dinner and enjoyed a *soju*-sodden night with the guides. After the meal, Lee had stood up to make a speech, which I had managed to write down:

We want to become a member of world society. Inside of DPRK there are so many people. We don't like sanctions, we don't like hostile policy against our country. We are not guilty. So when you go back, please tell the truth. What have you done, what have you seen? Let them come to our country. We are 20 million people, we are not guilty. There is a very big gap between Western mass media and DPRK reality, so please make people understand. And even though there are so many problems of 'no photos', I think you've seen and felt what is life in DPRK. We are developing step by step, in our own style and at our own pace.

He'd finished by downing his *soju* then brandishing the glass. Alice's eyes had filled as ten days' worth of suppressed emotion finally erupted.

As I reread his words, I wondered what to make of them. I kept hearing Victor's voice saying: 'Don't drink the Kool-Aid.' Was the speech a part of the show? Or had the *soju* loosened his tongue? One thing was certain, with the exception of a few dedicated reporters, the Western media did propagate a horrible stereotype of North Korean people, stripping them of their humanity. Yet how much of what Lee wanted us to tell was 'the truth'? Until the day the regime fell, no one could ever know precisely what went on. Closing my notebook, I looked out at the countryside retreating into the distance. Owing to the state of the tracks, which had fallen into disrepair, the train crawled along, offering plenty of opportunity to absorb the gentleness of the journey. There was an enviable peacefulness about the scattering of thatched villages where a couple of oxen stood tethered to trees, radishes dried in the sun, and women bent over their allotments. In a few hours we would be back in the smog and grind of Beijing, clogged with cars and angry people, and I wondered who really had the better lifestyle. Knowing – or at least being told – that most of the country lived in abject poverty was at odds with what we could see, and I didn't know what to believe, wanting desperately not to be duped.

Nick and Jem had gone in search of the dining car, and Sarah, bunged up and coughing, was reading in her berth. Feeling braver without the guides hovering around, I asked her what she had made of Lee's after-dinner speech.

'They usually make a closing statement at the end of a trip, but he's never said anything like that before,' she replied. 'I was quite taken aback actually. That was something very special.'

'How much do you think they buy into the official story? He's lived abroad so it seems a bit odd that he wouldn't know what goes on.'

'It's really hard to know. You can glean a bit from their body language and their general attitude towards visiting monuments and stuff. I used to work with this guide who would deliberately dirty his shoes before we went to the mausoleum, and wear them in defiance. You would never hear him praise the Kims the way the others do, and it was his way of quietly protesting against them. From my years of knowing him, and from what he's told me, he somewhat resents his situation and feels frustrated. He'd experienced a great deal of freedom growing up abroad and I felt like he never really adjusted properly to being back in North Korea.'

'Would they ever say outright what they think?'

Sarah shook her head. 'No. It's just not in their interest. I mean, some of them read BBC news and various other bits of coverage that aren't censored and they don't bat an eyelid, so whether it's because they don't believe it or they just can't say anything …' she trailed off. 'On one of the tours I did, there was a guide who carried a small picture of Barbara Demick in his wallet. Obviously, I was quite taken aback, and asked him why he had it and he said it was so that he would never forget her face.'

Immigration and customs officials always have a way of making me suddenly wonder if I've got a kilo of heroin in my washbag, as they eye my passport, looking back and forth from my ten-year-old photo to my casual countenance. By early evening we had reached Sinuiju, and as the sound of boots and voices approached our compartment I began to sweat with anxiety. A guard ordered us to hand over our phones and cameras, writing down the brands and models of each one. Within minutes a second guard arrived with cheekbones that could carve rock, and gestured for all the iPhones. There had been no access to wi-fi, 4G or any kind of mobile network for the previous ten days, so I'd been unable to send off the photographs I suspected would be deleted by the guards. Thinking myself a genius, I had already saved the photos I wanted to keep in the trash and was perplexed to see the guard go straight for that folder. I also had a bundle of Korean won – rolled up in the dirty socks in my rucksack – which foreigners weren't allowed to own, let alone take out of the country, but that we'd managed to exchange in a department store for a wad of sought-after euros. The guard's eyes moved sideways to meet mine as he carefully scrolled through the selection, deleting anything he considered inappropriate. Handing back my phone, he barely touched Jem's before going through Nick's camera and ordering him to delete a selection of photos that featured local people. Disappointed that my favourite shots had gone, I sulked by the window and waited for the passports to be checked. More than an hour passed until we were cleared and on the move towards the border, my dirty socks untouched.

Together, we gathered at the window to see the two countries flanking the Yalu river, and watched the sun cast its tired rays across the water, around silhouettes of fishing boats. As we crossed the bridge into China our compartment glowed as if with pleasure. At the end of the bridge my phone buzzed across the table and the first messages began to come through as we officially re-entered China. Nick beamed.

'Now that we're out, I'm slightly euphoric and hysterical,' he said, rubbing his thighs. 'Imagine though, we're all feeling so free and liberated in *China* of all places. It's all relative isn't it, when you think about it. Now come on, who's ready for dinner?'

Hot and smoky, the dining car was packed with North Koreans, Chinese and a mass of tourists from various other tour companies who were sizing each other up over bottles of local beer. Sarah was napping, and Nick had joined Tommy and Anna, so Jem and I slid into a table at random, next to Ed from Utah, and Jacek from Poland. Curious as to whether or not Ed was a Mormon missionary, I let Jem initiate the usual traveller chat, while I judged and made assumptions. Tanned like a Benidorm granny, bearded and wearing a couple of leather bracelets that frayed at the knots, Ed had obviously been away from home for a while. This wasn't just a one-off trip to North Korea. He looked to be in his late-forties, which made me suspicious: there was nothing wrong with middle-aged, professional holidaymakers who often devised laudable ways to contract for six months, make a fortune, and then jet off for the rest of the year. But on the whole, they could usually be grouped under the same umbrella. I had encountered a number of them while on backpacking trips to Southeast Asia and while inter-railing around Europe: they always travelled alone, yet attached themselves like limpets to groups of people at least ten years younger than themselves whom they could then patronise while expertly rolling a spliff on the beach. They always carried a worn Camus paperback in their backpocket, knew *the best* stall to find pad thai in Ko Phangan, and had almost died in the jaws of a python/crocodile/wild boar. They usually had the meaning of life all figured out, despite having pissed away most of their years, and amounted to nothing more than being a creepy bore sitting on a pebble beach in Biarritz with a group of eighteen-year-olds and a box of Desperados from Monoprix. Their peers were probably married with children, driving a Lexus, and holidaying in Costa Rica.

I smiled to myself, realising that I had now become that same judgemental traveller. It must be a rite of passage. Tuning back into the conversation, I asked Ed where he was off to next.

'Vietnam, Laos, maybe Cambodia.'

'We haven't been to Laos, but we took the Reunification Express down the coast of Vietnam and then went across Cambodia,' I said.

'Yeah, but you can't beat Laos,' Ed said, emphasising the 'oh' in La-oh. 'I spent three months there last year and I've taken that Vietnamese train.'

'It was a lot of fun, but probably one of the worst compartments I've ever travelled in.'

'The worst?! Try taking the Tazara to Zambia. Or the one to Kigoma or Angola. Man, Asia's got nothing on Africa. Derailments guaranteed.'

The guarantee of derailment was hardly a selling point to a seasoned train traveller.

'Where did you travel in Vietnam?' Ed continued.

'From Hanoi to Da Nang. We spent a couple of days in Hoi An, then went back up to Da Nang and took the train down to Saigon. It was okay, though not as comfy as this one,' Jem replied, following a bean around the plate with his chopsticks.

Ed smirked. 'You travelled sleeper class? That's a shame. I find it kinda fun to travel with the Vietnamese people.'

I was about to tell Ed that 'the Vietnamese people' also travelled in sleeper class when they weren't flying Vietjet Air, when Jem flashed me a look from across the table and stepped on my foot, signalling that he was ready to break free from traveller one-upmanship and head to bed. Whether or not Jacek could speak English was debatable as he'd stayed silent for the entire dinner, but I suspected he was playing a wily game and I bade goodnight to them both. Nick was pink in the cheeks and had evidently made good on his promise to begin drinking as early as possible, so we left him with the others and swayed back to our compartment.

Though red-eyed and drained, with the obvious beginnings of the flu, Sarah was still looking a lot more relaxed now she had fewer people to manage, and was closer to home and her own bed. It turned out that a few days earlier another group at the Yanggakdo had gone in search of the fifth floor, got caught, and been forced to write letters of apology, which Sarah had had to oversee. Having cleaned teeth and washed faces, we slipped under our blankets and began chatting with Sarah about Beijing life, how often she got to see her family in England, and whether or not she tired of traipsing in and out of North Korea every fortnight. Eventually, we got onto the topic of how she had left school and moved to Australia. She was midway through a story when the others arrived, bringing a strong smell of garlic oil and beer. Tommy parked himself on the end of Jem's berth.

'I was probably about nineteen,' Sarah went on, 'and living in Canberral with this guy who was in his forties. We lived in this really small studio room and he was quite mean to me.'

'In what way?' I asked.

'Well, I thought at the time that he might be selling drugs, and then one afternoon he went out and sold our mattress.'

'What?!' Nick looked appalled.

'Yeah, he was quite horrible. And then after I came back from a trip to Perth, I realised I'd picked up scabies, and he threw me out saying the scabies creeped him out. I had to spend the night in the garden. I didn't have any money, so he paid for my bus fare to this farm in Victoria where I worked pruning vineyards. The farm was full of Chinese illegal immigrants who lived in the back garden in two caravans, and I had to stay there until I had enough money to move on. It was pretty dodgy, but they were all so nice and they helped me to get rid of my scabies.'

Tommy had been listening with his mouth slightly open. 'Was that your gap year?'

Once the others had gone back to their own compartments, Nick lay on his back, playing peekaboo with the curtains.

'Had a few beers, Nick?' I asked, as he wrapped his bedsheet around his head.

'I didn't have any beer! Had one and a half bottles of wine, though.'

Nick was beginning to sniffle, and I could tell he had the beginnings of Sarah's flu. One night sealed in this Petri dish of a compartment was guaranteed to make us all ill, but there was no way of escaping it. Nick picked up a bottle of Tylenol and started wrestling with the childproof lid, until Jem eased it away from him, popping it open and rationing him a couple for the night. He soon quietened, and Jem flipped off the light. That night we tossed and turned amid a chorus of coughs, snores, and clearing of phlegm, waking in Beijing with runny noses, sore throats and churning stomachs.

A different Beijing was waiting when we woke the following morning. Clean blue skies revealed a modern, arty-looking skyline that had until now been obscured by the smog. With a Midas touch from the sun, the colours of shops, clothing, trees, cars and people had brightened and deepened, casting the city in a fabulous light. It was a national holiday, and over the previous week the government had simply ordered the factories to shut down, and forced cars to drive on alternate days to limit traffic pollution. Amazed that it was so simple to reduce the pollution levels, we were, however, housebound by illness and unable to enjoy this brand-new Beijing.

My friend Adrian and his wife Hannah were from Wimbledon, but had spent the last ten years living in Beijing. She worked for the British embassy and he'd given up journalism to join the company that had taken us into North Korea. We'd briefly crossed paths at the Yangakkdo, where he and his group were finishing their trip as ours was just beginning, and now that we were all back in Beijing, Hannah and Adrian had generously thrown open the doors of their spare bedroom for as long as it took us to mend. Falling ill was part of the adventure, a minor setback that required little more than good books, patience and sachets of Dioralyte. But it was a blessing to be infirm in someone's home, rather than on a moving train or holed up in a hovel with bad TV and scratchy toilet roll. Before leaving for work, Adrian pointed out the tea, the washing machine and the wi-fi code, before explaining that Ayi would be coming by lunchtime.

'Ayi?' I asked.

'Ayi's our cleaner.'

'Oh, okay. Do we need to let her in or does she have a key?'

'She has a key, so you'll probably just find her wandering about.'

'What's Ayi's name?' I asked, thinking it sounded a lot like ayah, the Hindi word for a nanny or maid.

He frowned for a moment. 'I have no idea. She's just … Ayi. *Ayi* is the Chinese word for aunt or auntie. She's cool, but she breaks stuff and then doesn't tell us that she's broken it. And if we ask her about it she says we have too many things.'

'How did you find her?'

'We didn't. She sort of came with the flat. I don't actually have a number for her. Hannah might. In fact, we've never seen her papers or anything so if we ever went away she could clear out this place and all I'd be able to tell the police is that Ayi did it.'

Ayi turned out to be a wisp of a lady with cropped hair, who didn't seem at all bothered by two strangers wandering around in pyjamas. She politely refused my offer of tea, washed the dishes, scrubbed the bathrooms, and sat down at half time to have her own cup of tea and a mantou bun from a blue plastic bag. The culture of instinctive trust placed in hard-working elderly people was something I was used to seeing in India, and it was heartening to see the same here in China. There was no way I'd hand over my house keys to someone in London without knowing their name or where they had come from. While Ayi pottered around, I put on a load of laundry and we spread out our map to see what remained of our route. From Beijing, we planned to board the bullet train down to Shanghai then swoop across the country to Xining where we would take the Qinghai railway to Lhasa. This was set to be one of the highlights of the trip. While tracing the line, the very thought of travelling to Tibet on the highest railway in the world sent tingles through my finger.

I put the kettle on as Jem began to check timings for the onward journey from Lhasa, when my heart thumped to a halt. The washing machine was sloshing our clothes, and with them, the rolled-up bundle of North Korean won that I'd forgotten to retrieve from my socks. Almost in tears, I switched off the machine and peered inside; everything was soap-covered and drenched. This was Kim Il Sung's divine retribution for taking the notes in the first place. With a consolatory cup of tea, I sat down again and examined the official outline of Tibet's present-day borders, which China had chewed off with such ferocity over the last sixty-five years that the region was barely a fragment of its former self. It was another pin on the map that raised a red flag on my conscience. I had interviewed Tibetans who had escaped to India; I'd joined in Free Tibet protests outside the Chinese embassy in London, and was acutely aware of the plight of Tibetan monks and nuns who had taken to self-immolation as a means of protesting against Chinese rule. However, I had also heard the Dalai Lama speak, and witnessed him encouraging foreigners to visit Tibet and to describe their experiences on their return. His approval had lessened my guilt as I booked our stay in Lhasa. Much the same as North Korea, we had to secure visas from China and were unable to travel without an approved guide, but it was a small price to pay to scale the roof of the world.

Folding away the map, I heard Ayi close the door behind her, leaving as quietly as she had arrived. On the kitchen table was a small pile of our books and pens that she had tidied up, along with one stray sock that she had picked up on the staircase – inside of which was the bundle of won. Unrolling it with a yelp, I saw the beaming face of Kim Il Sung on a treasured 5,000-won note, and gave thanks for the stroke of luck. At that very moment, my phone alerted me to the day's second piece of good news: Marc had arrived in Beijing.

10

Ghost Cities and the Great Wall

Being on the road frees you from the burden of the everyday. Witnessing others' hardships and poverty puts first-world problems into perspective, slapping you out of misery and self-pity. Yet, before I met Jem, I had often had moments on my travels when I was overwhelmed by loneliness, and sank into troughs of depression deeper than those I had at home. Suddenly aware of the distance of my loved ones, I'd plummet into despair, watching sunsets alone, camouflaging myself in noisy cafes, convinced that everyone was laughing at my solitude. These dips would never last long, but there were periods of being alone in hotel rooms, where night and day blended into one, my thoughts turned to liquid, and nothing but a small miracle could save my soul. Five years ago, Marc was that small miracle.

I had just boarded the *Lifeline Express*, a hospital train run by an NGO in Madhya Pradesh in India. It was stationed for five weeks in a town called Umaria, a spot so desolate that connections from big cities ran only twice a week, and my fellow passengers from Katni had laughed in my face as I got off, enthralled as I heaved my bag across the tracks. I had recently fled from my travelling companion – under a dark, dark cloud – and was ill, depressed, and desperate for someone familiar to talk to. Aware that the best cure for my woes was to focus on someone else in need, I had arrived on the train to report on volunteer surgeons who operated on local people suffering from cleft palates, polio-related deformities, cataracts and ENT complications. The last thing I had expected of my first morning was to meet a photographer from Hackney. With a Welsh mother and a Sikh father, Marc had grown up in Scotland before moving down to London to be a railway engineer. But after ten years, he'd packed it all in to become a photographer. Like me, Marc had turned up in Umaria to document the work on board the train, and was equally pleased to find a journalist who could put words to his pictures. We'd worked well together and continued to do so once we were back in London, staying firm friends to the point that Marc and his camera had agreed to join me and Jem for the final six weeks of our trip.

Marc had flown in to Beijing pumped up and raring to go, only to find us deflated and dormant. While we recuperated, he had busied himself by wandering the *hutongs*, photographing the local residents, and getting to know his flatmate, Fish, before luring us out for a bowl of noodles, where he proposed we spend the afternoon climbing the Great Wall.

'Come on guys, we can't come to Beijing and not see the Great Wall.'

An Imodium between my teeth, I observed him with envy. His eyes shone with the anticipation of adventure, and his leg bounced with the energy of a man with culture pulsing through his veins. We had probably looked like this five months ago. But at this stage, I hadn't passed a solid stool in six days, selected my daily wardrobe based on what smelt the least, and was perfectly happy to accept that my time in Beijing had been spent shopping for cardigans in Zara, being ignored by taxi drivers, and having a back massage. All three experiences had been unique to the Chinese way of doing things, and as a result I'd broadened my understandings of the local take on fashion, racism and masochism.

Marc's eagerness reminded me of my parents during family holidays. My father would hammer on the hotel door at 8 a.m. on a Saturday, while my mother rang the bedside phone – at least three times – to inform us that they were going down for breakfast. Finally, my brother and I would surface at 9.55 a.m., just as breakfast was finishing, and then want to go for food, much to my father's chagrin, having paid for breakfast in the room. We'd get moving around noon and everyone would be sulking, my father striding ahead at the Hagia Sophia, or the Acropolis, or Disneyland. Nonetheless, we still ended the day with the middle-class comfort of having embraced some culture – even at Space Mountain. Keen, therefore, not to emulate teenage apathy in my thirties, and excited to ride another train, I gave in to Marc's demands, and we set off to visit the Badaling section of the Great Wall.

The train smelt of popcorn – hot, radioactive-yellow popcorn – carried by a man wearing a satchel and jeans. He appeared not long after the train departed, clutching an open bag that wafted buttery, salty pleasures up the aisle. Holding it out to a girl with pigtails, he offered her a handful, but she handed over a note, took the bag, and he wandered back the way he came. She hugged the bag, staring out of the window, mechanically chewing one piece at a time.

'Has she just bought his popcorn off him?' Jem asked.

'I don't know, but it does look like it.'

'It smells amazing, I want some now,' Marc said from across the aisle.

The man appeared again, holding another single bag. Curious, I edged past him and went to see if he had a stash in the next carriage, or a portable microwave, and found nothing but passengers scrolling through phones and staring at the expressway running parallel to the train. I returned to my seat as some students bought his second bag and shared it round their group. Within a minute, he came by with a third bag, so hot that he was tapping it between his fingers. Convinced that the carriage must have some kind of Narnia-like doorway, I bought his bag and settled back as the popcorn squeaked between my teeth like buttery bits of polystyrene. Five minutes later he came through with two bubbling bowls of noodles.

The S2 service to Badaling took just over an hour to Yangqing county, about fifty miles northwest of Beijing. The section of the wall at Badaling is the most accessible stretch, which means that it is also the most popular. More than 70,000 visitors are said to pass through every day – and it appeared that they were all here now, at four o'clock on a Tuesday, jostling to get up the hill. It was icy, and my eyes began to water as we climbed the paving slabs leading to the wall. Gusts of wind shoved me around, and a needle of air pierced my eardrums, but after a quick stop to haggle for a fake Burberry scarf, I was better equipped, and jogged to catch up with Marc and Jem. Unaware when we set out in the morning that this was to be our afternoon activity, I was wearing a pair of ballet pumps, and Jem was in flip-flops and socks, like a geisha, carrying a bag full of notebooks and tickets that were meant to be posted home. Tenzing and Hillary we were not. As the wall began to incline, my shoes began to slip off, and resignation set in as I eyed the curves rising in the distance, a dragon's tail being pulled across the peaks.

The Great Wall was as magnificent a sight as I'd hoped: the smog filtered the evening sun, allowing no more than a veil of peach light to drape the valley, softening the silhouettes of surrounding mountains. Conifers huddled together on the slopes, flecked with the maroons and reds of autumn, and the long shadows of walkers followed under our feet with the stealth of spectres from the past. After a couple of hours, the crowd thinned, the clouds drew together, and a stillness settled on the wall. Recognising that he was not travelling with two athletes, Marc had climbed ahead and Jem had gone to buy tickets for the last cable car down, leaving me with nothing but my thoughts for company. I wandered into a watchtower and crouched down to peer through a shooting hole, looking out to where one rogue ray of light had slipped through the cloud. From my spot, the wall looked like a stone roller coaster, looping over hills and plunging into valleys. Hundreds of years ago, a guard had stood at this very post keeping watch over the same valley. A tornado of leaves spun in the corner and for a brief moment I imagined being that guard. Had he watched the same conifers bristle in the breeze? Had he seen the stones turn pink in the light? For all the famous images of the wall – at sunset, at dawn, or powdered with snow – none could trigger the urge to transpose oneself quite as much as touching the stone, hearing the tap of woodpeckers in the trees, witnessing it first-hand. Travelling is synonymous with escape, the desire to create distance and observe differences, but for me it now meant the opposite. I took comfort in identifying with others, bridging distance and erasing the idea of otherness. I wanted to know who had stood on this spot, and if they'd felt the same chill I now felt in my fingers.

Of late, it was increasingly rare to find a corner in China that resembled its original form. Even this part of the wall – that had previously collapsed – had been reconstructed to look, ironically, like its former ruined self. Most of the country was being demolished, only to be rebuilt, demolished and rebuilt again. Like an ageing Hollywood actress addicted to surgery, the country seemed unaware that the endless facelifts, chipping, digging and filling had effaced an original, timeless beauty that would have aged with grace. A shout and wave from Jem brought me forward to the present and I crept out from the tower, climbing up towards the cable cars as the leaves continued to spin in the wind.

Beijing South railway station resembles a sports stadium. Like much of the city's newest infrastructure, the station was one of a number of projects whizzed through in time for the 2008 Olympic Games. It took 40,000 workers just two and a half years to complete, replacing the Yongdingmen railway station, a piece of architectural beauty that had dated back to 1897. With more than 300,000 people passing through its halls every day, the station was designed across three floors to separate arriving and departing passengers. It certainly lacked the fever and intensity of the city's other stations: flashing with sunshine and dotted with palm trees, the station was also fitted with a glass, solar-panelled roof to provide electricity. This was the first of China's high-speed railway stations – the prototype for all future high-speed stations – but it looked more like an airport, with white, bottle-nosed bullet trains lined up and ready to shoot off around the country.

It was just before noon, and we'd arrived to take the G train down to Shanghai. The *gaotie* high-speed train covered the 819 miles between Beijing and Shanghai in just under six hours and was the preferred choice of business travellers and the wealthier middle class, who couldn't bear the tedium of an overnight service or the fuss of a two-hour flight. Between 7 a.m. and 9.30 p.m., more than forty of these trains travelled to Shanghai, so we'd had no problem reserving three seats, boarding and departing on time.

The romance of railway travel took a bullet to the heart on these trains. Most passengers ate out of KFC bags, then slept face down on the tray tables or chewed on sunflower seeds that they'd poured into their sick bags. After an hour, an attendant came by with a trolley stacked with mini tubs of strawberry Häagen-Dazs and bottles of Starbucks iced coffee. Like Japan's Shinkansen, the G trains offered no more than a means to travel from one destination to the other. Of course, this was no bad thing. Fewer people had the time or the inclination to while away a full day picking their teeth and staring at the countryside. Overhead, a digital monitor showed that we were travelling at 302 km/h. The train had a 350 km/h capacity, but after an accident near Wenzhou in 2011 that killed an estimated forty people, the authorities had lowered the speeds – even though speed was not the cause of the collision, but a lightning strike that had stalled one of the two trains involved. The Chinese government had tried to censor reporting of the crash unless it highlighted positive stories of blood donation or local heroes attending the scene, so strong was the government's fear of painting the new railway in a poor light. The crash led to a state investigation into the ministry for railways, which uncovered widespread corruption and resulted in suspended death sentences for two officials. However, in September 2017, a number of trains were once again allowed to run at their maximum speed and were renamed 'Fuxing' – the Chinese for 'rejuvenation' – to reflect improved monitoring systems that would stop trains automatically in the event of an emergency.

Looking out of the window for inspiration, I found nothing but concrete clusters of empty tower blocks and dormant cranes flashing past every few minutes. The skeleton structures looked like lifeless Lego cities sprouting up from the farmland. Most remained unfinished, the top few floors draped in tarpaulin. Dubbed China's 'ghost cities', these hubs had first emerged in Shenzhen in 1978, then mushroomed over the last fifteen years after a government push to boost GDP and improve the infrastructure in the country's more remote areas. The new developments contained sports stadia, shopping malls, schools and crèches, all of which were designed to attract rural communities or citizens from overflowing megacities in search of lower rents and a better quality of life. Yet most remained empty, gathering dust and notoriety: the foreign media had taken delight in the apparent failure of the scheme, pushing 'ghost cities' to the top of the folder labelled 'Wacky Chinese Stories for Westerners', but they had ignored the small print; most of the cities had been built with the aim of populating them by 2020 or 2030, so it was too soon to declare them a flop. The Chinese response was that they were simply in the middle of development. In reality, the term 'ghost cities' was a misnomer. 'Ghost' suggested that these cities had once thrived, before succumbing to desertion, but these stillborn cities had never had a pulse, and were waiting for people to come and pump life into them.

Government officials claimed that some cities were already populated, but the numbers seemed disingenuous; they included construction workers from the site, and people who had had no other choice for accommodation after their rural homes had been wiped out to make way for the cities, buying the properties with the compensation money. However, that didn't detract from the fact that some cities were beginning to see other residents move in. I hoped they succeeded, if only to wipe the smirk off the face of Western press.

Although I despaired about the annihilation of ancient sites and the bulldozing of history to rubble, there was still something enviable about the Chinese attitude to construction, whether it was cities or railways; they thought, they planned and they built. The high-speed railway programme began in 2003 with a 251-mile line between Qinhuangdao and Shenyang for trains running up to 155 mph, and in just fourteen years China had completed construction of more than 12,500 miles of high-speed track, with trains running at a capacity of 217 mph. To put it into perspective, that was almost a third of the entire length of India's railways. The proposed plan was to extend the passenger lines to 18,600 miles by 2020. While we were still dithering over plans for a third runway at Heathrow, and HS2 was set to be ready by the time most of us were dead, the Chinese had already resurrected the old Silk Road route and were running weekly freight trains from Beijing to London.

Turning away from the window, I looked around for someone to talk to. Jem was reading Andre Agassi's autobiography, and Marc had wandered off to try and photograph the flatbeds in business class. This wasn't the sort of train journey conducive to the natural striking-up of conversation. Headphones were in and eyes were closed. It would have been inappropriate to start sliding into empty seats and tapping strangers on the elbow for a chat. Another option was to stand in the vestibule in the hope of ambushing passengers on their way to the toilet, but that was about as attractive an option as being punched in the head – which would probably be their response to a weirdo hovering outside the door with a notebook and pen. Besides, maybe this journey was their only quiet time of the day, the time for parents to savour the silence and the absence of children, the time to switch off before morning meetings, the time to disengage from the speed and roar of the city. Entering that precious space would be as criminal as trying to talk to someone on the Tube. Still, I felt restless – almost enough to start kicking the back of the seat in front. The quicker the journey, the more antsy I became. Such is the paradox of high-speed travel. On the other hand, the prospect of a fifty-six-hour journey barely registered on my radar as an inconvenience. But right now, it was imperative to arrive in Shanghai on time, as I had made plans to eat dumplings and sit in my pants watching rubbish telly.

Giving up on unearthing stories, I dug out my Kindle and began to click through the selection of books I'd optimistically loaded before leaving London. I hated my Kindle, not because I loved the smell of paper, but because I liked knowing exactly where I was at all times. The percentage was available if I looked, but it was all relative: reading 20 per cent of *Fahrenheit 451* was very different from reading 20 per cent of *War and Peace*, and I couldn't thumb through the pages, or wedge in a bookmark. The Kindle was also starting to look like an ugly, outdated piece of kit that was destined for the back of a bedside drawer along with my MiniDisc player and a couple of old cheque books. Incidentally, I'd given up on *War and Peace* on the Trans-Mongolian, and had little to no intention of going back to it unless I had a long period in hospital. Along with *Catch 22* and *The Satanic Verses*, it was just one of those books with which I was not fated to have a positive relationship. I had almost reached the end of *The Dinner* by Herman Koch, when the battery died, renewing my hatred for the device. But at that moment, I noticed passengers stretching, pulling on shoes and re-tying their hair. It was just before 7 p.m., and after only six hours we were already slowing into Shanghai's Hongqiao station.

'I don't like Shanghai.'

Marc sank into the sofa in the lobby and scowled as he took in the opulence. 'It's like one big shopping mall. Just glass and neon. I hate it.'

Unsure how to respond, I ordered a pot of jasmine tea and tried to look understanding. On the contrary, Jem and I had fallen in love with Shanghai overnight. At the station, Marc had hopped into the first taxi and zoomed off to his Airbnb, while Jem and I had taken the taxi behind, deciding to treat ourselves to a night at the PuLi, a luxury hotel in the Jing'an district. After checking in, we had gone out looking for the city's best *xiao long bao*. The doughy, porky mouthfuls – otherwise known as Shanghai dumplings – were plumped up with hot, silky stock, and in keeping with the status quo, were not hand-pressed by a wrinkly *ayi* down an alley, but mass-produced at a Taiwanese chain called Din Tai Fung in a big shopping mall made of glass and neon. It had taken a while to find the place, after a shop assistant had appeared to know where we wanted to go and then started showing Jem hairdryers, which we could only assume was a misunderstanding of *feng* meaning 'air' and our pronunciation of Fung. Sated, we'd had a long soak in the bath, overlooking the skyline's fairground madness, then slept under a cool white duvet while the city flashed and strobed below. Little did we know that across town, the serendipitous nature of hailing taxis had resulted in two rather different first impressions of Shanghai.

'It's not so bad,' I said. 'Did you get to your place okay? Our taxi driver couldn't figure out how to get here and kept ringing an English-speaking friend of his and asking her to translate "PuLi". Got here safely in the end though.'

'My taxi driver crashed.'

'What?!'

'Yep, we had a crash on the motorway after we left the station.'

'Why didn't you call?' Jem asked.

Marc shrugged. 'No point, I'm all right and I don't think my SIM card's working properly.'

'What happened?' I asked.

'It was like something out of Grand Theft Auto. He was weaving from lane to lane at about eighty miles an hour while everyone else was doing about forty. It felt like a car chase, but we weren't chasing anyone, and no one was chasing us. I don't get scared that often, but there were no seat belts in his beat-up old car, and then suddenly we went sideways into another car and bounced off it. The cabbie stopped, literally in the middle of the motorway, on the central reservation bit. I thought there was going to be a massive fight but they weren't arguing, just swapping details, so this kind of thing probably happens all the time. In the

UK you're supposed to get out and I suddenly realised that I was still sitting in the back, in the dark, and that any second someone could plough into the back of us. So, I got out, and my driver was standing there chatting for about ten minutes. He didn't stop the meter or anything and then he got back in and we kept going. When I got to my Airbnb I told him I wasn't paying for the journey after he'd crashed into someone, and we had a big argument that neither of us could understand. Then he grabbed a guy off the street to translate, and got him to tell me that he was going to call the police. He started getting more and more irate and I just thought: "This is brutal and not worth the seven quid", so I just paid him and then went into my jail cell.'

'Jail cell?'

'My room is like a little underground prison cell. The host is nice but she's got this windowless room that's like the servant's quarters or something. And it's got nothing in it apart from a single bed and a DVD player, and she keeps trying to give me DVDs, and I keep telling her I don't want to watch DVDs, I just want some sunlight in my room.'

'I wish you'd called us or come over for dinner,' I said, pouring out the tea.

'Nah, it's fine, I went out into the street just to get away from the room, and these two Norwegian students went past on mopeds, so I stopped them and asked where I could get some food. They told me they were off to some proper little party street, so I hopped on the back of one of their mopeds and they drove off, and then said that it was a street where I could get burgers and pizza and there'd be no Chinese people, and I was like: "Mate, I don't want that at all! I want some proper Shanghai Chinese food," and the guy said: "Oh, I don't know where to find that, we're going to an Irish bar," so I got off and walked around a bit on my own. I found this wee place, but then I made the mistake of ordering, you know, that nice-looking chicken in soy sauce with coriander, and it turned up fridge-cold and dripping with blood. I knew when I sent it back that the guy was thinking "You fucking foreigners." I don't like Shanghai.'

Our hotel room was bigger than our London flat, had a sunken bath, a bed that could fit four people, and complimentary beer in the fridge. I quite liked Shanghai.

'It's not like Beijing. Beijing felt like Glasgow, it had that raw, working-city feel.' Marc sipped his tea. 'Anyway, it ended up being quite a decent evening. Anything was better than sitting in my jail cell feeling depressed.'

I had thought of asking Marc if he wanted to come up and check out the view from our room, but suspected he might smash his camera over my head. Instead, we finished the tea and decided to get as far away from the glass and neon as possible, winding our way across the city to the ancient water town of Zhujiajiao.

On my travels, it had become apparent that development and modernity posed a direct threat to the enjoyment of many travellers, disgruntled that the world should adapt and progress at the expense of their own pursuit of the exotic. This was no criticism of Marc's loathing of Shanghai – which was swift to change after we ran him a bath, handed him a beer and left him to wallow in salt crystals while we went for a swim at the spa – but the realisation of a distinct trend that had emerged from eavesdropping on other people's conversations. Granted, most of us don't travel 5,000 miles for Starbucks and KFC, but it was abhorrent to some that Chinese people might like the odd Frappuccino and some hot wings. While I could have ridden on trains with chickens and farmers who would make for a great Steve McCurry-style Instagram post, I preferred the new trains and their soft mattresses. I liked riding alongside families watching soaps on their phones, and chatting to students in English. One was no less China than the other, and both had their own stories to tell. But there was a constant yearning for the authentic – whatever that meant – and a need to seek out the China of movies, where old men with catfish moustaches smoked opium pipes in antique shops to the sound of mandolins. Like Marc, I baulked at the idea of arriving in Shanghai and heading straight to The Tipsy Fiddler to neck a pint of Guinness with Erik and Andreas from Oslo, but I couldn't see the offence in a city's pursuit of its own dreams. 'Modernised' was a dirty word for everyone but the inhabitants of that city, for whom modernisation meant employment, prosperity and greater peace of mind. The modernised city didn't lend itself to the sexy narrative that travellers needed to recount on their return, but the modern was as key as the ancient when it came to understanding the evolution of a place and its people.

Zhujiajiao was built on canals running off the Yangtze river. Wooden bridges looped from one bank to the other as boats glided below, dragging wisps of willow in their wake. Dating back to the fourteenth century, when the town was a trading hub, it was still very much a place to trawl for knick-knacks – from gold-tipped chopsticks and fridge magnets of the late Bin Laden, to live hairy crabs and floral fans. A confusion of alleyways tricked visitors into getting lost down lanes, where women flash-fried fermented tofu and steamed mountains of *char siu* trotters, the slam of cleavers sending flecks of honeyed skin to the walls. Pet shops sold fishy-smelling terrapins crawling over each other in buckets, and hamsters burrowing in sawdust, while a few lanes along, a jeweller laid out freshwater pearls still stuck to the goo in their shells. Down one backstreet was a shrine to Michael Jackson featuring two photographs of him from the 1980s, his silver glove in a silk-lined box, and an 'I Love MJ' coffee flask, all of which was guarded by two stuffed wolves snarling at onlookers. Fat corgis waddled around in the sun, gnawing at scraps of pig ear from the gutters, and nipping at tourists. Elderly women wearing conical straw hats and loose, mid-calf trousers, wheeled their bikes along, grocery bags swinging from the handles. Zhujiajiao was the antithesis to the techno-fizz of downtown Shanghai.

A few twists and turns brought me past a temple and onto a quiet street of guesthouses hung with cages of coloured birds, tweeting and beating their wings against the sides. Peering into a pair of open shutters, I saw a man as old as the earth wearing a baseball cap, preparing his lunch. He caught me spying, put down his bowl of rice and potatoes and shuffled to the window, his skin soft like silk and his mouth missing all its teeth. A number of residents still lived here, their laundry drying in courtyards parked with cycles, which endowed the little town with more spirit than if it had been preserved solely as a relic for tourists to enjoy. And yet I had an uncomfortable feeling that this had all been carefully curated to appeal to nostalgia. The town was a popular spot for newly-weds, a number of whom were posing on the bridges and enjoying the novelty of quaintness in a city like Shanghai. It would come as no surprise if every evening, after the last visitor had left, the bridges were dismantled, the canals drained, and the sound of birds switched off in a control room.

After loading up on suede notebooks, chopsticks, and a stash of hand-painted postcards, we took a boat along the town's canals with a middle-aged Chinese couple. It was a warm day, and the lady's white make-up had begun to run in rivulets down her cheeks and neck. Worried that her face was melting, I looked on in sympathy as she pulled out a handkerchief and began to dab her upper lip. Seeing me stare, she began chatting, and asked if we'd tried the fermented tofu, a speciality that smelt like a foot infection.

'It's very famous in the south, they eat with spring onion and congee in Guangdong province.'

'Is it a delicacy?'

She waved her hand and screwed up her mouth. 'Have you heard of Three Squeaks?'

'Three squeaks? No, what on earth is that?'

'New-born mice. Tiny, tiny,' she said, pinching her thumb and index finger together. One of her eyebrows had now begun to slide away.

'They cook new-born mice?'

She laughed. 'No cooking. They alive. First squeak, you pick up with chopsticks. Second squeak you dip in chilli. Third squeak you put in the mouth.'

The gruesome image made me feel suitably ill, but also strangely hungry, so we disembarked for lunch before heading back into the city. While stepping out of the boat I asked the lady if there was a special name for the boat in Mandarin. She turned and asked the boatman.

'Tourist boat,' he replied.

'Tourist' is a bad word. Covering every cliché – from wearing Crocs and bumbags, to travelling by the coachload – 'tourist' is a label from which 'backpackers', 'travellers', 'wanderers', 'adventurers', 'explorers' and 'vagabonds' are quick to distance themselves, most of whom are usually men. But ultimately, if you're visiting a place for pleasure and interest, you're a tourist. I had no qualms about being labelled a tourist. Nor, presumably, did the millions who descended upon my home city every summer, to whom I took a natural and instinctive dislike. It was in every Londoner's DNA to feel the surge of rage – and pleasure – at spotting a tourist standing on the left of the escalator who simply *had* to be ploughed out of the way with a 'sorry, could you stand on *the right*, please'. At its core, the problem the world over wasn't the presence of tourists so much as the way in which they chose to embrace their new surroundings. Wearing plastic bags over feet so as not to catch anything from a temple floor, fondling in a hotel pool in front of children, and referring to locals as 'natives', wouldn't curry favour, but a vague attempt to blend in and observe wouldn't go amiss.

Now, as we stood on the platform at Longyang Road station, waiting for the maglev to approach, I had no shame that we were about to embark on a ride to tick a tourist box. To onlookers, it was obvious that we were the only three passengers travelling to the airport without luggage. The magnetic levitation train to Shanghai Pudong International Airport was the fastest train in the world, and we wanted to ride it for the thrill of travelling at 268 mph. I couldn't think of a better reason. It was the same reason why Space Mountain had the longest queue at Disneyland. In the absence of wheels, the train was pulled upwards by powerful magnets, leaving a gap of around 8–12 mm between the magnets and the guideway that essentially allowed the train to fly, owing to a lack of surface friction. As the train entered the station, I edged towards the doors, nudging a few kids out of the way, before darting in and trying to figure out which seat would feel the greatest impact of the speed. Scrambling around, I eventually settled on a forward-facing seat by the window and waited. Like an aeroplane, the train tilted up ever so slightly and began its seven-minute journey across the city, the force pinning me to my seat. From the window, I could see the track curving above the motorway, and felt a pang of horror as it swooshed around the bend, blocks of flats blurring past. It was impossible to look at any building or car for more than a split second before it was gone. A lady sitting across from us looked up from her phone as we took photos of the overhead speedometer. As we sailed into the station, she waited by the door with us and smiled.

'A lot of Chinese families come on a Sunday afternoon to do the same thing.'

Stepping down, we hovered around on the platform until our fellow passengers had vanished into the terminals, before boarding a different carriage – much to the amusement of the train attendant, who smiled and waved. We were soon hurtling back into the city having discovered the best way to pass fifteen minutes in Shanghai.

Marc was furious. Dumping his rucksack on the floor, he yanked the sleeve of his T-shirt and wiped the sweat from his face, which was now the same hue as the rose in our compartment.

'Guys, this is not good enough.'

We had arrived at the station with just over ten minutes to spare before the train to Xining, and still had to collect tickets, go through security, find the platform, and board. Having caught trains for almost six months, we had breezed in, safe in the knowledge that it wouldn't be a problem – and it wasn't. Admittedly, I could barely breathe, and needed a bottle of water after having belted down the platform with less than two minutes to departure, but we were on board and on the move. Catching trains had become second nature to us now and I enjoyed spicing up the day with the thrill of a chase. But Marc was not amused, and was now drenched in sweat and loathing. Looking at the floor, we took a stern telling-off, which ended abruptly when Marc finally stopped to look around the compartment. 'Wow, this is nice, man.'

So far, Marc's Chinese train experience added up to nothing more than the train to the Great Wall and the bullet train to Shanghai. He was yet to ride the long-distance trains with their soft-sleeper berths, carpeted floors and pretty gold curtains. There was even a pair of towelling slippers for each passenger. The long-distance trains he'd taken in India aimed for a similar set-up, but the most they managed was four berths, grime-ridden floors and broken fans. This was luxury by comparison. Forgetting his rage, he turned around a few times, patting the berths and pulling back the curtains, pleased with his surroundings. It was just before 9 a.m. and the train was due into Xining at 5 p.m. the following day. Covering almost 1,550 miles, the train would arc across the country through Nanjing, Xi'an and Lanzhou, before arriving in Xining. This was the sort of train journey I lived for – a mobile camping trip. Under normal circumstances I hated everything about camping: the lack of showers, the lack of sleep, squatting in the dark, spiders in my shoes, and grass in my tea. But somehow train travel adapted the best bits, and from within the cosy confines of my berth I could change into woolly socks, unpack bottles of stewed peaches, sip hot tea and watch the landscape swell and shrink. Jem had put on his dad's old long johns, I'd pulled on my thermal leggings, and Marc, watching us both, had eventually given in and got into his own thermals. We looked like a third-rate cycling team.

An hour into the journey, the fourth berth was as yet unclaimed, and filled with potential. It lay there as a question mark, waiting to be answered by an unknown protagonist in our story. Whether it was to be occupied by a cast of characters, or one sole hero of the tale, whoever came along would change the fate of our journey. The door slid open – and we all looked up as the conductor came in. Wearing prim white gloves, she took our tickets, slotting them into a leather case and handed over three plastic cards for us to keep until Xining.

Over the previous six months, my brain had become conditioned to expect certain sounds and sights, and any anomaly triggered a short circuit of confusion. Now, as I looked out of the window, I could feel sparks fly. Most trains originated in the heart of a city and were pumped out to the peripheries past shopping complexes, office blocks and high-rise apartments, while the city peeled away in layers; graffiti-covered concrete and stacked living thinned to low-rise suburban housing and green spaces, then flattened to countryside and miles of emptiness, before the layers reassembled and we drew into the next city. But over four hours, this train passed through a single, unending megacity that refused to shake free from Shanghai. Whenever the countryside drew into view, a chain of apartments appeared, then a shopping complex, then a ghost city, then a car park, and then another string of apartments. According to the timetable, we were travelling through a number of discrete cities: Kunshan, Suzhou, Wuxi, Changzhou, Zhenjiang and Nanjing, yet each melded to the next with a haphazardness of construction I'd never seen before. For those who disliked the modern face of Shanghai, or who couldn't afford the property prices, these extended cities threw up the perfect answer for commuters. They just needed to come.

I speared a peach slice, wondering if our fourth roomie would ever appear. Marc was editing photos, and Jem was reading up on altitude sickness, paranoid that the few hours we had to wait in Xining were nowhere near enough for us to acclimatise before the overnight train to Lhasa. There was no question about it, four hours was definitely nowhere near enough to acclimatise, we needed at least two days, but the train timetable and our own schedule meant that we had no choice.

'We need to drink as much as possible to stave off headaches,' Jem read off his phone. 'And don't forget what Yuhan said about falling asleep.'

After staying at the PuLi we had also dabbled with Airbnb, and spent three nights in the home of a pleasant young woman named Yuhan, who owned a three-bedroom flat in the former French Concession. She slept in the single room, rented out one room to a couple who only emerged to take breaks from rampant sex sessions, leaving a post-coital fog in the corridor, and the third room was used for short stays. Each time we bumped into Yuhan she had wet, freshly washed hair and was wearing new pyjamas. It was a pity that she didn't apply the same rigorous levels of cleanliness to our room, which had a mucky Hello Kitty duvet cover with no duvet inside, a pair of unwashed pants at the top of an unemptied bin, and a sink so clogged with hair that I wondered if I pulled it all up I might find the last guest still attached. Yuhan had recently visited Tibet with a group of friends and had shown us a number of photographs that could have been taken anywhere in the world that had a bit of blue sky. Each one was a photo of Yuhan, or a photo of Yuhan with reapplied lip gloss, or Yuhan holding up two fingers with a monastery in the background. As she flicked through photos of herself, she warned us about the dangers of altitude sickness: 'Don't go to sleep if you have sickness, you could slip into a coma and no one will know if you die in your sleep'; and the dangers of eating fish: 'I travelled with a group of twenty doctors and everybody fell sick. The only one who didn't fall sick was the one doctor who did not eat fish. Fish are sacred.' Her final warning was not to haggle with Tibetans. 'They all keep knives on their person that they're given as children. And they will use them.'

Just as I was considering going for a recce down the train, the door opened and a tubby man with glasses peered at the number on the empty berth.

'Ah, this is me,' he said, glancing around at the three of us with a weak smile.

I felt bad for him. As much as I was excited about our new arrival, the poor man was clearly dreading spending the next twenty-four hours with three tramps wearing their underwear on the outside of their clothes. He unpacked his things, tucked away his bag, then disappeared into the corridor to make a phone call, nodding on his way out.

'He seems nice,' Marc said. 'And he doesn't stink of cigarette smoke.'

Our compartment was right next to the vestibule, where most smokers gathered in a haze that drifted through the door every time someone came up the corridor. Technically, smoking wasn't allowed in the compartments, but no one cared to observe rules, and the sour smell of cheap tobacco hung in the air. The door opened again and the man came back in and sat down next to me.

Gerry was a retired high-school teacher who had spent the week at his sister's, and was now heading back home to Lanzhou. He picked up my notebook and ran a finger down the list of trains, letting out a low whistle.

'You are very lucky people,' he said. 'I would love to travel like you.'

'Do you always travel by train to see your sister?' I asked.

Gerry nodded. 'I love it, it's relaxing and I can sleep well.' He pointed out of the window at the cranes and viaducts dotted with engineers in high-vis jackets. 'The speed train from Lanzhou to Urumqi is in operation since last year, now they are making the breakthrough with this region. Less than a hundred kilometres is mountainous, so they will complete this construction by 2017 and all the speed trains will be connecting. Shanghai to Xining will take eight hours after this.'

'This route? Just eight hours?'

'Yes. So, when I go to see my sister I will definitely take that one. Of course, I won't take this one any more.'

'Will anyone still use this route?'

'People will still need the cheaper trains, the high-speed train in future is going to be more expensive than airlines. But like the Shanghai region, as you see, the fast trains are everywhere and they are almost putting the airlines out of business.' Gerry had a pronounced stutter that made me feel guilty for badgering him, but it was unusual to find a bilingual passenger so willing to chat that I continued to probe, figuring he would shut down the conversation as he saw fit.

'I thought that was just a myth.'

'For not very long distances, people prefer to take the speed train because otherwise you have to go to the airport, there are delays, the travel time, the check-in, the weather, the queues. It is changing very fast here in China. Everything is changing fast in China. You see this kind of train, this soft seat? When I was young it was only for the high-ranking government officials, so ordinary people couldn't buy this ticket, you were not supposed to take it. You could travel but the people didn't have the money. Train tickets compared to today were much cheaper, but the whole society was very poor.'

'Did everybody travel in hard sleeper?'

'No hard sleeper. Just hard seats,' Gerry laughed, thumping the berth.

'Isn't that quite similar to how North Korea is now?' Jem asked, swinging down from his berth.

'China was similar to North Korea, thirty years ago, in the sense that there was restricted travel. And at that time, we admired North Korea. We thought that North Korea had the much better life, the best life in the world. We saw the North Korean movies and at that time China was really messed up. Now China is a totally different nation. Thirty years ago, the common people couldn't hardly put food on the table. We are the luckiest generation in history.'

'Why do you say that?'

'When I was a boy I never dreamt I would have this kind of life. No, never. At that time it was crazy, the Cultural Revolution was very oppressive. It was very strange, every morning the whole family got up, first thing you are supposed to do is talk to Chairman Mao's picture and give the report to Chairman Mao about what I have done, what I did yesterday, and what I am going to do today. You had to give a report saying: "Today I will follow your instruction and do your work", and of course everyone kept their door open so that all the neighbours can see the political show-off. That was a crazy time.'

'What did your parents do at the time?'

'My father was a government official, and my mother, she was the school headmistress.'

'Did people agree with it or do it out of fear?'

'My parents, they were complaining, and we were young. At that time, there was not many industry, we were close to nature, we didn't have much schoolwork to do and we just played from dawn to dusk.' He smiled. 'Even though we didn't have much food to eat we were happy. We had many adventures and the parents didn't have time for us. We just played everywhere in mountains, rivers, many dangerous places. Very different from today's life. Today's kids they learning and studying all the time. That time was the late sixties and early seventies.'

'When did everything change?'

'After Chairman Mao died, we thought: "Wow, it is the end of the world."'

'Were people frightened?' Jem asked.

'Yes, people frightened, we didn't know what we were going to do. Mao's wife was almost in power but later she and three guys in the top position were arrested and a couple of years later Deng Xiaoping came to power and he started reform and opening up. That was the Thirty Years' Miracle. Life changed, everything changed very rapidly, very dramatic. His first policy was to allow the farmers to have their own land, to produce their own food, before that everything was collective. He just released the power back to the people.'

'How did things change for your family?'

'During the Cultural Revolution my father was persecuted and that time he was released back to power again, and he was the vice governor of this province so everything started to change and life got better.'

'Did people adapt quickly?'

'Oh, absolutely. Now it's getting better, two years ago before Xi Jinping took the power, the corruption was very serious.

People complaining, still some of them were saying: "Ah we miss Chairman Mao's time", and we ask them: "You want to go back? You don't like today's life? You don't want your car, your comfortable apartment and your life now?" and they say: "Oh no, no, we want that. Today's life is better than Chairman Mao's time.'"

The train slowed past yet another ghost city and I asked Gerry what he felt about them.

'It is difficult to say. Even if we don't like, the government will clear everything that is here and they build what they want. Most people here, even if they own the property, they do not own the land. The government owns the land, so they demolish anything, anytime, and the people, they have no say.'

'Aren't people compensated?'

Gerry looked at me blankly.

'Aren't people given money for their old house and then given a new place to live?'

Gerry smiled. 'That would be very nice. But that is not what happens for everyone. People have no rights, and they make protests and they try to get money, but often the government ignores this.'

He pointed out of the window. 'You see, China's landscape is like one big construction site. Every day they build, they build, they build. The farmers' homes, they are destroyed, all these apple orchards you see, they will all go soon. This is very common all over China.'

Gerry's phone began to play a techno dance tune and he glanced at the screen. 'It's my daughter, I must answer, this. Please excuse me.'

I looked out at the stepped hillside, great mouthfuls of which had already been devoured by bulldozers. In ten years' time, this train route would showcase a different China, one that I wasn't sure I ever wanted to see.

The following afternoon Gerry got off at Lanzhou, a few stops before we arrived in Xining. He'd called up a number of hotels close to the station and found a room for us for a few hours so we could shower and nap before the next leg of the journey to Lhasa, and unknown to us, had pre-paid the bill. These gestures of goodwill only ever came from train encounters. As Gerry waved from the platform, I knew we would never see him again. He owed us nothing, yet had extended a kindness that we could never repay, nor have the opportunity to repay. But Gerry was now sewn into our narrative and there he would stay. He could never be unpicked or dropped or forgotten. He could never age or change or fall foul of us. He would just be Gerry, the kind teacher from Lanzhou.

At Xining station, we followed the signs to the basement taxi rank and were encircled by more than forty drivers wearing blue blazers and ties, waiting by a fleet of polished Nissans – and one hackney carriage. There were no other customers, and their jubilation made me wonder if we were the first people they had seen all week, if not all year. I almost felt that the three of us should take three separate taxis just to give the drivers something to do. Still, I admired their confidence that people would come, and I hoped that one day the stations would be filled, the taxis hailed, and the ghost cities brimming with life.

Later that evening we returned to the station showered and refreshed, ready for the journey to Lhasa. It was devastating that half the journey would take place in the dark, but no matter which train we took, a large portion would have to be spent travelling overnight, leaving the magnificence of Qinghai province to be admired by no more than my imagination. Under Marc's dictatorship we had more than an hour to spare at Xining station – another glass expanse that echoed with emptiness. The upshot was that there were no queues at any of the fast-food outlets, so we loaded up on fried noodles, fresh from hot woks, and pork buns as soft as clouds, collecting a feast for the night train that was already waiting at the platform. Stashing bags and unrolling duvets, we got comfy as the train began to move.

'I can't find my trainers.' Jem began to look around in a panic, zipping and unzipping pockets.

'Where did you last have them?' I asked.

'On the Xining train.'

'You didn't leave them in the hotel?'

Jem yanked open a carrier bag for the third time, as though some sorcery might magic them into existence, but to no avail. His face collapsed. 'I think I left them under the seat in our compartment.'

Both Marc and I looked down at Jem's flip-flopped feet with deepest sympathy. Havaianas weren't the finest choice for Tibetan climes.

'Do you think I'll be able to buy some new ones in Lhasa?'

'I'm not sure you're going to find New Balance outlets in the middle of Tibet,' said Marc.

To console himself, Jem unwrapped his dinner. Almost immediately, cigarette smoke swirled into the compartment, so I went out to investigate the source. The culprit was in the compartment next door, smoking under the covers. Holding a hand up in greeting, I gestured to the door, and he waved for me to slide it shut.

Ducking back into the safety of our compartment, I bolted the door, and turned around to find Marc and Jem wearing towelling slippers, sharing pork buns and deciding which film to watch before bed. Since Marc's arrival I could see a change in Jem. While I worked, he had busied himself, but I knew the last few weeks had taken their toll and I could feel his endurance wavering. But Marc had jolted us both into action, pulling us back on course. Pushing the curtains to one side, I cupped my hands to the window as the train's lights lit up the flats that sped by. The ground appeared to be covered in snow, but perhaps it was wishful thinking. No one else was due to take the spare berth, so we made up our beds, set up a film on the laptop and slid under our duvets. With the lights off, and our stomachs full, we snuggled in for the night. In the warmth, I could soon hear deep, even breathing. Both Jem and Marc had nodded off, the blue light from the screen revealing their sleeping faces. Closing the laptop, I climbed up to my berth as the train tilted and beat on into the night.

11

Viva Lhasa Vegas!

Someone was sitting on my head. I tried to get up, but my skull was clamped in an invisible vice. I lay in the dark, listening to the hiss from above. Purified oxygen was supposed to smell faintly sweet, but the air being piped into the compartment had the dankness of cigarettes. Waking Jem and Marc, I inched up the blackout blind, allowing the blaze of light to rouse us from the coma of altitude sickness. The Tibetan plateau resembled a Rothko painting: a slab of yellow rose halfway up the window to meet a slab of blue, separated by a squiggle of mountains, dusted with snow. The expanse of desert and sky galloped so far off into the distance that somewhere along the horizon it was already next week. Few sights have taken my breath away, but at more than 3,800 metres above sea level – and climbing – the air was struggling into my chest, making me faint. Marc sat up to photograph the view, while Jem lay slumped against the pillows apparently experiencing the early stages of rigor mortis. My own nails had turned blue, and a glance in the mirror confirmed that I had indeed died overnight; my lips had cracked and my skin had paled to a couple of tones shy of jaundice. Digging out scarves, gloves and knee socks, we passed around Marc's flask of jasmine tea in an attempt to hydrate and stay warm, sharing a squashed Snickers bar that Jem had slept on and salvaged from his pocket. In the corridor, our fellow passengers weren't faring much better. Perched on the pull-down seats by the window, our neighbour was sucking at an oxygen nozzle, his lids closing over watery eyes. I felt no sympathy: in spite of signs instructing passengers not to smoke beyond the city of Golmud, when the cabins became pressurised, he'd been puffing away in his berth.

Over the previous two weeks I'd adjusted to the Chinese penchant for spitting and throwing sunflower seeds on the floor, but I couldn't tolerate the smoking. One in every three cigarettes smoked in the world is smoked in China, with one person dying every thirty seconds from tobacco use. I was sure I'd be next. For that reason alone, travelling in hard-sleeper was now out of the question. The air was a cancerous blue, and men with gold teeth strolled around in singlets and flip-flops presenting with what appeared to be stage-four emphysema. Soft-sleeper was marginally better as smokers usually gathered in the vestibules, but, like our neighbour, a number of them hid in their berths with the door locked. I hadn't given it much thought, but I now realised that in a country with one of the worst pollution levels in the world, it probably made no difference whether or not people smoked, given that the day was spent inhaling noxious levels of particulate matter. By contrast, a packet of Panda ciggies was quite the treat.

With a surgeon's mask in place, my asthmatic lungs and I found a seat in the corridor and looked out at this new earth – the rest of the world as I remembered it had fallen away. But for a few breaths of cloud, the sky sang arias of joy, lakes shimmered like molten metal and Tibetan antelope sprang in and out of sight. The higher we climbed, the more dreadlocked yaks lumbered into view, nibbling at tufts of grass or tethered by nomad tents strung with rainbow-coloured prayer flags. Higher and higher still, the yaks faded away and mountains sharpened by ice closed in around the train as it pushed into places no railway was ever meant to go. Opened in 2006, the Qinghai railway from Xining to Lhasa was considered a feat of engineering impossibility. Passing through earthquake zones, the highest railway in the world peaked at 5,072 metres above sea level at the Tanggula Pass, and contained more than 300 miles of elevated track built on permafrost that could melt at the slightest increase in temperature. In a region where temperatures ranged from -35°C in winter to 30°C in summer, engineers had circulated liquid nitrogen below the rail bed to keep it frozen throughout the year. Magic though this was in terms of pioneering technology, the new railway had posed an ecological threat to natural reserves and endangered species such as snow leopards. It was received with dismay by most Tibetans, who saw the railway as nothing more than a means by which Han Chinese – the largest ethnic group in mainland China – could pour in with renewed vigour, and continue to colonise their home, while others living close to the proposed stations were cheered by the business and employment prospects for their towns. At the time the Qinghai railway was announced the then president of China, Jiang Zemin, declared: 'We must absolutely not allow separation of Tibet from the motherland and must absolutely not continue seeing Tibet remain backward.'

For all the border controls and efforts to police the region, writers have always managed to worm their way into Lhasa and document everything from the colour of the skies and the sound of monks at prayer, to taking tea with the Dalai Lama. But in recent and turbulent times, the shifting of borders and people – and with them their stories – meant that from one day to the next, Tibet's soil kept turning into fertile new territory for exploration. At this moment, the only thing I was interested in exploring was the underneath of my duvet. My temples had tightened, and mindful of Yuhan's warning that if I fell asleep I might slip into a coma, I fell asleep, waking more than two hours later as we descended into the Lhasa Valley, having missed the best views of the journey. Soft suede mountains had moved into the foreground, and the clusters of tents had turned into stretches of grey concrete houses, each with a red Chinese flag in the front yard – a sinister omen. As the train approached the Tibetan capital, Marc stood at the window, his eyes widening as a Mitsubishi garage and a Buick showroom sailed past on a street lined with a parade of Chinese flags. A shadow cloaked our carriage as we drew into Lhasa station, and passengers began to gather their bags at the doorway. The wind whispered in our ears as we breathed in air as sharp as shards of glass, and looked around the station. Police with rifles wandered around as though a terrorist attack were imminent, and military guarded the exits, scanning bags and diverting passengers for searches. No one smiled and I already felt like I'd done something wrong. We were the only foreign tourists on the train and were ushered into a police station to have our permits stamped before being waved off to meet our Tibetan guide, who stood at the end of the path waiting with a sign saying 'Welcome US guests'.

There are certain faces that are so imbued with goodness that it's impossible to look away. Warmed by the kindness of their thoughts and lined by moments of mischief and laughter, those faces compel the beholder to come closer and to trust. Jhampa had such a face. Alert and amused, his eyes lay within soft folds and his smile carved dimples into his cheeks, revealing one overlapping tooth. Jhampa wore a hoodie and a baseball cap and carried three white *khatas* – ceremonial scarves – that he held on upturned palms before placing each around our necks in welcome. Thrusting bottles of water into our hands, he gestured to his car: 'Come, let's go to your hotel and make sure you keep yourselves hydrated.'

Jem sat in front chattering away with Jhampa while Marc and I sat in the back, muted by the sight of Calvin Klein, Siemens, and fake Apple stores lining the streets. Posters of President Xi Jinping and Chairman Mao appeared on every other corner, and a billboard stretched over two lanes of traffic with a tacky tourist-board painting of the mountains that read: '*Welcome to prosperous, harmonious, legal, civilized and beautiful socialist new Tibet.*'

We drove on in silence, not wanting to look at one another. At the traffic lights, boxed in by taxis, motor scooters, a brand new Audi A3 and a Porsche Cayenne with blacked-out windows, I looked from the 'China Post Office' to a 'Bank of China' ATM, next to which a young woman wearing New Balance trainers was buying a drink from a Coca-Cola vending machine, gripping a smartphone between ear and shoulder. Jem would have no problem replacing his trainers. A recurring roadside advert featured a whitewashed Chinese woman with one of her eyelids annotated. Two pairs of eyes showed the before and after images of an eye-lifting procedure to make the lids less hooded and slanting. Overhead, the road sign pointed to Central Beijing Road and East Beijing Road. As we approached the Gang Gyan Hotel, an old Tibetan lady shuffled along the pavement, her purple-ribboned hair divided into two plaits, and tied together at the bottom. She wore an ankle-length skirt and a multicoloured apron, her walnut cheeks a wind-burnt red. She looked completely out of place.

The altitude sickness was proving hard to shake off. I'd woken in our hotel room in the middle of the night with my head clamped back in the vice and had to call for room service who had delivered a standard order of water and a canister of oxygen. In the morning, Jhampa arrived with an antidote to the sickness, producing a box of tiny vials containing a burgundy tincture called *Rhodiola rosea*. Sitting on the bed with the vials laid out, the three of us stared at what looked like a pile of blood samples and wondered who should go first. After a quick Google search, we learnt that the herb was used to improve cognitive function and fatigue, and having readily ingested far worse in the past, we poked in straws and sucked up the liquid, which tasted like rose-flavoured tea. Grabbing a handful of the vials for my pocket, we set off for a day of sightseeing, buoyed by the herbs, or at least a much-needed placebo.

Our first visit was to the Potala Palace, the home of the exiled Dalai Lama. Sitting atop the Red Mountain and overlooking the Lhasa Valley, the palace was visible from all over the city – one of the few reminders of where we really were. Like rows of fallen dominoes, two sets of stairs zigzagged up a fortress of whitewashed walls and wooden windows. This section of the palace was government-owned, while the red and yellow complex rising from behind belonged to the monastery. The beating heart of Tibetan Buddhism, the palace was a place of pilgrimage for Tibetans, particularly nomads, who could be seen prostrating themselves on the pavement. Wearing what looked like old oven gloves, they raised their arms in the air before falling to their knees and stretching towards the palace with a sweeping motion. Most pilgrims arrived wearing knee pads. Looking up at the palace, I relaxed. This was more like it. This was Tibet. With the exception of the Chinese flag that poked out of the top like a tiny middle finger.

During the military-grade scan to enter the palace, I noticed a bucket of confiscated cigarette lighters, which was no doubt to prevent Chinese tour groups from smoking around the palace, though the cynic in me wondered if it was to avoid spontaneous acts of self-immolation. In 2012, two Tibetans had set themselves on fire outside the Jokhang Temple in the centre of town, where monks had previously taken part in anti-Chinese riots, and the Chinese government had ramped up security to ensure it didn't happen again, turning Lhasa into an Orwellian nightmare of CCTV, road blockades and pop-up police stations. Even inside the palace courtyard, Chinese guards wearing orange, flame-retardant jumpsuits and heavy boots shoved their way through crowds, snapping at anyone pausing for too long at the shrines. As we took the stairs at a geriatric pace, elderly Tibetans speeding past with grandchildren on their backs, I asked Jhampa why the flame-proof guards were around.

'Too many candles,' he said, smiling.

'Candles?' Marc replied, roaring with laughter. 'These monks have been lighting candles for hundreds of years and never needed Fireman Chan on standby.'

Travelling with Jhampa as our guide was a treat, but it presented similar problems to those we'd faced in North Korea. The difference here was that Jhampa knew what we wanted to ask, and we knew what he couldn't tell. He needed to keep his job and we didn't want to get him into trouble, but we still had four days to extract what we could.

Climbing the stairs was proving a task for Jem, whose altitude sickness was manifesting itself by paralysing him from the waist down, whereas mine focused on the neck up. Yogic Marc, on the other hand, was bounding ahead and looking back at the pair of us with the patience of a dog off its leash. Citing 'years of rugby' that had given him 'too much muscle' in his thighs, Jem was picking each leg up the steps and struggling to breathe. Fishing out my inhaler, I handed it to him and suggested he have a puff to ease his breathing. He looked at the Ventolin with suspicion, as the three of us crowded around, as though watching him drop his first E.

'Go on man, try it,' Marc urged.

Jem frowned. 'Are you sure?'

'Honestly, it will be fine,' I promised, 'it can't make you feel much worse.'

That's where I was wrong. After taking two puffs, he spent the next hour not only unable to walk, but riddled with palpitations and panic.

Once inside the palace, Jhampa took us directly to the main room, which housed the Dalai Lama's throne. Propped up by red pillars carved with peacocks, trees and roses, the room was packed with loud Chinese tourists in anoraks jostling to see the throne, and throwing white *khatas* in its direction. The throne itself was almost invisible under the scarves, which had collected like piles of old laundry. Threads of smoke curled off crumbling sticks of incense and I stood back against the wall, breathing in their calm and waiting for the crowd to move along. Two crinkled monks in robes were sitting to the side and watching a video on a gold iPhone, giggling like schoolboys, before one of them saw me staring and began asking Jhampa about me. He gestured for me to come over to the monk who clasped my hands and began talking in rapid Tibetan. Jhampa translated: 'He has been guarding the Dalai Lama's room since 1991 and is delighted to see you here because you are Indian. Tibetans are grateful to India for keeping his Holiness safe.' The monk continued to smile and natter in a way that made me want to both hug him and weep on him, when Marc and Jem came over to see what was going on.

'I'm half Indian,' Marc said. 'That must count.'

'And I could be Indian,' Jem added.

Seeing that there were more of us, the monk handed his iPhone to his friend and signalled for us to wait. We watched as he waded through the scarves and climbed up to the Dalai Lama's throne, retrieving three golden silk scarves from the seat. He came back and knotted one around each of our necks. His eyes moistened and I stared at the cloudiness of his cataracts as he talked at us, then squeezed our hands again. Jhampa said: 'He is very touched that you have come so far to see Tibet. And he would like you to take these scarves back to your home as a blessing and to remember his Holiness.'

I stroked the scarf and thanked the monk before striding off to sniffle in peace. For the next two hours, we wandered around the palace, peeking into tea rooms, the Dalai Lama's bedroom, and marvelling at the tombs where the previous seven Dalai Lamas were all mummified. Jhampa explained that the current (14th) Dalai Lama would have to decide with the support of UNESCO and the exiled government if he could also be laid to rest here, though it was unlikely that China would allow the creation of such a site of pilgrimage. Copying the other visitors, I had been taking care not to step on the threshold every time we entered a new room, until Jhampa whispered that it was a Chinese superstition, not a Tibetan one, and I immediately stopped. Even the smallest gesture of defiance felt worthwhile.

'Do you reckon they give these scarves out to loads of tourists?' Marc asked, as we left the throne room, but over the next two hours, not once did we see anyone wearing a golden scarf.

Owing to its position and its rich, natural resources, Tibet's history is pitted with battle scars, but in 1950 events took a turn for the worst when China led a full-scale military assault on the region, coercing its leaders into signing a treaty that resulted in military occupation. In 1959, a major uprising against the Chinese led to thousands of Tibetan deaths – an incident that China's government denies – and forced Tenzin Gyatso, the Dalai Lama, to flee the Potala Palace and seek sanctuary in

Dharamsala in India, with more than 80,000 Tibetans following at his heels. China's Cultural Revolution unfolded in the mid-1960s, driving the desecration of almost all of Tibet's monasteries, destroying libraries and paintings. Han Chinese swarmed into Tibet under the guise of developing the region, moving swiftly to mine its wealth of copper, gold and silver, with no concern for the pollution and devastation wrought across the land. Anti-government protests and self-immolations by monks, nuns and local Tibetans led to the Chinese pushing a 'patriotic education' programme, which forced all Tibetans to publicly denounce the Dalai Lama. Today, images of the Dalai Lama are banned and Tibetans undergo regular searches of their homes, where the discovery of any sign of His Holiness can lead to brutal punishment.

The Chinese, however, see things rather differently. They argue that Tibet has never been an independent state and that the West has laboured under a misapprehension, romanticising the Buddhist culture and deliberately ignoring the fact that, until 1959, Tibet was operating under a feudal system with more than 95 per cent of the population living at the mercy of an elite 5 per cent, which comprised corrupt lamas and rich landowners who brutalised their subjects – though there is little evidence to support this claim. According to the Chinese government, the events of 1959 brought about the peaceful liberation of Tibet from its cruel overlords, and China has since set about modernising a backward society, pouring billions of dollars into the region, developing its infrastructure, building housing, pushing education, creating tourism, boosting GDP, and dramatically raising the standard of living for local Tibetans.

After a quick stop for noodles, Jhampa took us to the Drepung monastery. Built into a rocky hillside and dating back to 1416, it is one of the last strongholds of Tibetan Buddhism, where monks continue to live a traditional lifestyle, praying, cleaning the monastery, schooling young monks and generally keeping to themselves. It had once housed more than 10,000 monks but now there were fewer than 500 in residence. The monks were preparing for the annual festival of Lhabab Duchen, celebrating Buddha's descent from the heavens back to earth. It is a time when everything is given a new coat of paint, and they were slapping the walls, pathways, trees, and their own hair and robes with a mixture of paint and milk, causing the sun to ricochet off the white surfaces. A young monk, no more than ten years old, stomped past, the laces of his Nike trainers coming undone. I smiled at him and he scowled in return, glaring at the phone in my hand.

'No!' he barked, making a beeline for Jhampa. After a short exchange, the monk threw me a fierce look and disappeared through a wooden door.

'He wanted to know how to say: "Don't take pictures of me" in English,' Jhampa said. 'Reincarnation is important in Buddhism and some Tibetans believe that when you take a photograph it captures a little piece of their soul and traps it on earth after they die.'

I didn't blame the monk for being annoyed. Photography wasn't allowed inside the Potala Palace but here the Chinese were out in force with their long-lens cameras and selfie sticks. It was impossible to turn a corner without finding some narcissist brandishing what looked like a broken-off wing mirror and grinning with the belief that an image of an ancient monastery was somehow enhanced by their face in the foreground. I didn't understand the obsession with selfies. Were they taken as proof that you were really there? Was it for those suffering from amnesia, to remind them where they had been during the day? I rarely took photographs while travelling, other than to use as memory aids when writing, which normally included road signs, information on monuments or snippets from local papers and menus. These made for a dull set of holiday snaps, but I preferred to enjoy the moment for what it was. The last thing I wanted to look at when I returned home was my own face wincing in the wind, with a runny nose and a few angry monks in the background.

Leading us through huge timber doors, Jhampa guided us around the shrines, keeping well out of the monks' way. I tried to merge with the shadows in the hope of being less conspicuous. Visiting Tibetans brought plastic containers of butter and oil that they poured onto the lamps to keep the thousands of wicks and candles flickering in the dark. Here, the interiors felt safe and cocooned from reality. By the glow, I watched the monks busy themselves carving sculptures out of butter, shuffling through the piles of small denominations that littered the floor like dry autumn leaves. One monk crouched down in front of a little girl whose hair was pulled into a number of bunches, and blessed her with a smudge of ash on her nose. I'd seen a few young children with it and had wondered what it was. The injustice of brutalising such a harmonious culture rang hard in my ears as we walked through the halls, redolent with burning butter. Epic tales of Buddha and monks covered the walls in the form of floral, curly brush strokes, outlining temples, lotuses and mountains, all of which were painted in the richest reds, oranges, greens and blues. Knowing that hundreds of monasteries like this one had been reduced to rubble to make way for real estate was deeply depressing. I hovered for as long as possible with the dread that in the not-so-distant future the last candle would melt and these walls would collapse, leaving nothing but smoke and memories.

Jem was standing on the edge of a wall looking out over the city. 'What's that veil of yellow in the sky?' he asked Jhampa.

'Factories,' he replied, his hands in his pockets. 'Lots of mining companies here now.'

Marc slung his camera over his shoulder. 'It's just China now, isn't it? This whole place is just China. Tibet's never going to be free. You'd need a full-scale, UN-backed military invasion to undo all of this. It's so far gone. It's like Lhasa Vegas.'

Jhampa smiled at the ground, kicking a pebble at the wall. A Chinese couple wielding their selfie stick had moved to within reaching distance of Jem, and I thought he was going to push them over the wall. Whereas foreign tourists like us had to jump through hoops to obtain special permits, and could travel for only a limited number of days with an organised guide – and journalists were banned – China's domestic tourism push had gone into overdrive. Chinese tourists filled the city, hankering after sightings of these quaint little people with their bright clothes and red cheeks; it wasn't unusual to see an elderly Tibetan holding beads and cowering from a group with video cameras. Tibetans had been commodified by the Chinese, their home turned into a zoo-like compound for the curious. To add insult to injury, Han Chinese migrants now ran most shops, cafes and hotels, depriving Tibetans of the chance to at least eke out a living and find some benefit from the boom in tourism. We'd had a stroke of luck with Jhampa. Tour groups were often assigned Chinese guides who had no concept of Tibet's history and made up facts as they went along. In the year the Qinghai railway had opened, Adrian, my friend in Beijing, had travelled to Tibet without a permit, and wandered around freely with local Tibetans helping him avoid security checks. He'd seen no more than a small Chinese quarter in Lhasa but could sense that the railway link had been built to serve as a catalyst for the 'Hanification' of Tibet, as he called it. It had taken less than nine years for his prediction to come true. The Chinese government already had plans for a second service, a high-speed train between Chengdu and Lhasa that would cut the journey time to fifteen hours. There was no hope of Tibet ever shaking off China's clutches.

Security cameras on the street clicked and swivelled as a group of pilgrims went by swinging Mani wheels – wooden prayer wheels fitted to spindles. The lady at the front was wearing a pair of red New Balance, much like the pair Jem had left on the train. Marc read my mind.

'Everyone's got to wear shoes. What they going to wear? Yak skins?'

I realised that, despite my brownness, I was veering dangerously close to developing a white saviour complex. Most of the monks wore branded trainers and used iPhones, but then, so did I. What gave me the right to text and tweet and stroll about in a pair of Adidas Superstars, then lament that they were doing the same?

Perhaps I was just as guilty as the Chinese, willing these doll-like people to live in the past in some sort of colonial quest to find an authenticity that no longer existed. Before I had a chance to consider it further, a dog leapt up from where she had been sleeping and launched herself at Marc, who was leaning over a pair of her adolescent pups. Her teeth just made it through his Gore-Tex trousers, leaving a tiny scratch, but it was enough for him to spend the rest of the afternoon convinced he'd contracted rabies.

On a beautiful morning, the prayer flags fluttered wildly as we walked through the main marketplace. Lacquered windows twinkled in the light and chocolate mountains peered above the rooftops. In the centre of the square, a crowd of traders wearing skullcaps and pinstriped suits with jumpers underneath had gathered around baskets brimming with what looked like dried yellow chillies. Descended from Kashmiri Muslims who had arrived in the seventeenth century, these men were predominantly butchers selling caterpillar fungus to buyers from Guangzhou. Picking up a broken one, Jhampa pinched the caterpillar between two fingers and held it up. One end was just a brown stalk, while the other was covered in a fungus that had devoured the body of a caterpillar larva. Known as *yartsa gunbu*, which translates as 'summer grass, winter worm', the caterpillars are hunted by nomads on their hands and knees on the most fertile heights of the Tibetan plateau, and bought cheaply, before being sold at market in China for more than their weight in gold. *Yartsa gunbu* is believed to alleviate all kinds of ailments, ranging from heart disease and asthma, to HIV and erectile dysfunction. A pound of the top-quality grubs can sell for around £30,000.

With so few work opportunities for ethnic Tibetans, the lucrative trade had caused in-fighting between villagers, keen to make the most of their resources, but also between Tibetans and Han Chinese poachers looking to cut out the middle man. The haggling process involved a ritual from the buyer who moaned about how terrible the samples were, and the seller shouting back. It ended with the exchange of money through a sleight-of-hand movement, and looked quite a fun way to pass the morning.

The rest of the market featured the usual suspects: butchers selling curtains of purple yak meat hooked to rails, the mournful head of the yak covered in flies; greengrocers with shiny pomegranates; jobless men in leather jackets; and a number of mannequins that looked like Brigitte Nielsen – one of which had been doodled with a miniature goatee. Sidestepping puddles of meaty water, I wandered around the corner and came face to face with a lovely old bookshop. If there was anywhere in a new city that felt like home, it was a bookshop. After definitely not looking for my own book – which no writer ever does – I gazed at the covers, like a big kid in a sweet shop, wondering which world to open up. The shop was lit by paper lamps and stocked with an unusual amount of Lonely Planet guidebooks that a number of young people had taken from the shelves and were reading in the window seats. Foolishly, I approached the man at the counter and asked if they had a copy of Heinrich Harrer's *Seven Years in Tibet*. A young woman browsing nearby looked up and came over.

'They don't keep that book here,' she said, pushing her huge glasses back on to her nose. 'The book is not allowed. How to say … the police, they do not allow that book. They don't approve.'

Surprised by her honesty, I thanked her and backed away. I hovered around the shop for about ten minutes, pretending to look at the postcards, before approaching the woman and asking if she wouldn't mind talking to me for a few minutes. She agreed to go for a drink to a nearby bar that served Belgian beer and spaghetti. Two students were watching a show on a MacBook Air as we took a seat and the woman ordered a *po cha* – butter tea. 'Lucy' felt safer with a pseudonym even though she gave me her Tibetan name and talked far too loudly for comfort. Born in the north of Tibet, the twenty-five-year-old was half Tibetan and half Han Chinese, explaining that her

Chinese grandfather had come in 1959 to 'help encourage the Tibetan people to go to university'. I asked her outright about book censorship.

'They have some English books, but ... how to say ... they have a special company that edits the books and they allow some, but not the other books. Before we travel to other countries, if they don't understand something or if it is about Buddhism or the Dalai Lama, they take the books away.'

'Do you follow the Dalai Lama?'

'I am Buddhist because I am Tibetan. It is according to your heart, if you believe or not. But you can't keep pictures of the Dalai Lama. In people's homes they have a room to pray and we have the photo of the Dalai Lama, but we cannot show people, especially the government. I think old people still believe in the Dalai Lama, but now most of the monks are very young so the government teaches them to not believe.' She took a sip of her tea, which gleamed with spots of butter.

'How do you feel about the monks who have burnt themselves in protest and all the police in Lhasa?' I asked her.

'Last time was maybe 2008 in Lhasa they burn, but most people don't know what happened. At that time the government took all the monks up to the mountain for one month, but the government would not allow them to take food. After 2008 everywhere they put the police to watch everybody. In the beginning the people felt: "I was living here, I was born here, why you want to check me?" They check the ID if I went to the temple. At the beginning, we feel very uncomfortable. It seems like I am a bad person. I am not a bad person but after few years it becomes normal. Otherwise it is very safe in Lhasa. Especially in the night, if a girl is just one person walking around the streets it is very safe.'

Lucy's glasses were slipping down her nose again and she pushed them back up, tucking her bobbed hair behind her ears.

'Is it difficult for you, being part Chinese?' I asked.

'Now it is very mixed, it is very normal. I have a lot of friends who are half Chinese and half Tibetan. Tibetans begin to learn

Chinese when they are very small in school so it's not very difficult.'

'But how do you feel about people coming into Tibet to visit if you are not allowed to leave?'

'The people coming to Tibet? For us it is okay. Tibetan people like foreigners, they like talking to you, because the government not allow us to go outside. For young people, they are very angry for this. Before, I met a friend, a boy who was nineteen, and we drink the tea together and he was very angry because of this. The old people they don't care about this. We have a door controlled by the government. They let a few foreigners come in, but we cannot go out. The most important reason is they are afraid the people will go outside and follow the Dalai Lama. But it wasn't always this way. Deng Xiaoping allowed Tibetans to go out.'

'Do you think the Dalai Lama will ever come back?'

Lucy shook her head. 'No, never. So now we are talking about when he die, who will be the next one? Will he be chosen by the Chinese government or by the Dalai Lama? If chosen by the current Dalai Lama the next Dalai Lama also not come to Tibet. If chosen by the Chinese, he will be allowed to come to Tibet.'

The Dalai Lama had issued a statement in 2011 that if the reincarnation of the Dalai Lama should continue, and there was a need for the 15th Dalai Lama to be recognised, 'no recognition or acceptance should be given to a candidate chosen for political ends by anyone, including those in the People's Republic of China'. So there was no chance of a new Dalai Lama ever coming to Tibet.

'If you can't leave, how do you find out about the outside world?' I asked.

'We have the Lonely Planet, so we read many. Some people come in just to look and read them.'

Remembering the young people in the bookshop, I felt suddenly depressed. They came in to read the Lonely Planet guides just to learn about countries they would never get to visit. Then Lucy told me something that cheered me up.

'Some Tibetans, we can go outside to university. I have studied French in France. I lived in Nice. We can apply to other countries' universities, and if we have a letter of acceptance, then we take that to the government, then we can apply for passport. I have a passport as a student, but when that passport has run out I cannot have a passport again.'

'Do you feel like Tibet is a part of China?'

'For us Tibet is a part of China. For you it is very difficult to understand. Foreigners they think that Tibet is a country. China took the Tibet for themselves. Foreigners think that it is a country and it will be free, so the government is worried about these foreigners who come here. When I was in France, they don't think I'm Chinese, they think I'm Tibetan. Tibet is one part of China, we think like this. I don't know why the foreigners think that Tibet is a country. Now for us we live with very peace. It's much more better than before. My grandma tell me before is really bad. Now the old people their living is very peaceful, very good.'

I wasn't sure how much Lucy was brushing over Tibet's history, and I wanted to ask what she thought had made living in Tibet so very bad, and why it went through a period of unrest, but the moment didn't feel right and she was too kind to antagonise.

'What do you think of the Free Tibet movement?' I asked.

'I was talking with my friend with this problem. We think Free Tibet is not a good thing. We need things from other cities. Like before in Tibet, people don't know how to grow the fruits, so all crops are from Chengdu. Now people know how to grow that. Also, some skills like how to use washing machines and things, also internet. In my family, the first washing machine my father brought from Guangzhou. Before that we don't have that. There are many good things.'

Lucy's final answer frustrated me. Having a washing machine, knowing how to grow fruit, and using the internet didn't have to come at the expense of thousands of lives.

Despite Lucy's insistence that they now all lived in peace, I struggled to reconcile my feelings. Jhampa's sister had fled in the 1980s and he hadn't seen her since, nor had he ever met his nephews and nieces. He couldn't speak freely for fear of reprisal, and there was no hope of seeing his sister again, when he, like almost every other Tibetan, was forbidden from leaving the country and she wasn't allowed to return. Within a year, Lucy herself wouldn't be allowed to leave Tibet once her student passport had expired, nor could anyone else in her family. That was not living a life of peace. That was living with Stockholm syndrome. Since our chat, I'd become obsessed with making sure everything we bought was Tibetan, that our money went only to Tibetans, and that every yak momo that passed our lips was pressed and steamed by Tibetan hands. That afternoon we'd insisted Jhampa take us to one of his favourite restaurants for lunch. Looking a bit surprised, he'd driven us to the edge of town, parked down a quiet lane and led us to a barber shop, next to which was a discreet doorway hung with an old curtain, where a girl and her mother brought out steaming metal plates of yellow yak curry that made us sweat. It was the best meal of our whole Tibetan trip.

On our final evening, Jhampa walked us to the home of a Tibetan couple who ran a restaurant from their two-roomed apartment, known as Tibetan Family Kitchen. A couple of hand-painted signs on crooked arrows took us down Dan Jie Lin Road, with a sharp turn into an alleyway, through a courtyard, up some stairs, past a few old people with missing teeth, and into a kitchen where a couple wearing bodywarmers and jeans were making tea and tossing greens in a wok. We'd come for a cookery class with Lumbum and his wife Namdon, who originated from the region of Amdo. They had worked there as English-speaking tour guides for eight years, before moving to Lhasa in 2009 where there was more business. But after tourism dried up, they decided to open up their home as a restaurant.

While the couple finished clearing away after their previous customers, I wandered through to the next room, where the walls were scribbled with messages from happy diners; I'd just begun nosing at them when I was suddenly aware of something moving on the table. A fat bundle of baby extended a tiny arm from where she was sleeping while her parents worked. She started to cry, so I gathered the blankets together and brought her into the kitchen while her mother balanced their other daughter, five-year-old Tenzing Yandon, on her hip, flash-frying yak meat that roared in the flames. Lumbum put a cup of ginger milk tea in front of me while six-week-old Tenzing Wampo drooled in her slumber. Jem and Marc rolled up their sleeves and began chopping spring onions and celery while Jhampa kneaded the flour for the momos, which would be stuffed with yak meat and steamed. With the altitude, there was no need for a pressure cooker as water boiled at around 70°C. The atmosphere was like that at my parents' home on a Friday night: the men were busy dicing with Namdon, Jhampa was rolling out dough, and Tenzing Yandon was playing with an Acer laptop on top of a rice cooker, while trying on a new pair of socks. She checked her sleeping sister from time to time and shot me coy looks from behind her computer. The couple were also catering for a group of ten German diners in the next room and had had to turn away another group. Foreign tourism was no bad thing for them. I asked Lumbum how he felt about the controversy over foreign tourism, and described to him some of the comments I'd had from friends who disapproved of my visit.

'No, you have to come, you have to feel,' he said. 'This is the twenty-first century, you have to be open, you have to have communication. You can't just read the media and believe. You come here and you feel. Life is happy, it won't make us rich, but we are happy.'

It reminded me of Lee's speech on our last night in Pyongyang.

'Yes, it is true that life is not great for everyone here. And there are troubles. But this is a great job for us,' Lumbum said, 'because we can be at home with the children and we really want people to come and learn about our culture and our lives.'

He picked up a platter of momos and a dish of fried noodles, and disappeared into the next room.

Jem was thrilled with his dumplings, which, although misshapen, were delicious. After passing around small bowls of steaming rice, Jhampa ladled out the curry, which shimmered with fat and screamed with chillies. Sitting around the table in the warmth of this family was a fitting way to end our time in Tibet. But the ache of imminent departure had already settled in my stomach, and no amount of good food could ease the pain. Seeing Tibet in all its naked hopelessness had crushed me, and I welled up thinking about what it would be like next year, the year after and the year after that, its essence diluting and draining away. Jem took my hand under the table and I saw that he too had red eyes. I gave him a doleful smile and Marc looked across at us.

'Don't you two start or you're going to make me cry, too,' he said, helping himself to the last of the momos. We walked back to the hotel in silence, our breath curling on the night air. A low moon followed until we passed the golden roof of the Jokhang Temple, where it came to rest. The square was still open to prostrating pilgrims, banging their wooden blocks and sweeping along the ground. On we walked, the sweep growing fainter until we turned a corner and could hear them no more.

12

The Old Silk Road

'*Um Gottes Willen! Da schläft ja ein Mann hier!*'

A German woman with a side plait and hooped earrings pushed past me as I wandered out to see what the commotion was about. She was now dragging her guide behind her and shoved past me a second time, pointing into the compartment where Marc was sitting up in his berth looking confused. He took off his headphones.

'What's she yelling about?'

'She's complaining that there's a man sleeping in her compartment.'

'It's not her compartment. I was here first. It's my compartment.'

'*Keineswegs!*'

Making an educated guess as to the gist of her rant, I pieced together bits of GCSE German, trying to remember the minefield of datives, genitives and accusatives, before resorting to English to reassure the angry fräulein that Marc wasn't going to do anything to her.

'Is that so?' she snapped, her face flushed with fury.

'God, don't flatter yourself, love,' Marc said. He gathered up his things. 'And don't worry, I'm not staying in here with a bunch of uptight Germans.'

Annoyed that he now had to drag his bags round into our compartment, Marc hauled himself up into one of the spare berths and took out his computer. 'If someone comes I'll just pretend to be asleep and they can share with her – or she can stand in the aisle for the next thirty hours.'

Leaving Lhasa Vegas just before noon, we'd boarded train seventy of the journey to find Marc had been booked into a separate compartment, which implied another couple would be joining us at some point along the route back to mainland China. Much like our journey up to Lhasa, the return service carried only Chinese passengers – and now the German tour group. A smattering of Tibetan nomads had disembarked within the first few stops of the journey, standing on deserted platforms in oversized coats, their cheeks aflame in the bright cold. Guilt-ridden, I pinned back the curtains allowing the last we'd see of the Tibetan light to flood into the compartment. Contrary to China's relentless propaganda machine, the train did little to help Tibet from remaining 'backwards', and everything to help Han Chinese move forward in eroding Tibetan indigenous culture and extracting what they could. Apologists who championed the construction of the train, arguing that it had modernised and revolutionised the lives of Tibetans, were the same ones who insisted the British had gifted the railways to India, ignoring that building the railways was hardly an act of benevolence towards the Indian people, rather a fast-track plan to govern more efficiently, facilitate the plunder of loot, and line their pockets at the expense of the Indian taxpayer who had footed the bill for the railways' construction. Emerging like an umbilical cord, the proposed new high-speed line from Chengdu would help to further feed off the region. And here we were, hopping on for the ride, keeping the train in business and justifying its existence. Plugging in my earphones, I stared at the shades of navy and turquoise blending through an expanse of lake, a whisper of waves lifted by the breeze. Nothing but water and sunshine, the view was extraordinary in its beauty. Playing back my conversation with Lucy, I felt somewhat relieved by her admittance that foreigners in Tibet provided eyes and ears for Tibetans who, maimed of their own, devoured guidebooks to gain an understanding of what lay beyond their reach. And even if they couldn't leave Tibet, it was imperative that their stories did.

Kneeling up on the carpet, Jem pulled out a map and spread it open across his berth to examine our onward route. After almost seven months on the rails our adventure was winding down: from this point on we were heading back to London. Although Marc hadn't travelled on the Trans-Mongolian, we'd vetoed taking that train for the second time. The thought of spending another eleven days eating dill and dried noodles was too painful to consider. Instead, we'd plotted a route via the old Silk Road, climbing up to Xinjiang province in northwest China, then crossing the border to Kazakhstan, travelling up Russia, and home through Europe. Our original and more ambitious plan was to travel down from Kazakhstan to Uzbekistan, Turkmenistan and Iran, where the Trans-Asia Express would have taken us from Tehran to Tabriz, and across to Ankara and Istanbul, from where it was easy to wind through Eastern Europe. But days after we'd made enquiries, a spate of terrorist attacks by Isis and Kurdish separatists along the southeast Turkish border had suspended the service indefinitely.

That night, we left the curtains open, unwilling to shut out the Qinghai skies. Wherever I travelled to, I always left knowing I could return, but there was a finality to the way in which we were sweeping across the soundless plateau, as though we were the last audience to catch the show before it closed. The moon was at its fullest, rolling along the ground, illuminating the origins of the Yangtze river, which shone like strands of silver against the black. I'd fallen asleep knowing that someone else was likely to arrive during the night, and woke the following morning to find a heavily pregnant Chinese lady lying in the berth below. Easing down the side of the bunk so as not to wake her, I peered out into the corridor and found her husband asleep, upright on a hard seat that he'd pulled down from the wall. The couple had boarded in the middle of the night and the German woman had refused to let him into her compartment, locking the door. After patting the poor man awake so he could move into her now-empty compartment and claim his berth, we took ourselves off to the dining car where we found the German group eating

Knäckebrot and cheese. Every crunch of the flat dry bread sent a spasm of sadness through me, as I watched them reject the fundamentals of what made travel so wonderful: surrendering to the unknown; forging relationships; relinquishing home comforts and discovering new ones. What had kept our journey alive and moving was the constant clash of the familiar with the unfamiliar, catching us off guard and keeping us alert. As I spooned up my bowl of congee and pickles, I saw now that those fundamentals mirrored my relationship with Jem. When we got engaged we thought we knew everything there was to know about the other, but over the previous seven months we had constantly surprised ourselves, as we adapted to changing surroundings and tackled new challenges, discovering traits in each other's personalities that could only be invoked by the dynamics of travel.

Coming from a country as small and insular as England, it wasn't surprising that we were still unable to gauge the sheer size and scale of China. Refusing to leave the country without visiting the Terracotta Warriors, Marc had insisted we travel from Lhasa to Xi'an – instead of back to Xining, from where we could have connected to Turfan and Urumqi in the northwest. Arguing that it was insanity to come this far and not visit the sculptures – 'It's just two stops after Xining' – he'd convinced us to double back on ourselves to get to the city, which had looked on the map like it was a couple of thumb-widths away, but had added an extra ten hours to our journey – about the same time it would have taken to fly home to London. From Xi'an we set off in drizzle, driving for an hour out of the city before arriving in rain, to find a traffic jam of taxis, coaches and guided-tour groups, which further dampened my mood.

In 1974, a group of villagers were digging a well when they discovered fragments of the first warrior, unearthing one of the archaeological wonders of modern history. Concealed in subterranean structures made from earth and wood, the warriors were gathered together in partitioned corridors paved with bricks. A light wooden roof was then covered with fine soil, which had kept an estimated 8,000 warriors and their horses, chariots and weapons hidden for more than 2,000 years. The construction of the mausoleum was thought to have been ordered by Qin Shi Huang, the first Emperor of China, to guard him in his afterlife. Housed in three different buildings, the warrior pits were now essentially active archaeological digs. To get to them required walking through a village selling plastic replicas of the warriors, along with warriors on mugs, warriors on T-shirts, and warriors on aprons, with models of the warriors guarding the doors of each shop. Self-defeating in its layout, the village did nothing but lessen my enthusiasm at each step until I arrived at the pits, with no interest in going in.

Our plan was to save the main pit until the end to guarantee the wow factor, and we began at the second and third pits, unsure what to expect. Dimly lit, they echoed with the babble of visitors and lost friends waving and yelling at each other across the room. Edging towards the perimeter, I peered down over the wall, expecting to be floored by the sight of thousands of figures, only to find four pottery horses and a few headless warriors in a ziggurat. Wandering around, I came across Jem, then Marc, looking as confused as I was. Moving off to the next pit, we found piles of limbs and faces covered in sticky notes, and some plastic sheeting. We agreed that the main pit was probably the place to be. Contained within an aircraft hangar, the entrance to the pit was bottlenecked with hundreds of tourists in wet weather gear, shaking off umbrellas and pushing the smalls of each other's backs in a futile attempt to move closer; in a country of 1.4 billion, every inch was important. The Chinese had succeeded in earning a universally bad reputation as international tourists, with one of their own vice-premiers – there were four for some unknown reason – bemoaning the way they conducted themselves abroad, carving their names into heritage sites, crossing roads at red lights, and stealing airline cutlery. But as we waited among the crush of visitors, it was clear that this behaviour wasn't saved up for their holidays – it was standard practice.

For more than half an hour, we shuffled between pushy children and grandmas as vicious as they were small, all the while looking down at our feet and trying not to glimpse the warriors before the big moment when they came into view. As we neared the front, I kept my eyes low, then whipped my head up and looked out across the clay corridors, only to find we'd been funnelled in through the back of the hangar by a member of staff trying to manage the crowds. The vision was certainly impressive in its ability to be anticlimactic beyond the realm of all expectation. Furious, we were now shoved up against a barrier, looking onto a patch of decapitated figures wrapped in cling film and a few numbered plastic boxes. The other thousand or so warriors stood with their backs to us. It didn't bode well that I was standing witness to apparently one of the greatest modern discoveries, but wishing I'd stayed in bed at an inner-city Ibis. But it was better to have come and leave disappointed, than to have not come and be disappointed, imagining I'd missed something worth being disappointed about. The warriors weren't fully unearthed, so it was really one of the greatest modern half-discoveries, the rest covered in soil and maybe buried underground. Nor were the warriors terracotta; they were more a washed-out peach colour.

Pushed along by the crowd, I tried to pinpoint what was so underwhelming about the figures. For a start, looking down on the six-foot-tall warriors did them a disservice as it made it impossible to see them eye to eye, and appreciate the delicacy of their faces – each one unique. Every photo I had seen had been taken from within the pit, cropping out the sections that were under construction, suggesting the site was in a state of completion, and the warriors taller and more imposing than they were.

'Imagine,' said Marc, cradling his camera against his body, 'two thousand years ago the Chinese were building the Terracotta Army and the Great Wall while we were scrabbling round in the dirt.'

The discovery of the Qin emperor's warriors made for a compelling tale, but to me, the more intriguing story was what had happened to the small group of farmers who had stumbled upon them. Swooping in to claim their land, the government demolished the village, displacing the residents with meagre compensation, most of which was alleged to have been swiped by officials. Four of the original farmers were hired to sign books for tourists at the gift shop, earning a monthly pittance, with some of the men deemed to be imposters. But it wasn't a story that anyone around me would have cared for. Piling up books, mugs, postcards, coasters and wind-up toys, every visitor had made their mark with a selfie and a V sign, taking away souvenirs of their visit that they'd look at for no more than a day before it would all be shoved into a drawer and forgotten about.

Nowhere is out of bounds. No matter how remote or dangerous a destination, you can be sure to meet someone who has not only been there, but has married a local woman, fallen foul of the police, spent time in prison, and has the scars on his upper arm to prove it. AJ was one such person: the Shantaram of Xinjiang province.

We first saw him sitting at a table on his own, eating a bowl of hand-stretched noodles, when we stopped at a roadside joint for dinner. More precisely, he was chewing on one long noodle that was coiled beneath a scattering of coriander. With the exception of the emperor's mausoleum, which was the only reason why most tourists came, Xi'an was a gritty, friendly city, where everyone went quietly about their business, whether it was selling boxes of puppies at market or pouring pints of Boddingtons at a pub. Marc and Jem had left me writing in the hotel, and had gone off on their own for the afternoon, confessing when I arrived for dinner that they'd almost bought a bulldog puppy, but realised we wouldn't get him over the Kazakh border where he would inevitably be left behind – or eaten. During this discussion about whether or not we could have hidden the puppy in a rucksack, AJ had interrupted to ask if we were going to stay in Xinjiang on the way.

'It can get kinda edgy round there,' he said, holding his chopsticks with the claw that only Chinese people used, and I was desperate to master.

'In Urumqi?'

'Urumqi, Turfan ...'

'What do you mean by edgy?' Jem asked.

'You're foreign, you'll get stopped. They'll ask you for money, bribes, tell you they're going to take you to the police station. You need to keep a wad of cash on you to, basically, pay people off.'

'Would you advise against going to Xinjiang then?' I asked, biting into a dumpling that exploded between my teeth sending hot stock dribbling down my chin.

'No, I mean, I lived and worked around there for five years, spent a couple of nights in the cells sometimes. Just be prepared to be stopped and asked all kinds of things, and you should just say yes to everything.'

'Even if they ask if I want to go to jail?' Jem asked, rubbing his hands in the cold.

AJ ignored him. 'Don't drink. Don't carry alcohol, but do carry cigarettes cos, y'know, they're great currency. I was always kinda poor, handing over cash, but you know it's just how it is there. And your beard,' AJ said, pointing his chopsticks at Marc, 'that could get you some attention.'

'What's wrong with my beard?' Marc asked, his hand going protectively to his face.

'They have a no-beard policy there now, it's a clampdown on the Muslim-minority Uighurs. It's not like an open thing, but the government is definitely putting a stop to the call to prayer, and headscarves, and so on.'

'Most people just think I'm Israeli.'

'I am Israeli.' AJ finished his noodles, wiping his mouth and throwing an orange-stained napkin into the bowl. 'It's a pretty cool place, you guys stay safe.'

The three of us sat staring at the table, waiting for our noodles, which were still being stretched and swung in the open kitchen.

'Mon, you need to get yourself arrested, I could get some great photos of you in jail,' said Marc.

'Or maybe you could get us all arrested with your beard.'

'I don't want to shave off my beard. I quite like my beard.'

'Are we still going to go?' Jem asked.

Previously reluctant, I realised now was the time to come clean about my misgivings on travelling through Turfan and Urumqi. 'I read that there had been a combined bomb and knife attack in Urumqi last year.'

'Where in Urumqi?' asked Marc.

'Um ... the ... train station. Apparently, it was an attack by Uighurs who then stood at the exit with knives after people fled the bomb.'

'That's so messed up. What are we going to do? Which route are we going to take back?'

'We could flip a coin,' said Jem. 'Heads we get blown up by Isis, tails we get stabbed by a Uighur.'

For the next two days, Marc wavered between wanting to shave off his beard and not wanting to shave off his beard, eventually deciding that if we were going to get stopped, arrested, mugged or stabbed, it was unlikely to be the result of his facial hair and more because we were three wealthy foreigners carrying expensive cameras and equipment. On the train to Turfan we were sitting quietly in our compartment, a cosy little hub with camels embroidered on net curtains. Marc was editing his photos, while Jem was reading Colin Thubron's *Shadow of the Silk Road*, and I was typing up some notes, when a big, round face appeared at the glass. Pulling back the door, the woman walked straight in, pointed at my computer and started chatting away, smiling so hard that the apples of her cheeks looked like two actual apples.

'What's she saying?' Marc said, taking off his headphones.

'I have absolutely no idea, but she seems to be in a good mood.'

'Is she a nun?'

Looking at the lady, whose soft brown scalp was showing through her shorn hair, I saw that she was wearing burgundy robes beneath her mustard overcoat and concluded that she was indeed a Tibetan nun. She was still talking, clutching a flask of tea in one hand, and gesturing towards me, breaking into giggles and evidently asking me some sort of question. Slapping her thigh and laughing in frustration, she turned to Jem and Marc for help, asking again the same question until I caught the word 'Indian'.

'Yes, Indian!' I said, pointing to my chest. 'And he's half Indian,' I added, pointing to Marc.

The nun grabbed my finger, erupting with joy. Waving her hands and chattering, she pushed Marc's pillow to one side and sat down. The revelation had inspired another monologue.

'What on earth is she saying?' Marc asked, sitting up and trying to slow her down.

Jem had disappeared to the next compartment and returned with a nervous-looking, heavily pregnant young woman – the trains were full of heavily pregnant women, and I realised now it was because it wasn't advisable to fly after a certain point. 'She speaks English,' Jem said, 'she's offered to translate.'

Perching warily on the edge of the berth, the young woman listened for a few moments then turned to me.

'She wants to know if you are from India.'

'Yes I am,' I said, deciding that it was safer not to complicate matters by throwing English into the mix and disappointing the nun, who I could see wanted more than anything in life for me to be from India. Translating, the young woman started to laugh as the nun bounced on the seat, threw her hands in the air and then lurched forward to grab my arms.

'She is very pleased you are from India. India is kind to Dalai Lama. You are the first Indian she meets. You are special, she says.'

'We've just been to Tibet,' said Jem, showing her a photo on his phone.

This was too much for the nun who broke into infectious laughter, her eyes disappearing into creases. Marc opened up his computer to show her the rest of the photographs of the Potala

Palace as she sat on her hands and chuckled like a child, pointing at the screen with delight.

'I love how happy this woman is,' Marc said. 'It's amazing. She's only got happiness.'

From the time the nun had poked her head in through the door, the compartment had radiated with warmth and laughter. We had no idea what she was saying, and she had no idea what we were saying, and the poor pregnant woman was struggling with all of us, but through gesture, facial expression and touch, we had managed to establish a mutual understanding. The nun took out her iPhone 6 Plus and began scrolling through photographs of young monks in training, and elderly monks taking selfies outside the Drigung Til monastery in Lhasa. Marc leant forward to look at the screen.

'She's on WeChat! I love it, Tibetan nuns on WeChat, having a conversation with another nun.'

WeChat was the most popular Chinese messaging service, and the three of us had been using it instead of WhatsApp since our arrival. Picking up my phone, the nun signalled for me to add her as a contact. Unsure how to search for her username, which was in Chinese script, I handed her my phone and she instantly opened up the settings and showed me how to scan the QR code, before handing it back to me with a nod and a laugh. She pointed at my phone, and I looked down to find she had already sent me a message – an emoji of a golden Buddha that exploded with light – turning everything I knew on its head. If I had to rely on a Tibetan nun to show me how to use my iPhone, nothing could ever surprise me again.

Before getting off at the next stop, the nun gestured for us to follow her to her compartment. There she rummaged through her bags, pulling out three red threads strung with gold amulets. Tying one to each of our wrists, she then placed a little black seed in our palms, indicating for us to eat it. Normally, I would have questioned ingesting strange black seeds from strangers, but I had moments of blind trust when travelling, and crunched down on its smoky sweetness, hoping it was the source of all her joy. Wrapping her shawl around her shoulders, the nun hurried to the door as we drew into the station, leaning in to give me a hug before she got off. As she let go of me, Jem reached out to hug her and she recoiled with shock, ducking like a boxer.

'Mate, you can't hug a nun!' Marc exclaimed. 'They've taken vows against that sort of thing.'

Sweetly patting Jem on the shoulder, the nun was still all smiles as she turned and got off the train, waving from the window as a group of her fellow nuns came to greet her on the platform.

After another thirty- or forty-hour journey – five hours here and there no longer registered on my radar – we arrived in Turfan, a sandy expanse that smelt like a spice market, owing to the enormous spice market just behind the station. Emerging from the exit, we were immediately encircled by taxi drivers wearing suits over jumpers, and embroidered felt skullcaps, colourful and flat on top, instead of fitted round white ones. Knowing our rucksacks made each one of us look like a mobile ATM, we strode off, fanning away the drivers until I checked the map on my phone and realised we needed a taxi. The station was not actually in Turfan, but thirty miles outside the city in a town called Daheyan, so I slowed down, trying not to look too keen as I haggled with the one driver who'd had the persistence to tail me into the middle of the street. The others had gone back to standing around. Knowing he'd got me as soon as I stopped, the driver took out his keys and pointed up the street to his car.

At the side of the road, a baker was shovelling frisbees of speckled cumin bread out of a kiln, which smelt too good to ignore. Buying a couple twisted into a brown paper bag, I climbed into the back of the taxi, warming my hands on the soft, sweet dough. Jem and Marc were trying to load our bags into the boot, which was full of gas canisters, when a chubby man wearing a sweater vest and sandals got into the back and closed the door. I looked at him, confused.

'Friend,' said our driver.

'Wait, hang on,' said Marc, sliding in next to us, 'what's this guy doing in here?'

'Friend, Turfan.'

'He's your friend? Is he getting a free lift with us to Turfan?'

The chubby man sighed and scratched his face, tightening his grip on the grab handle.

'I'm sorry, are we delaying your journey?' said Marc. Tapping the driver on the shoulder he leant forward. 'Mate, we can't all fit in the car if your friend is coming with us. There are three of us, and there's no room in the boot for our bags.'

'We've got to keep at least two of the rucksacks in the front,' said Jem, doing his best to squash them down.

The driver was now on his mobile, calling a friend who could speak English, and he handed the phone to me.

'Hello?'

'Hello, you go Turfan?' said a voice.

'Yes, but there are three of us. Three. No room for bags.'

'Yes, room.'

'No, no room.'

'You pay small fee.'

'For what?'

'You pay 30 RMB.'

'For what?'

'You give phone to driver.'

Passing the phone back, I tore my bread into three parts, handing one each to Marc and Jem as I realised that we could be here for a while. So as not to appear ruder – we were already trying to throw him out of the car – I offered my third piece to the chubby man, who had settled himself in. He nodded and took a bite, his green eyes darting back to the driver on the phone. Marc was barely visible behind his camera bag, nibbling at his bread, and Jem was standing by the car waiting for the chubby man to move. More than twenty minutes had passsed when Marc lost his patience.

'This is ridiculous,' he said, 'let's just get out and get another cab.'

Realising he was about to lose his customers, the driver opened the back door and removed his friend, who sighed as he heaved himself up, crumbs all over his sweater vest. Calling his interpreter back, the driver passed the phone to me for a second time.

'Hello?'

'Hello, extra 20 RMB, you go, you three.'

'Twenty RMB? For an extra twenty he'll leave his friend here?'

'Tell him we're going to pay it,' Marc said. 'But relay to the driver that we're very disappointed and that we're not going to haggle because we can't be bothered.'

The chubby man, who hadn't said a word since he got into the car, now sauntered off into a tea shop as the car started up, and we drove through the town and out into the countryside.

'Consider it a comfort tax,' said Marc. 'We've just paid not to have the big guy in the back with us.'

After this initial tussle, no one tried to extract money from us in Turfan. No one tried to stop us, arrest us or knife us as we walked around the city eating freshly grilled kebabs and looking at mosques – none of which were sounding out the call to prayer. It was one of the few elements of AJ's scaremongering that proved to be true. Originally a nomadic tribe who'd ruled in eighth-century Mongolia, the Turkic-speaking Uighurs were at one time the dominant ethnic group in Xinjiang province, which had long encountered bloodshed during China's civil war. Backed by Russia, the Uighur population had briefly declared the region the independent state of East Turkestan in 1949, but lost control a few months later after the communist takeover brought it into the firm grip of the central government. Although deemed an 'autonomous region', Xinjiang province had remained under Beijing's control, sagging beneath the weight of Han Chinese flooding into the region, taking over jobs and diluting the Muslim culture. After 2001, the discovery of Uighurs in al-Qaeda camps, and a spate of horrific knife and bomb attacks on civilians, had spurred the government to clamp down on Islamic practices, blaming the population for fomenting unrest. However, human rights groups and analysts of China's ethnic politics had accused Beijing of exaggerating the number of attacks, and explained the surge of violence as a response to China's unprecedented actions to subjugate the Muslim minority: allegedly forcing women to remove headscarves; prohibiting beards; banning young people from going to mosques; restricting their employment prospects; replacing Uighur with Mandarin at schools; outlawing Muslim names; and offering cash subsidies for marriages between Uighurs and Han Chinese in an attempt to annihilate the culture. A number of critics had gone so far as to draw parallels with the Tibetan plight, but it was impossible to know where the truth lay. Almost every report of violence originated from China's state-run Xinhua news agency, while witness accounts on Weibo, the social media platform, were rapidly removed. Local people were unwilling to speak on record to foreign journalists who were increasingly restricted from moving through the region.

With our Chinese visas on the brink of expiring, we had barely a few days to stroll around the oasis town's covered markets and open bazaars stockpiled with melons, dried apricots and raisins, the atmosphere cloying with the smell of open pomegranates. Under the glow of a single bulb, slender chickens were being smoked and turned on spits, elderly Uighurs beckoned us over to sit with their young customers who shuffled up to make room, carrying on with their tea and gossip, unbothered by our presence. With the help of an English-speaking guide, we managed to spark up conversations with some of the young people, who initially avoided our questions, then warmed up over tea and bowls of mutton dumplings. It helped that we looked like nothing more than a trio of hapless tourists buying tat and eating noodles, which allowed us to coax out a number of depressing stories that aligned with many of the allegations of government suppression. The young Uighurs were regularly stopped and asked to hand over their phones for examination, and CCTV cameras above mosques ensured they didn't try to enter to pray. Most Uighur men had pencil-thin moustaches, but no beards, and the women covered their hair with nothing more than small silk scarves, which was as far as they could go without reprisal.

One afternoon, we drove across the Taklamakan desert to see the Flaming Mountains, trudging for hours across the spectacular red dunes, not another soul in sight. From the outside looking in, this region was usually deemed exotic and arcane, rarely visited and often feared, when it was once the centre of the world, channelling civilisation out to the west and east. This northern branch of the old Silk Road route was rich with indicators of the origins of modern-day food, art and infrastructure – from the locals deep-frying triangular *samsas* stuffed with fatty meat, to the *karez*, a subterranean irrigation system hand-built more than 2,000 years ago that continued to sustain Turfan's vineyards. Over the past seven months, I'd come to appreciate the depth of Britain's diversity, and the way in which we took for granted the spectrum of colours and creeds who lived in relative harmony. With the exception of New York, most of the world's major cities were visibly dominated by their own ethnic majorities, leaving us to wander around feeling exposed and sometimes vulnerable. But here in Turfan, we moved freely among local people whose slim eyes were hazel, green, and even blue; black and blond hair sticking out from under skullcaps. The fluidity of their features implied how we all might look one day, once we'd pooled and diluted our genes.

Just as Turfan had begun to settle in under my skin, we had to leave, driving in a haze of disappointment through the desert to the brand-new high-speed railway station. Like the ghost cities, the station soared out of the middle of the desert, having been built with the same optimism: less than a year old, the mega-station looked as though it was expecting thousands of travellers – or soon-to-be new residents – to pass through every day. And perhaps it had already started. A shiny white bullet train was waiting for us on the platform, one of fifteen departures a day, and in just over an hour a packed train pulled into Urumqi.

Unlike air travel, which eases you into a city, weaning you from the plane through the airport, and eventually onto the street, train travel parachutes you in. And from the moment I stepped off the train, I had a sense of foreboding. In the absence of the usual flurry of meeting and greeting, nothing but footsteps echoed through the building. People moved with care, their heads low, their eyes averted. No one spoke as we made our way to the exit where we were met by the ominous sight of soldiers and tanks in the forecourt. As though in the throes of a military coup, the immediate area was lined with barricades and police behind shields. Scanners beeped, boots trudged too close for comfort, and red lights spun panicked beams around the station's perimeter. This was not like Turfan – which was a Garden of Eden by comparison.

'Has something just happened?' Jem wondered, as we joined the line waiting for taxis to draw up to the kerb.

'Maybe, though I'm not sure I want to hang around too long to find out,' I replied.

In silence, we drove through the city, taking in the armoured vehicles, riot police, and cameras bunched on lamp posts.

'This is really sinister,' said Marc peering out of the window and turning his camera onto a parked tank. Through the top, a single army officer held aloft a machine gun. As we'd witnessed in Tibet, open-backed lorries packed with troops rolled down the streets, pumping black diesel fumes into the traffic. Local militia carrying metal rods roamed in front of mosques as pedestrians crossed the roads to avoid them. What should have taken less than twenty minutes took more than an hour, as our taxi faced roadblocks and barricades, reversing down streets, circling newly devised one-way routes. Resigned to what was evidently a daily but relatively new situation, the driver finally deposited us at our hotel.

Determined not to feel threatened, but struggling to resist the urge to hide in our rooms, we spent the next few days venturing no further than a one-mile radius of the hotel, depressed by the military presence, and seeking comfort in nearby restaurants.

Gravitating to the same place every day, we set up camp in a warm front room with an open kitchen run by a family of Uighurs. Much like a local pub, we began to recognise the same customers who came in to eat fried mutton noodles, and watch soaps on the overhead TVs, kissing each other's cheeks and drinking tea. Bringing us free bowls of bone broth and bread, the owner saved us the same table every morning; his kids kneeling up with colouring books, occasionally trusted to serve small plates of kebabs. Out on the pavement, sheep carcasses hung from the trees. The temperature was below zero, and the air served well in the absence of freezers as the owner's brothers grilled cumin-scented kebabs on coals, the men rubbing their fingerless-gloved hands and waving through the window when our food was ready.

'Are we supposed to be scared of these people?' Marc asked, winding his noodles around his chopsticks. 'They're so lovely.'

'The only thing I'm scared of is the tanks and machine guns,' said Jem, turning around and tapping on the glass for another round of kebabs.

Between here, Turfan, and on the trains, the Uighurs we had encountered had come across as peaceful, softly spoken people with a warm and welcoming manner. They didn't seem to want for anything more than to be allowed to live among themselves, practise their faith, and earn their livelihood. And the Han Chinese were the same. Two doors along was a Sichuan hotpot restaurant where the young staff were as helpful and kind as any we'd come across. It was too simplistic to wonder why the two couldn't live side by side, the idea reminding me of Sir Harold Atcherley's words that equal proportions of good, indifferent and lousy people existed in any group, and any country. But collectively labelling Uighurs as one oppressed minority was naive. No doubt there were a number who did subscribe to extremism, and it was a tragedy that the entire community was suffering as a result. The extent of the military presence was evidence that the government was not going to allow the Uighur community to exist in peace until they conformed and came round to the Han Chinese way of life.

'Are you anyone's girlfriend?'

'Sorry?'

'Do you belong to one of these men?'

Looking from Jem to Marc and considering the idea of belonging to anyone, like a slave or a blow-up doll, I pointed to Jem. 'He's my fiancé.'

Making smart-mouthed comments to border officials ranked low on my list of priorities, least of all on the Dostyk border between Xinjiang and Kazakhstan, the only feasible route home. After more than nine hours on board the weekly train, and another twenty to go, I was not about to risk being turned around and sent back in the name of feminism. Bringing a shock of cold air into the compartment, two male officials in long grey coats and furry hats looked in, snowflakes on their shoulders. Extending gloved hands for our passports, they looked at each one of us in turn before summoning an English-speaking female colleague who pushed and prodded our rucksacks before asking Marc to open his. He unpacked his cameras, rolls of film and balled-up socks, tipping the remaining contents onto the floor as one of the male officials nodded and moved on to the next compartment.

'You didn't have to do that, but thanks,' said the woman, rummaging around the pile of pants and unwashed T-shirts. Pulling a brown package out of a trouser pocket, she handed it to Marc.

'Open this up.'

'It's nothing, just a little clay thing from Tibet.'

'Open it.'

Reluctantly unwrapping the parcel, Marc pulled out a hand-carved Buddha that he'd bought from an elderly woman sitting at the side of the road.

'May I see this?'

Handing it over, Marc frowned as the woman turned it around, giving it to her colleague, who examined the piece.

'This may not be authentic,' she said.

'What do you mean?'

'We do not want you to take fake goods out of the country. Sometimes the Tibetans sell fake items and it is illegal.'

'Please don't confiscate that. It's just a little thing that I got for my gran as a souvenir. It's real, it's so small, please.'

As I watched the scene unfold, my heart sank into my shoes. In the middle of the floor was a red cloth bag containing an exquisite hand-carved serving dish. Jhampa had taken us to a Tibetan-owned shop selling handicrafts, in particular wooden bowls and serving dishes that nomads used in their homes. Varnished and painted in curly, floral strokes, the wooden dish was so huge I'd been carrying it in both arms since we'd left Tibet, and it was now about to be confiscated, too. Avoiding Jem's gaze, I smiled at the official who had finished going through Marc's things, finally handing back the figurine. Patting the side of my rucksack, she slid her hand into a pocket and pulled out a tiny bottle with a gold lid. She held it to the light.

'What is this?'

I'd completely forgotten about the holy water from Lourdes that had stayed in my bag for almost seven months, unbroken and tightly sealed.

'It's a souvenir,' I said, reaching for it and putting it in my pocket.

Pulling open the main compartment of my bag, she peered inside for a moment before fanning it away, as a warm, musty smell emerged.

'What's the worst part of this job?' Jem asked, as the woman pointed to his bag.

'I'm not sure chatting her up is going to help us,' Marc muttered.

'I once put my hand into a used diaper with no gloves on,' she laughed.

'Or maybe it is ...' he said, raising his eyebrows at me.

'Are you a couple?' Jem asked, pulling out his clothes.

'No, we're not a couple,' said the man, whose name was Qian. 'We're just boyfriend and girlfriend.'

'I knew it!' said Jem, looking smug and folding his arms, having made an entirely random guess.

'You can say "couple" even if you're not married,' said Marc.

'Oh, okay,' said Qian, touching Ling on the arm. 'And lover?'

'Well, yes, assuming she is your lover, but you don't generally introduce someone as your lover.'

'Do you not get married yet?' he asked Marc, leaning against the door.

'Me? No, I'm not married. These two are going to get married.'

'No? You don't have one person close to your heart?'

'Not yet,' said Marc hugging his bag.

'But you're very handsome,' said Qian.

'Now look who's chatting up who,' whispered Jem, delighted at the frisson of impending romance.

'What's this?' asked Ling, pulling out a foil-wrapped parcel.

'Oh, that's my ... gas mask,' said Jem, who had forgotten about the mask he'd stolen from the hotel in Moscow.

'Please open it.'

'Oh no! I've managed to keep that for more than five months and I wanted to take it back to London.'

'Jem, it looks like a brick of heroin,' said Marc, with a shout of laughter.

The four of us leant in closely as Jem unzipped the pouch and unwrapped the mask. I was as curious as they were to see what it looked like. Unfolding the gas mask, Jem held it up over his face. Satisfied, Ling and Qian seemed to have forgotten about the rest of our bags and moved on to the next compartment as we sat back with relief, the Tibetan dish sitting in full view in the middle of the floor.

Wandering up the corridor, I looked into each compartment, amused by the women applying eyeliner, removing rollers and rubbing in Nivea cream. I couldn't remember the last time I'd applied make-up, carrying nothing more than a pot of concealer the size of a ten-pence piece, and a tub of Vaseline, which

I knew the boys had dug into, after catching them sitting around with glossy lips. A rotation of five different T-shirts had seen me through seven months, each one barely held together by its threads. But until now I hadn't considered how little it bothered me. Before leaving Vancouver, we had stocked up on thermals knowing that temperatures in Kazakhstan had highs of minus seven, and as I looked out of the window at the guards' breath, I shivered in anticipation. Touching the cold glass, I watched as China rolled away from the window, and we were shunted across the border into Kazakhstan, and a little bit closer to home.

13

Azamat and Marzhan

Snow billowed around the train. Soft as cotton, it swooped at the window in panicked flurries, a Christmas-card frame building along the edge of the glass. Through the blizzard, the Tian Shan mountains were just visible, their wizened old heads greyed with ice and veiled by rolling cloud. Curving away from the mountains, the train swept across the dry grassland towards a fresh army of thunderclouds gathering force on the horizon. After crossing the border, we'd stopped at a small station cafe for a breakfast of lamb and tomato noodles, and mugs of builder's tea – a gift from three off-duty Kazakh officials who were drunk on Russian vodka. No longer the green-leaf kind, the first cup of regular tea I'd had in a long time marked the beginning of our shift from East to West. Presenting me with a carton of grapefruit juice, the officials showed us photos of Gennady Golovkin, the Kazakh middleweight boxer. One of the men took out a ballpoint pen and wrote 'Triple G' on the back of my hand, before offering us a photograph with them to post on our 'English Facebook'. Our first Kazakh encounter was a positive indicator of things to come. Like all good drunks, the group apologised on a loop for their drunkenness, before doling out hugs and leading us back out to the forecourt where the train had returned with its new engine. 'Forecourt' was generous; the station was more like someone's old house with a railway shed in the back garden.

Now, as we strained across the extremes of terrain to Almaty, I watched as the expanse seemed to double every hour. The snow had melted away, spotlights of sunshine lighting up the ground like a stage. Lagoons shone between bright yellow banks of sand as though we'd arrived on the coast. Until darkness streaked the skies, eclipsing the sun, which swirled like a beady eye, I sat in the warmest corner of the compartment, feeling a distinct sense of place. My mental clock had finally adjusted to the marathon stretches of time spent on these trains, and I now understood how far we would travel in twenty hours, thirty hours – or even five days. I could gauge the distance we were moving, and know how my body would respond to the rhythm beating beneath my feet. It had taken just under seven months, but after much fine-tuning I'd finally located the precise wavelength where I could sit in peace, my thoughts at rest, and time ceased to exist.

In the harsh pre-dawn cold, Almaty station woke briefly with the thump of boxes and cases being dragged and rolled along the ground. Boots crunched through sludgy ice, and coarse voices blew steam into the air. Following the Kazakhs as they ignored the footbridge and traipsed across the tracks, children sleeping on their shoulders, we passed beneath the grandeur of the station, then found ourselves alone as they got into taxis, kissed friends and family, or walked on with purpose through the unlit streets. It was just after four o'clock, and guessing that we wouldn't want to wait for first light in the emptiness of the station, I'd booked a hotel a few streets away. Trudging down the middle of the road, none of us said a word, unnerved by the stillness of our new surroundings. Each clearing of a throat or rustle of a bag was deafening, and I wished I could silence our footsteps and blend into the dark. A broken strip light flickered above the hotel door as we wandered in to find more darkness, wincing as we pressed a silver bell, shrill in its announcement of our arrival. Scuffling up from the floor behind the desk, a member of staff yawned and rubbed his eyes, handing over our card and sending us straight up to the room without checking passports or checking us in. Fumbling up the corridors, we found the door by torchlight, dumped our bags and crawled straight into three hard beds.

★

'What did you think? That Almaty was like small village?' Azamat burst out laughing, wiping away a foam moustache. 'You thought it was like Borat's TV show, with one goat and a cart?'

I was sitting in a Costa Coffee drinking a latte with an ecology student named Marzhan. I'd found her on Instagram, after trawling a forum for English-speaking students wanting to practise their language. Marzhan and I had been struggling along, Katy Perry playing in the background, when Azamat had stuck his head over a wall of plant pots and called out to me in perfect English. Announcing that he'd studied linguistics at Southampton University, he asked if he could join us. Relieved, I waved him over, having learnt nothing from Marzhan other than she was an ecology student who wanted to practise English, at which point we'd both smiled in silence as though on a bad date. Azamat was in the middle of having coffee with a young woman with green eyes and a sleek black ponytail; abandoning her without a moment's hesitation, he grabbed his leather jacket from the back of the seat and came over. Thirty seconds was all it took for me to see that it was less my English prowess and more Marzhan's rose-pink pout and soft eyes that had lured him across. Azamat was a trainee secondary school teacher who had spent a number of years in Hampshire and London, but had returned to Almaty to finish his training and start work. With thick eyebrows, perfect teeth and eyes that turned up at the corners, Azamat had one of those faces where you instantly knew what he'd looked like as a child, causing trouble and smiling his way out of it.

'No,' I lied. 'I didn't think it would be like that, but I wasn't expecting a Costa Coffee next to a KFC and a Hardee's.'

'Usually Kazakhs drink tea, proper black tea with cream or milk and sugar like in England, but recently coffee shops have become trendy. You know, in our tradition if you are bright, you should know how to make proper tea. When you get married for the first time, the other family will taste your tea to see how well you make it, and they give you money afterwards.'

Kazakhs sounded like English Northerners.

'Seeing as you brought him up, how do you feel about Sacha Baron Cohen,' I asked carefully, worried about offending them.

'He's a super comedian,' Azamat said, edging closer to Marzhan. 'Most people here didn't understand that metaphorically he's actually making fun of Americans, not us. I like him, he's so funny, and actually I'm sure he made people like you want to visit the country, no?'

Azamat was prodding me in the shoulder and laughing, while Marzhan looked on in confusion at the exchange. Feeling guilty that she had no idea what we were talking about, I asked Azamat to translate for her, which he was only too pleased to do as her knight in shining leather, while I waved over Marc and Jem, who had just arrived from trawling the bazaar next door.

'What language are you speaking?' I asked.

'We speak in Kazakh, but we also use some Russian words. We are, how do you say, switch-coding.'

'Do children still learn Russian at school?'

'Yes. They teach both languages at school. We only got our independence from the Soviet Union in 1991, and things have been slow to change, but we are getting our identity back. Some Russian people think we are trying to discriminate against their language, but we are not, we are just trying to get our own language back. For example, we don't have many media channels in Kazakh – maybe 30 per cent – and that will change. Some families speak only Russian, but most Kazakh people are bilingual, I'd say around 90 per cent. And from the first grade they now teach English here. Our government is changing the formation at school, we have a multilingual education system. Most people aren't ready for that, they think it's overloading children, but our president, Nazarbayev, suggested changing to English language in tenth and eleventh grade, and he thinks that in university everything should be taught in English.'

'Do you?'

'After studying in the UK, I think we should if we want to catch up with the rest of the world, and catch up with research – which is always in English.'

'And does everyone get on? I've seen such a mix of Kazakhs and Russians.'

'Yes, we are friendly, they are our neighbours, but we don't want to be under their system. Of course, there were many advantages of being a part of the Soviet Union, but the Russian people claim that when we were a part of the Soviet Union they helped us build a lot of the infrastructure. I don't agree, because they used our resources, 90 per cent of our resources went to Moscow. Oil is the first thing, but we have gold, silver, coal, we are a really rich country.'

Almaty was no small village. Not that I had ever thought it was, but it was hard to visualise a country that I knew little about other than from a London comedian with a penchant for bad moustaches and swimwear. Moving out of our far-flung hotel and into the centre of town, we had walked for more than an hour down the four-lane avenues, as though drifting through a brutalist nightmare. Passing expressionless Russians in stonewash jeans and stilettos, and Kazakhs wrapped in fur, it was hard to tell what they thought of us. They were neither friendly nor unfriendly, with the exception of a drunkard who had tried to throw a punch at Marc, then chased me up the road until I'd hidden in an ammunition shop behind a counter of handguns. Veering away from the bare woods and speeding cars, we'd taken a detour through the university and its gardens, one of the few regal-looking buildings in a city that was architecturally stuck in the 1970s.

Over the next week, I discovered that the post-Soviet dourness belied an energetic youth culture of techno clubs, Superdry T-shirts and Converse, which Azamat and Marzhan were quick to introduce us to. Taking us to a student party one night, they followed up the next day with cheeseburgers and ice-skating at the Medeu speed-skating rink. On the bus journey there, we'd discovered the other side of the city, driving up Almaty's answer to Beverly Hills, where boulevards were lined with designer fashion outlets, gated mansions, and shopping malls shining like Mecca. On the way back into town, we stopped to thaw out at the Bellagio, a restaurant and bar that resembled a grotto with fairy lights – the sight alone had warmed my gangrenous fingertips. Azamat and Marzhan hovered nervously at the gate as an attendant in a beanie and black jacket stepped out of his cabin and trudged across the snow.

'Where are you going? What do you want?' he barked.

'I want a drink,' said Marc.

'You cannot come in here.'

'Why not?'

'You do not have the money.'

'Maybe we go,' said Azamat.

'No, no way,' said Marc, getting riled up into a frenzy. 'Who are you to tell me I've got no money? I've got loads of money,' he said, probably wishing at that moment that he wasn't wearing hiking gear.

'I think it's because he just saw us get off the bus,' Jem interjected.

For all our bravado, I had a sinking feeling that we might be arguing our way into the most expensive restaurant in Kazakhstan. Ushering in Marzhan and Azamat, I knew it was too late to back down now, and racked my brains for the PIN of our emergency credit card. The bar was like Austin Powers's living room, with open fires and suede corner sofas amid an atmosphere of après-ski. Surrounded by the gurgle of shishas, Azamat glanced over his shoulder and gave a low whistle of amusement at women slouched around in white fur boots and pink sunglasses, chewing on the pipes, their husbands dressed like Tony Montana. Moneyed kids with slicked-back hair smoked cigars, snapping their fingers at the staff. Over a pair of Irish coffees, Jem and I pretended not to watch as Azamat continued to 'interpret' for Marzhan, staring at her glossy hair and flashing us grins, while she blushed into her mint tea. Thrilled to discover a range of single malts, Marc soon calmed down; when the bill came he was pleased to see that the Bellagio was cheaper than a Wetherspoons.

By day, Almaty station was far from the threatening expanse we'd first encountered. Lit by the glare of winter sun, the enormous pillared building was packed with passengers shuttling around its hallways, and fringed by the usual nondescript figures who furnish every station in the world: never travelling, collecting or seeing off passengers, they can always be found loitering around as an integral part of the railway landscape. Our train to Astana was waiting on the furthest platform, the shadow of the station's roof throwing the reverse of KAZAKHSTAN across the side in Cyrillic. As we hovered waiting for Marzhan and Azamat to arrive so we could say our goodbyes, I felt like we were in the middle of a wartime evacuation: families were hurrying down platforms wheeling barrows of boxes tied in string; wailing mothers clasped their sons to their breasts, and women gathered their skirts and children, picking their way across the tracks, rushing back for cartons of fruit and carrier bags.

Watching the clock tick closer to the minute of departure, we gave up on the pair and crossed the tracks to our train, which had a bright blue engine and a big red Soviet star on the nose. Climbing the ladder to our carriage, I came upon the familiar sadness of premature departure, like a kid being dragged home early from a birthday party: if only we'd been able to say goodbye to Marzhan and Azamat. Throughout our journey, we'd been scooped up and looked after by wonderful people. As though adding pearls to a necklace, I'd now gathered a priceless string of friends that extended around the globe. Pacing down the carriage and pulling open the windows, Marc was taking photographs of a man standing in the doorway of the train across the tracks, while Jem stacked our bags. Stifling heat was already blasting from the air vents, along with clouds of dust, so I wandered down to the vestibule for some fresh air, just as Azamat leapt up the ladder in a huge fur-lined coat, and landed on both feet, his fists raised in celebration.

'I made it!' he shouted, Jem and Marc cheered and grabbed him in a hug. 'I was not going to let you leave without saying goodbye.'

Livid, our *provodnitsa* screamed at him as he turned around, and he replied in Kazakh: 'It's okay, they are all celebrities.'

'Where's Marzhan?' I asked, hearing the engine rumbling.

'She is coming,' he said. 'I just spoke with her.'

'You got her number then?' Marc said. 'You should ask her out.'

'I am not taking advice from you. You're thirty-six and still single.'

'Thirty-seven.'

Losing her patience, our *provodnitsa* dragged Azamat out of the door by his collar, just as Marzhan came running down the platform, her cheeks pink. The ladder had been pulled up and the train was on the move as she ran alongside, reaching up with a soft, cold hand. As I crouched down, she managed to kiss me on the cheek, the sweet smell of strawberry on her lip gloss. Our fingers came apart as the train picked up pace, and the three of us huddled in the doorway watching the pair wave, until the train began to bend and they were no longer in sight. If the romance of train travel was still alive, it survived in moments like this.

With less than a day in the Kazakh capital, we'd chosen to be kind to ourselves and spend the time lolling around in the hotel's spa in preparation for the fifty-eight-hour journey up to Moscow. It had snowed the previous night, which wasn't so remarkable as Astana spent a third of the year covered in snow and ice, but the latest precipitation had surprised even local Kazakhs, for whom a daily snowfall was as normal as drizzle. Venturing out into the drifts, we'd gasped for breath in the sub-zero temperatures. Unlike damp cold, though, which made my joints ache, this was a bearable, dry cold, made all the more pleasant by the blue sky and sunshine. Attempting to go for a walk, we'd realised that Astana had no pavements, and any pathway that may have existed for pedestrians was at least a foot below. Making it no more than twenty metres out of the hotel car park, we decided we'd seen enough of the city and hurried back inside, foot-long icicles hanging like daggers above the doorway.

With no incentive to venture out, we had every incentive to stay indoors, where we were currently being treated like royalty – as the only guests in residence at a hotel that resembled a run-down stately home. Pleased to have something to do, the staff had laid on a full banquet for lunch, the three of us sitting at a round table for eight in the centre of a ballroom, while several waiters stood at the edges watching in silence. Featuring doughy breads, noodles, indiscriminate cuts of meat – and many cups of tea – the Kazakh diet was geared to suit the weather, slabs of fried fatty meat and thick soups providing insulation from the cold. After devouring a delicious plate of sweet horsemeat and lambs' hearts in a bourguignon sauce, we decided to sweat it all out in the steam room. Pacing the dungeon of corridors, we climbed a number of spiral staircases before giving up the search and seeking out the receptionist for guidance.

'Where's your steam room?' Marc asked the young woman at the desk, who had just applied a new layer of eyeliner using the camera of her iPhone, and had smudged it so she now looked like a tearful clown.

'No steam room.'

'No steam room? Then where's the sauna?'

'No sauna.'

'What? Your website says you have a sauna and a steam room,' I said.

'Yes.'

'Do you have them or not?'

'No.'

'So, you've just stuck it on your website for the sake of it,' said Marc.

The woman now looked not only tearful, but guilty.

'The only reason I booked this hotel was because your website said you had a steam room and sauna,' I said.

'Can we have some money back, then?' Jem asked.

'Yes.'

Taken aback by her compliance, I watched as she pulled open a drawer, counted out a few thousand tenge and pushed the notes across the table.

'Well, this is useless currency, I can save it as a souvenir,' said Marc, folding it into his wallet. He looked back at the woman. 'I'm assuming you don't have the Jacuzzi or gym then? No, didn't think so.'

Just then, I received a message from Azamat.

'Azamat says he's given my number to his friend Asem who's going to come and pick us up and take us out for the afternoon.'

'That's amazing, I love that guy,' said Jem.

'Asem? Is that a dude?' asked Marc.

'I have no idea,' I said, just as my phone buzzed with a second message from Azamat. *Asem is my girlfriend* read the message, with a winking face on the end.

'Player,' said Jem.

We'd barely put on our jackets and hats when Asem pulled up outside in a Mercedes C-Class sedan.

'Such a player,' said Marc, as we shielded our eyes from the glare of the snow, and slid into the warmth of her car.

Astana's skyline looked as though someone had gathered together the contents of a giant geometry box. After moving the capital from Almaty in 1997, President Nazarbayev had guided the city's development towards showcasing the country's post-Soviet independence and economic power. Its modern architecture had a delightful insanity, enhanced by the vast dry steppe from which it had emerged in just under two decades. Between the gold, dalek-shaped skyscrapers, Norman Foster had had a field day, designing the Palace of Peace and Reconciliation, a 62-metre-high pyramid with a stained-glass apex, and his most recent creation, the Khan Shatyr Entertainment Centre, a 150-metre-high translucent tent that looked as though it was melting into itself. Packed in by ice and snow, Astana was a futuristic vision of Dubai once climate change had taken hold.

By Asem's own admittance, there wasn't very much to do in one of the coldest cities in the world, where most activities centred on making the most of the cold, or hiding indoors from the cold. She and her friends went ice-skating and shopping, or spent their days in the myriad communal baths where most of the city migrated to in winter, staying inside until spring. On her recommendation, we were driving to Keremet, one of Astana's biggest public baths.

'Oh, it is not so cold today,' she said, glancing at the dashboard.

'It's minus fourteen,' I replied.

'Yes, that is not cold. Usually we have anything below minus twenty.'

'What's there to do here when it's that cold?' Jem asked.

'It is not a very interesting city if you are from here,' she said. 'For others who come from around the country there are many things to see and to try, like the indoor running track, bowling alley, and the opera house, but for me it is boring. I am going to leave to study in Dublin.'

'Why Dublin?' Marc asked, leaning in from the backseat.

'I have many friends who have gone away there, and they are having a good time.'

'Are these your school friends or university friends?'

'University friends,' said Asem, checking the rear-view mirror as she overtook a BMW and deftly wove us around the patches of ice on the road.

'Most of my friends are studying postgraduate degrees, others went to join Isis.'

'Ah, okay … wait, what?!'

'Mmmm,' she said, glancing over her shoulder. 'They pay well.'

'So does banking,' said Jem.

'Hang on, your friends went to fight for Isis?' I asked, pulling my seatbelt to breathe better, and turning to face her.

'Well, not so much my friends, but yes, some of the guys I studied with. They are paid very well, and they are able to save more money in one month than they can make in one year working here, so they go and send the money back to their families. We are here,' she said brightly, snapping off her belt.

Asem got out of the car as the three of us sat stunned, taking in the impact of her casual chatter. She'd made it sound as normal as going to Thailand on a gap year.

'Imagine being that bored that you want to go and fight for Isis,' said Marc, shaking his head as we entered the baths.

Asem had insisted on dropping us off at the station, and we were huddled in her car just before 9 a.m. listening to Ja Rule and psyching ourselves up for the big push. The 1,854-mile journey through Kazakhstan and Russia was the missing link that would carry us back to the other side of the world. From Moscow, just five trains would take us home to London. Getting out of the car, I took a moment for myself, picking my way through the snow, the wind burning my ears. The muffled hoot of a train rang through the numbness in my head. Not so long ago, the journey along the railways of the world had lain ahead of me, an open railroad leading to the unknown, and now it was almost over. Almost.

14
Homeward Bound

No one spoke. For the first few hours, Jem read in the dining car, and Marc leant against the window staring into low-hanging cloud like the spurned lover in an eighties power ballad. Propped up on my elbows, I lay in my berth watching the Kazakh landscape deteriorate into snow-covered steppe littered with miserable housing. Corrugated-iron roofs were barely nailed into place, and thin sheets of plastic billowed across broken panes of glass. The glitz of Astana had died a swift death, decrepit farmhouses and abandoned homes rolling past the window as we crawled northwest, stopping for two minutes at a time at Soviet-era stations, nothing more than pastel-painted concrete boxes. The scenes reflected our mood as we slumped around with the Sunday-evening feeling of school the next day. Jem and I were carrying on back to London, but Marc was meeting friends in Moscow, and we had only two days left together. As a child, I'd had a 'Peanuts' calendar with a picture of Charlie Brown carrying Snoopy on his shoulders with the caption 'In Life, It's Not Where You Go – It's Who You Travel With', which I'd never given much thought to. I didn't care for famous quotes by famous people: they were usually reeled off by the emotionally incontinent, but this one was as simple as it was true. It wasn't easy to spend weeks confined to a space the size of a shoebox, stacked one on top of the other, battling hunger, tiredness, and toe jam, yet we'd survived by tapping into the spirit of *gezellig*, and coming together as a train family.

Moving towards the window, I spotted a bundle of blankets and tins in a doorway where a rough sleeper had made his home at the edge of a ramshackle barn. A small fire smouldered where he sat rolling a cigarette. As we inched past, I stared at his bowed head wondering where he had come from, and what had happened to bring him here. This was the very essence of what drew me to trains: for a few seconds at a time I was privy to strangers' intimate actions; a vagrant rolling a cigarette, a mother nuzzling her baby's head, a banker checking his breath. Exposed, they would walk on, unaware that someone had shared their moment. On a day-to-day basis, the insularity that comes with living in a big city means that we don't see each other. Sometimes we look over, but usually we keep going with no more than a cursory glance at the other person's hair or untied shoelace, but we don't really see or listen to each other any more: empathy is fading from existence. For so long, I'd taken for granted having a front-row seat to unedited, unscripted footage of other people's lives, that I wasn't sure how I'd adapt to the isolation of life off the rails.

Sliding open the door, our *provodnitsa* appeared with two cups of tea with string hanging over the rim. Mostly Russian, the staff on board this service were an unusually friendly group, with more gold teeth than a rap video. There were few passengers on board, and like Oksana on the Trans-Mongolian, the staff had taken to mothering us, bringing tea, biscuits, and extra blankets – despite the tropical temperatures on board. Like the Kazakhs, we'd taken to wandering around in the universally accepted train gear of flip-flops and vests, sweating in our compartment, then darting about on the platforms in the snowy wind to avoid passing out in the soporific heat. A sip of tea lifted my mood, and I looked out to where the evening light had softened the landscape, black, naked trees outlined against a warm peach backdrop.

Unfolding our map, I traced the line that Jem had been updating since London: starting with a tangled mess around Europe, it arced across Russia, Mongolia and China, unravelling down Vietnam and tailing off in Thailand. Curving through

Japan, it then formed a plough shape around North America. From North Korea, the thread then extended up and back into China, looping like a lasso around Tibet, before running off through the northwest and into Central Asia. Digging out a pen, I drew in the latest segment of the journey, pausing at Tobol, where we were now around five hours from the Kazakh–Russian border. Until now, I hadn't absorbed how far we'd come: hopping on and off had become second nature to me and I'd taken each day as it came. Balancing my tea as it splashed across the map, I counted up the countries we'd crossed, tracing the hundreds of fine blue capillaries of river, darkening as they flowed towards the seas. Branches of blood-red railway arteries pumped up mountains, ran along coasts, and cut across borders. With just the odd break here and there, they threaded thousands of towns and cities together, binding countries, and breathing life into the furthest corners of the world. As much as I'd developed a taste for falling asleep in one country and waking up in the next, the richest flavour of train travel lay in the joints and hinges that held countries together: it was deep inside, buried into the bone marrow of these no-man's-lands, where cultures swirled together, currencies doubled up and languages overlapped. Invisible to others, these oases were the preserve of train travellers who were permitted a glimpse as they rolled from one side to the other.

When I left London, I set out to discover what train travel meant to people around the world, and to determine once and for all if the naysayers were right to sound the death knell for long-distance train travel. The romance, they said, was dead – shot down by bullet trains and high-speed rail. But it wasn't dead, just reincarnated, living on in the passengers who would always tell their story to strangers, offer advice, share their food, and give up their seats. It could never die, any more than our interest in people could die. After my journey around India, I came away in thrall to Indian Railways, convinced that no other country could emulate its spirit and vigour, and that I would be disappointed as I travelled this time, searching for something that didn't exist. Instead, I'd unearthed something greater: to some, trains would never be more than a convenience, but for others, trains were symbols of strength, weapons of war, and political tools. Trains provided salvation for the poor, and a lifeline for commuters. They offered the chance to escape, and homes for the lonely. Trains were a link to the past, and a portal to the future. And to me? Trains would always be an open window into the soul of a country and its people.

Beyond the Kazakh border, the train ran almost parallel with the Trans-Siberian route, dipping in and out of the more southerly regions of Russia. For two days, we pushed through the hinterlands, and I sat by the window watching passengers skip around in towelling slippers, smoking on frozen platforms. As though on the brink of death, miles of mournful trees sped by, spaced out by emptiness and snow. Gradually, dirt tracks appeared, furrowed by tyres, and houses emerged through the woods. Spirals of smoke greyed the skies, and gold-domed churches shone like beacons through the gloom. Farms turned into villages, the villages into towns, until the dismal sprawl of suburban Moscow caught up and began to run past the window. Tiered like an elegant wedding cake, Moscow Kazanskaya station drew into view. Rolling with one last gasp of effort, the train drew under the roof of the covered platforms, hissing to a standstill. Marc looked out of the window.

'Fifty-eight hours. We made it. But now I really do need a drink.'

Moscow is one of those cities that looks better under snow. In fact, most of Russia looks better under snow, its brutalism buried beneath drifts, leaving its domes and spires to dominate the skyline. Gathered on a rooftop bar overlooking the Kremlin, we each clasped tankards of Moscow Mules, wishing we'd worn gloves. Like celestial orbs, the uplit domes of St Basil's Cathedral shone through fat flakes of snow, fresh powder shifting and crunching under our feet. The leathery sweetness of cigar smoke drifted across the terrace and I took deep breaths of the sharp air, staring at the domes in the hope of making the moment last.

Six months before, I'd stood on the same rooftop anticipating the journey ahead. From where we were, Mongolia, China and Tibet had seemed so otherworldly, the space between us so vast. Now, though, I could journey back in an instant. Like a time-lapse video in my head, I could see the route unfold from where I stood, running past trees, farms, lakes, mountains, rivers, steppes, horses, villages, towns, stations, and cities. I could hear the hawkers, smell the dried omul and feel the Siberian heat. The earth was much smaller than I'd realised, and nothing was that far away. Taking comfort in the thought, I felt for the first time since we'd set off, that I was ready to return home. And there was only one train that could take us there ...

15

The Venice Simplon-Orient-Express

'Can I ask a silly question?'

'Yes, of course.'

'Would you like a glass of prosecco?'

With his thumb in the hollow of the bottle, the steward filled a crystal glass and handed it to me with a white-gloved thumb and forefinger.

'My name is Patricius, and I will be your steward for the duration of your time with us on the *Venice Simplon-Orient-Express*. If you need anything at all, please do not hesitate to call me.'

Thanking Patricius, I went back into our cabin, where Jem was running his hand over the mahogany panels, rapping them with a knuckle. 'I can see my face,' he said, crouching down and baring his teeth at the reflection.

'It's so shiny,' said Patricius, sticking his head around the door, 'because it has fifteen layers of varnish. They don't do that any more, though.' He raised an eyebrow at my glass. 'I won't tell if you won't,' he whispered like a pantomime dame, giving it one final top-up. Before he left, I tapped him on the elbow.

'Where's the washroom?'

Patricius pointed down the carriage.

'First door on the right. The toilets are charming, you have to lift up a lock and it folds out. It's utterly divine.'

In almost eighty journeys around the world, I was yet to discover a train toilet that could be described as 'charming' or 'divine'. Most were 'rancid' or 'unusable'. Finding a working lock on a door was luxury enough, finding toilet paper was a treat. Soap was out of the question. Intrigued by these water closets that had so charmed Patricius, I eased past our neighbours who were photographing each other in the aisle, and slipped around the door, sliding the brass lock shut, and turning around to inspect the fittings and solid mahogany walls. 'Divine' was a stretch, but the toilet was certainly more agreeable than any toilet I'd seen on our travels, lovelier even than most compartments we'd slept in. Washing my hands with the kind of soap that smelt and felt expensive, I suspected it had been created bespoke for the train, with base notes of teak, and top notes of velvet and pearls. Out of habit, I dried my hands on my thighs and nudged open the door with my elbow, as Patricius walked by and swooned.

After parting ways with Marc, Jem and I had taken the morning train to Warsaw, which connected to Berlin. From Berlin, we'd travelled via Munich down to Venice and spent three days getting lost, eating numerous plates of spaghetti *alle vongole* while trying to locate the route back to the hotel. Venice seemed deliberately designed for tourists to get lost. The city was fed up with them polluting the canals with their titanic cruise ships and clogging the streets in summer. Better that they gathered at dead ends staring at maps, than annoyed Venetians trying to eat dinner. That morning, we'd followed the curves of the Grand Canal, enjoying the slosh of vaporetti, and arrived at Venezia Santa Lucia station, where a blue-and-gold beauty was waiting on platform four, flanked by grubby, grey express trains. The *Venice Simplon-Orient-Express* gleamed from a recent polish, prompting passers-by to crane their necks with wonder. Built from sixty different types of wood – adorning everything from the wheels to the roof – it looked as magical as I'd hoped. Gazing up at the engine, I could almost hear the whistle pierce the air of a scene from the 1920s, where women wearing mink stoles boarded with leather trunks – a dreamy image deflated by the sound of my rucksack slumping sideways to the ground. While skimming the itinerary the day before, I had come across a line that had brought me up short: *In keeping with the spirit of the occasion, you can never be overdressed on board.* There was no risk of that, given our respective wardrobes no longer resembled clothing, but a bundle of limp rags. However, it had provided another excuse to get lost in Venice and eat *vongole* again, in between buying outfits. So genteel was the on-board service that passengers weren't expected to carry anything but prosecco: relieved of our bags at check-in, we were escorted up the platform and shown to our cabin.

Contrary to what passengers were led to believe, there was no 'original' Orient Express. Launched in 1883, the Orient Express was a regular passenger service – rather than a single train – incorporating numerous sets of rolling stock. This particular interpretation of the train was the brainchild of an American businessman named James Sherwood, who, inspired by the British nostalgia for luxury train travel, bought two 1920s carriages and some marquetry panels at a Sotheby's auction in the seventies. Over the next few years, he eventually acquired twenty-five cars, enough to string together a train, moving the collection to workshops in Bremen and Ostend, where the vintage carriages were carefully returned to their former glory – down to the last inch of marquetry. Even the cellulose in the wood was sourced from a tiny Italian company, the only designer in the world to manufacture it. Like a mobile museum, the train was so lovingly reassembled that it made me nervous to touch anything in case it broke off and could only be glued back together with Marlene Dietrich's tears. Slipping off my shoes, I stretched out on the sofa, as Jem sat down and pulled my feet across his knees, covering us both with a blanket. Rubbing in some complimentary 'palm balm', I looked around at the art deco lampshades and single lily. It was as though the previous seven months had built up to this moment, here in the sunshine, my prosecco fizzing on one side, my fiancé fizzing on the other.

At exactly five minutes past eleven, the train eased out of the station and I lay back watching the Venetian waters twinkle past the window. Finally, I could lie here in peace knowing that no one would enter the cabin. No one would ask me to move up or shift my bags. No one would hammer on the door and demand to see my ticket. No one would shine a torch in my face and check for stowaways. No one would smoke or grope me in the corridor. No one would make phone calls in my ear, throw sunflower-seed shells on the carpet or clear phlegm at 4 a.m. No one was here but the two of us.

There was a knock at the door.

'That didn't last long,' said Jem, throwing off the blanket and opening the door to find Paolo, resplendent in black tails with gold trimming.

'Good morning, sir, I have come to offer you a choice of two lunchtime sittings.'

'Just the man I wanted to see! Come on in.'

'What's a chicken oyster?' asked Jem, reading off the menu.

'I have no idea. Show me?'

'Here, it says *chicken oyster and foie gras lasagne with star-anise fennel.*'

'Shame, that sounded great until the fennel. It always tastes of liquorice.'

Surrounded by the Italian Dolomites, we were sitting in 'L'Oriental', one of three dining cars, waiting for our starters. Originally a Pullman kitchen car built in 1927 in Birmingham, its lacquered walls and blush pink decor made for a fine setting to dine in, the clang of pans coming through the swinging door. There were only three chefs in the kitchen, waking at 5 a.m. to bake and prep for the day. To avoid fires on board, they cooked without oil, and nothing was ever fried. Sunlight flashed through the windows, the fringes on the table lamp quivering as we jolted through the mountains, china rattling on the table. Steadying my wine glass, I looked around the carriage at our fellow passengers, who included families celebrating birthdays and anniversaries, retired couples, and a table of hedge fund managers wearing sunglasses, their wives at a separate table. The door swung open and our waiter arrived with the plates, swiping away the remaining glasses like a magician.

'Is this the foie gras?' Jem asked me, slicing open a delicately browned morsel of meat.

'I don't think so, it's layered through the lasagne.'

'It tastes a bit like thigh meat,' he said.

'Oh! I know what it is, it's that lovely juicy bit that you always push out with your thumb from the underside of the bird.'

'I never knew they were called oysters. They look more like mussels.'

There was always an element of suspense that accompanied fine dining, owing to a stray term or rogue ingredient that left a question mark hanging over an otherwise reasonable-sounding dish. Hispi? Dashi? Quenelles? Worse were the chefs who played around with menus to the point that it appeared they were serving the contents of their kitchen bins. No one wanted cheese crusts, shaved potatoes, or burned salsify. Scanning the train's menu, I was satisfied that I could expect 'purple potato puree' with my monkfish.

After pudding, we swayed back up to our cabin, reading trivia about the train that hung above the entrance to each carriage. Robert Baden-Powell had apparently used the Orient Express while spying for Britain, and Graham Greene had taken inspiration from it for *Stamboul Train*. I stopped beneath one panel and drew Jem's attention to the unsurprising statistic that there were thirty marriage proposals on board per year. 'See, *other people* propose on the Orient Express.'

'Yes, thirty unoriginal men. At least you're the only one who can proudly say you got engaged next to a bin outside the Tube.'

The *Venice Simplon-Orient-Express* travelled from Italy through Austria, to Switzerland and France, making several stops along the way. The technology for the signals varied between each country, so the train had to make adjustments before crossing each border. An engine was added at Verona to help pull the train through the Brenner Pass, then removed for the journey down to Innsbruck, giving us plenty of time to step out into the Alpine chill and admire the train from all angles. While Jem went out for a stroll, I stayed on board in the bar, listening to a pianist playing 'Moon River', and pretending to read *Murder on the Orient Express*, which I hadn't pretended to read since I was a precocious eight-year-old. From behind the pages, I watched the other passengers sipping gin and eating wasabi peas, in rapture at the scenery. Star-struck by the service, most passengers were unable to take their eyes off the grand piano and the brass fittings, stroking the sofas and staring at the walls, the romance of train travel igniting in their eyes.

That night, dolled up in a 1950s rose-pink dress, with a matching flower in my hair, I cupped my hands to the window of the 'Etoile du Nord' dining car and breathed in the sight of the Austrian Alps. In the almost-darkness, the snow appeared blue, sweeping down into the valleys where clusters of chalets glowed like golden orbs. Staring into the reflection, I could spy on men in black tie nuzzling into the perfumed necks of women wearing elbow gloves and flapper headbands. As authentic as the train was, this wasn't real. At least, not to me. This was a theatrical production put on for one night, and we were all starring in the show. Who didn't want to dine on champagne and truffles, or close their eyes in Zurich and wake up in Paris? The train was no more a representative example of train travel than a private jet was of flying. We were riding along in a hologram, a recreation of a time that no longer existed. It wasn't important, though. Reality was relative. To everyone around me, this was a dream realised and that was all that mattered.

After dinner, we shunned our fellow passengers and sought sanctuary in our cabin, where Patricius had made up the bunk beds, complete with damask sheets. Crawling onto the covers, Jem took off his tie and gestured for me to join him, and we lay there listening to the deep beat of wheels on steel.

'Doesn't the Reunification Express feel like a lifetime away?' he said.

'To you maybe; it's not easy to forget sitting up for seventeen hours with my feet on someone's crate.'

'I'd do it all again, though.'

'Really?'

'Well, most of it. Not sure I'd rush back to North Korea.' Jem turned to look at me. 'We're never going to be like those people, are we?'

'Which people?'

'All those retirees we met along the way who can't stand being in the same carriage as each other, let alone the same compartment. Imagine waiting your whole life to travel, only to find you can't bear each other's company any more. Or worse, finding yourself alone. Dad died before he and Mum could do anything like this. I don't want to wait to travel this way again.'

I moved towards the window and looked out as we neared Lake Zurich. Jem had stepped well outside his comfort zone to join me on a journey that would have made most seasoned travellers recoil in horror. He'd quietly shouldered the ups and downs for seven months, enduring stomach upsets, shingles, sleepless nights – and Robert De Niro – putting his career on hold to support me. The journey wouldn't have been the same without him, and I was confident we'd never be like those retirees.

'Then we won't,' I said. 'And thank you for coming with me.'

No one had slept – at least no one but us. Seasoned train sleepers, we'd fallen onto the pillows, sinking into deep, delicious sleep for the last time, waking in Paris to the smell of coffee and fresh croissants in our cabin. With a few hours to wander around the station, most passengers had disembarked while we stayed in bed, enjoying the peace of the stationary train. After pulling out of Paris, we were now being served brunch en route to the Channel Tunnel. Jem was reading through my notes, while I crunched into a chunk of sweet lobster tail soaked with garlic butter.

'Seventy-nine.'

'What?'

'Seventy-nine. We've only done seventy-nine trains.'

'That's really not funny. Don't wind me up.'

'I'm not winding you up. Look.' Jem turned my notebook towards me. 'I've counted every journey – twice. Have a look if you don't believe me.'

While Jem ran a piece of bread around my plate, I read through the list of trains, playing the journeys through in my head.

'You missed one. You jumped from 42 to 44.'

Jem was right. I'd scribbled in the numbers – probably on a moving train – and had miscounted them, reading 42 as 43, and leaving us with a grand total of 79 trains. My palms turned cold. I had planned the seven-month journey with surgical precision and care, but in the end, it wasn't a delay or a cancellation that had caught me out, or even a breakdown or a missed train: my own handwriting had failed me. Draining my prosecco, I pushed back my chair and fled back to the cabin.

'Don't feel bad,' said Jem, sitting next to me on the bed. 'It's an easy mistake to have made.'

'Would you have made it?'

'Don't be so hard on yourself. I didn't notice either. And besides, who cares?'

'You're right: *Around the World in 79 Trains* has quite a ring to it.'

'Maybe we can come back and do another train?'

'It wouldn't be the same.'

There was a knock at the door, and Patricius appeared, looking apologetic.

'I'm sorry for disturbing you, but this is just to let you know that we will be approaching Calais Ville station in around twenty minutes.'

'Thanks, Patricius,' said Jem.

Broken-hearted, I sat by the window, the misery of French rain dribbling down the glass. Staring down at my notebook, I re-counted the trains, hoping we were wrong. Jem had just finished packing our things when Patricius came by again.

'Madam, may I collect your bags? We will be sending them on to London Victoria for you.'

'Can we not keep them with us?'

'No, madam, the luggage will be transferred by road to London. It won't go with you on the Pullman.'

'The Pullman?'

'Yes, madam. At Calais Ville you will be transferred onto a coach to the terminal at Coquelles to travel through the Tunnel. At the other side, you will board the Belmond British Pullman. It's the sister train to this one.'

'There's another train?! I thought this train continued through the Tunnel and up to London?'

'No, madam, you have one more train journey to take.'

Jem wrapped me in a hug as I collapsed on the sofa in disbelief. 'I think it's very appropriate that our final train home is a good old British train.'

Once pulled along by the *Brighton Belle* and the *Golden Arrow*, the Pullman carriages had also been unearthed by James Sherwood, who had sourced them from a number of unexpected places. He'd bought one from a master at Eton College, two from a collector in Ashford who was living in one of the carriages at the time, and a baggage car that had been converted to transport racing pigeons in the north of England. Moved to a specially built workshop in Lancashire, the carriages had been restored but updated for modern-day travel: electric heating had been installed, and the antique glass replaced with safety glass, but otherwise the interiors were a perfect representation of their former selves.

Pushing back the Pullman's plush curtains, I bit into a smoked salmon sandwich and looked out at the Kent countryside. There was nothing remarkable about the scene that lay before me: the criss-cross of wonky wooden stiles, impossibly narrow lanes, and dried leaves coated with frost. But it was familiar. I didn't need to trudge across those fields to know how they'd sink underfoot or breathe the crisp air to know it smelt faintly of bonfires. Sipping tea, I leant back in a velvet armchair and looked down at the paper. My phone buzzed across the table. Swiping it open, I found a message from the Tibetan nun who had just sent another image of a golden smiling Buddha. As much as social media had its downsides, it was transforming the way we travelled. Where once I would have waved off my new friends, occasionally wondering about their whereabouts, now I could stay in touch with them all, from Azamat in Almaty, to Lucy in Tibet, Xué in Nanning, Bob in Boston, and Karen in Winnipeg.

As we swept up towards London, the last light dissolved into the horizon. Fields fell by the wayside, and stations flashed by, terraced houses backing onto the tracks. Burrowing into the south of the city, the train curved through Brixton, Stockwell and Clapham, the lights of Chelsea Bridge shaking gold into the Thames. Soon, the signs of arrival were all around: graffiti bulged from the walls, and parallels of track closed in as we approached Victoria Station. With a hiss and a jolt, the train finally came to a standstill. Stepping down onto the platform, I felt my city seep straight back into my bones: pigeons flapped through the rafters, engines slammed, and whistles blew. Commuters gathered on the concourse staring up at the screens, while others thundered down the stairs towards the Tube, shoving papers into plastic bins. Exiting the station, we walked towards the amber light of a rumbling black cab. For seven months and 45,000 miles – almost twice the circumference of the earth – this city, our home, had always been our destination, its invisible pull now as clear as the winter sky. Home was our beginning and our end, with the world lying somewhere in between.

Acknowledgements

In the days leading up to departure I often stared at my map covered in pins, strings, and scribbles, wondering what I was getting myself into. But my fears were soon allayed by the faith, support and endless enthusiasm from a circle of people who cheered me on from the moment I wrote my proposal until the morning the book went to print. To my brilliant agent, David Godwin, whose verve and spirit make this process an absolute joy, thank you for not laughing when I dropped in for a cup of tea and casually mentioned travelling around the world by train. Joining the Bloomsbury family has been a pleasure: my book has been loved and looked after in the safest of hands, particularly those of my editor Michael Fishwick who shares a thrilling obsession with dangling modifiers and without whom there would be far more descriptions of mucky toilets.

I owe overdue lunches to Professor Russell Goulbourne, Luke Doneghan, Shawna Pasquale and K. L. Kettle for their generous, patient editing, and to Adrian D'Enrico for forgetting to thank him last time. Along the journey we were housed and fed by Katherine Lambropoulos in Cannes, Adam Benzine in Toronto, Sarah Richards in Vancouver, Melissa and Anand Preece in Los Angeles, Matt Malarkey in Washington D.C., Arun, Rosie, Sean, Maya and Sam Naidu in Seattle, and Jamie Fullerton, Adrian Sandiford and Hannah Oussedik Sandiford in Beijing – much love and gratitude to you all. In addition, I am indebted to Azamat Abdullayev, Rod Beattie, Jean-Michel Filippi, Tomoko Maekawa, Hideo Nakamura, Professor Ulrike Roesler, Wade Shepard, Yuki Tanaka, Toshiko Yamasaki and Tetsushi Yonezawa for providing research, clarifying facts, arranging interviews, interpreting, and trusting me with their stories. A special thank you to Nick Bonner and Simon Cockerell at Koryo Tours for helping me in and – most importantly – out of North Korea, and to Sarah Davies and Geoffrey Cain for their guidance and expertise throughout the ten days.

It deeply saddens me that Sir Harold Atcherley passed away while I was still writing the book. His testimony, strength and unfailing good humour shaped my journey in a way I could never have imagined and I thank both him and Lady Sally Atcherley from the bottom of my heart for giving up their time and taking such delight in the book.

Marc Sethi deserves a gold medal. He and his flask of jasmine tea, sliders, and raucous laughter gave a much-needed boost to the final stretch and his beautiful photos capture moments in a way my words never could. Thank you for still talking to us. To my parents, Rekha and Rajesh, you embody the very essence of team work. Many thanks for your love, unflinching support and superior grandparenting skills. Jem read every chapter as I wrote it, helping me to relive an inimitable journey and make the book the best it could be; I couldn't have asked for a better travelling companion, editor, husband and papa to my little girl to whom this book is dedicated. Dear Ariel, the most wonderful writing distraction, please forgive me for spending the first nine months of your life hiding in a study so I could finish the book. But I hope one day when you read it, you will be inspired to have as many adventures of your own.

A Note on the Author

Monisha Rajesh is a British journalist whose writing has appeared in *Time* magazine, the *New York Times*, the *Guardian* and the *Sunday Telegraph*, in which she wrote a column about her journey around the world. Her first book, *Around India in 80 Trains* (2012), was named one of the *Independent*'s best books on India. Born in Norfolk and mostly raised in Yorkshire – with a brief stint in Madras – she currently lives in London with her husband and daughter.

A Note on the Type

The text of this book is set in Bembo, which was first used in 1495 by the Venetian printer Aldus Manutius for Cardinal Bembo's *De Aetna*. The original types were cut for Manutius by Francesco Griffo. Bembo was one of the types used by Claude Garamond (1480–1561) as a model for his Romain de l'Université, and so it was a forerunner of what became the standard European type for the following two centuries. Its modern form follows the original types and was designed for Monotype in 1929.